Taunton's COMPLETE ILLUSTRATED *Guide to*

Choosing & Installing
Hardware

ROBERT J. SETTICH

The Taunton Press

The Taunton Press
Inspiration for hands-on living®

The Taunton Press, Inc., 63 South Main Street, PO Box 5506, Newtown, CT 06470-5506
e-mail: tp@taunton.com

Distributed by Publishers Group West

EDITOR: Tony O'Malley
DESIGN: Lori Wendin
LAYOUT: Susan Lampe-Wilson
ILLUSTRATOR: Mario Ferro
PHOTOGRAPHER: Robert J. Settich

LIBRARY OF CONGRESS CATALOGING-IN-PUBLICATION DATA:

Settich, Robert J.
  Taunton's complete illustrated guide to choosing and installing
hardware / Robert J. Settich.
      p. cm.
Includes index.
  ISBN 1-56158-561-0
  1. Cabinet hardware. 2. Furniture making. 3. Woodwork. I. Title:
Complete illustrated guide to choosing and installing hardware. II.
Title.
  TT186 .S44 2003
  684.1--dc21
                              2003012094

Printed in the United States of America
10 9 8 7 6 5 4 3 2 1

About Your Safety: Working with wood is inherently dangerous. Using hand or power tools improperly or ignoring safety practices can lead to permanent injury or even death. Don't try to perform operations you learn about here (or elsewhere) unless you're certain they are safe for you. If something about an operation doesn't feel right, don't do it. Look for another way. We want you to enjoy the craft, so please keep safety foremost in your mind whenever you're in the shop.

To Barbara, my wife and best friend

Acknowledgments

I EXTEND MY DEEP APPRECIATION to the firms whose cooperation made this book possible. Supplying products for evaluation and photography was crucial, but even more important was their generous sharing of in-depth product knowledge. Special thanks to Rockler℠ Woodworking and Hardware who provided a large portion of the hardware shown in this book as well as invaluable technical advice. Thanks also to: Lee Valley Tools, Ltd.; Murphy Bed Company; Julius Blum, Inc.; Horton Brasses; Porter-Cable®; Kreg Tool Company; McFeely's Square Drive Screws; HEWI®; Doug Mockett Company; Woodhaven; Jesada Tools®; and Brownell's®.

I want to thank the many persons whose support set this project into motion and provided resources to bring it to a successful completion: Helen Albert, Tony O'Malley, Wendi Mijal, Jennifer Peters, Carolyn Mandarano, Diane Sinitsky, Joseph and Anna Settich, Frank Siudowski, Neal Harrison, Bill LaHay, John F. Settich, Tom Clark, Laura Greene, Diane Beers, Louis and Mary Arth, Francis Sidowski, Mara Martinelli, and Barbara Settich.

Contents

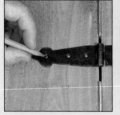

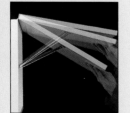

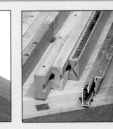

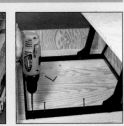

SECTION 7 Drawer Slides · 139

SECTION 8 Knobs, Handles, and Pulls · 153

SECTION 9 Glass and Panel Hardware · 165

Introduction

As one of the first research steps for this book, I contacted a long list of hardware manufacturers and suppliers and requested catalogs. As the catalogs arrived and filled one shelf after another in my office, I began to wonder how to compress all of that information into a single book.

It was immediately apparent that a single volume on the topic of hardware could not pretend to be absolutely comprehensive in scope—showing every piece of hardware available on the planet—and also utterly exhaustive in depth—demonstrating how to install each example.

Fortunately, the *Complete Illustrated Guide* format helped achieve a balance, delivering useful information in a concise manner that you can immediately put to practical use. In the overview portion of each section, you'll get a panoramic view of your choices in that hardware category, as well as tips on the key quality points to seek when you're choosing hardware. In the photo essays, you'll discover how to successfully handle even complicated installations step by easy step. Whenever possible, I've included insights as to why you're following a certain procedure so that you can apply the knowledge you gain to other projects.

Combining these two approaches gives you knowledge that is both extensive in range and intensive in application. As a result, you'll be better prepared and more confident in your approach to woodworking. You'll be able to maximize your time in the shop, building projects that are sturdier, better looking, and more functional. If you're an amateur, it can mean moving your abilities, work, and satisfaction to the next level.

Nails and Screws

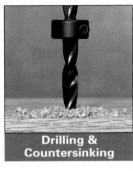

Drilling & Countersinking

➤ Drilling Holes (p. 13)
➤ Countersinking (p. 15)

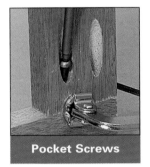

Pocket Screws

➤ Assembling a Face Frame with Pocket Screws (p. 17)

Removing a Damaged Screw

➤ Removing Broken Screws (p. 19)

COVERING EVERY TYPE AND SIZE of fastener would fill a hefty book. And frankly, that's probably more than you need or want to know. So this section focuses on the information that's most useful for cabinetmakers and home woodworkers: how to choose the right fastener for the job, and tips that will help you build stronger projects.

Choose Cut Nails for Historical Accuracy

Cut nails are made by slicing wedge-shaped pieces in alternating directions from a strip of steel: The width of the strip determines the length of the nails. Forming a head on the nail is a separate operation.

Four popular cut-nail forms are the rose-head common nail, available in sizes from 6d to 20d; the box nail that ranges from 4d to 10d; fine finish nails in sizes from 3d to 8d; and the brad, available only in 2d.

Because of their wedge shape, cut nails can split lumber across its grain. To minimize that, drive the nail so that the wedge parallels the grain.

Wired for Fast Production

Cut-nail technology represented a quantum leap in speed, but today's wire nail-making machinery produces fasteners quicker than your eye can see. Common nails are large-gauge headed fasteners used for house framing and similar heavy-duty tasks. Box nails have a similar design but are made from a

To minimize splitting, drive cut nails with the wedge shape parallel to the wood's grain. Four cut-nail shapes are (left to right): the rose-head common nail, box nail, fine finish, and brad.

smaller wire gauge to reduce splitting. Both casing and finishing nails are meant to be countersunk with a nail set.

Galvanized Vs. Stainless

Galvanizing is the usual cost-effective approach to stopping rust, but under that protective layer is a steel fastener that's eager to rust. If the zinc coating is damaged during installation or by later chemical attack, you'll start seeing rusty streaks. Stainless steel fasteners have rust resistance that isn't just skin deep. Stainless steel screws are a relatively common hardware store item, but stainless steel finishing nails and brads are more difficult to find.

Brads and Escutcheon Pins

Brads and escutcheon pins are the smallest driven fasteners that you're likely to encounter. Brads look like miniaturized finishing nails, and you can find them in most hardware stores in ½-in. to 1½-in. sizes.

The usual diameter is 17 gauge (0.0540 in.) to 18 gauge (0.0475 in.).

But even these small diameters can split tiny molding, especially if you try to drive the fastener too close to an edge. In some cases, you'll have to drill pilot holes, forming a makeshift "bit" by snipping the head off a same-gauge brad that's 1 in. or longer, then chucking it into your drill. This bit actually burns a hole instead of drilling it in the usual sense. You can use brads in a "hold-and-remove" role in glued assemblies by leaving the head proud of the surface, then pulling out the brads after the glue dries. Grab the brad with locking needle-nose pliers and pull straight out.

Escutcheon pins are meant to be seen. These little fasteners are usually round headed and are often supplied when you purchase hardware such as keyhole plates. Take a few moments to drill pilot holes. The alternative could be a frustrating search for an escutcheon pin to replace one bent by a glancing hammer blow.

When you drive an escutcheon pin into hardwood, drill a pilot hole to ease its entry. These miniature long-nose pliers were designed for precision electronics duty but are also the ideal scale to hold escutcheon pins. The rubber band on the handles maintains a firm grip on the pin.

Pneumatic Guns

Pneumatic tools can make your work faster, easier, and more accurate. But they also add an element of danger that demands respect. In fact, you should treat every nail gun as you would a loaded firearm. Never point it at anyone, keep all body parts away from the line of fire, and follow the manufacturer's directions for loading fasteners and clearing jams. Obviously, keep your hands well away from the muzzle of the gun.

Hammers and Nail Sets

When you're dealing with small moldings and tiny fasteners like brads and escutcheon pins, you need to change the scale of your tools to match the task. The Warrington-pattern hammer has a wedged head that hits the steel nail instead of your fingernail. Get the nail started with the finger-saving end, then switch to the business end. A relatively recent upgrade to the traditional nail set is the addition of color-coded grips. This seemingly small improvement adds several benefits: The grip prevents rolling, absorbs

This trio of pneumatic drivers will speed up production in the shop and on the job site. From left: a finish nailer with angled magazine, a brad driver, and a headless pinner.

shock, and also identifies whether the nail set is the $^1/_{32}$-in., $^1/_{16}$-in., $^3/_{32}$-in., or $^1/_8$-in. size. The Japanese-design nail set doesn't set small-diameter fasteners as well, but the off-set design of its second point allows access in tight quarters.

Screws

You can buy screws with a variety of head styles to meet specific project needs and can often select the fastener with your favorite drive system. Here's a quick rundown on the uses for the most popular types.

• Flat-head screws are probably the most common style and are used in a wide variety of applications, from general construction to fastening tiny hinges. The head is typically flat with the surface of the wood, or it can be driven into the bottom of a counterbore and concealed with a plug. It's

Lighten up on your pounding tools to drive brads or escutcheon pins. The 3½-oz. Warrington hammer combines ample power with plenty of control. The ¾-in.-dia. head of the midget hammer is another finger saver.

A set of traditional pencil-shaped nail sets has a size small enough to handle brads. The Japanese design (left) can be used in straight or offset applications.

► SCREWS AND NAILS

• Drive the fastener through the thinner board into the thicker one.

• When possible, choose a fastener that's three times longer than the thickness of the board being fastened. For example, if you're screwing on a ¼-in. plywood cabinet back, use ¾-in. screws.

• Countersink nails ¹⁄₃₂ in. below the wood's surface; flat-head screws should be flush with the surface of the wood or set into counterbores and plugged.

also the right choice to use with finishing washers.

- Oval-head screws mount with their smooth top just above the wood's surface. This gives a decorative look and also prevents the snags produced by flat-head screws that aren't fully countersunk. The oval head finds extensive use holding trim to boats.

- Trim-head screws look like finishing nails and can be used wherever you need the holding power of a screw but also require an unobtrusive look.

- Pan-head screws have a flat surface under the head that improves holding power when you mount hardware such as drawer slides. Using a screw diameter smaller than the mounting hole in the hardware gives you some adjustability.

- Round-head screws have the same flat surface under the head as a pan head but feature a higher domed profile that can be used as a decorative feature.

- Washer-head screws give you the broadened holding strength of a washer under a screw head but without the inconvenience of purchasing and handling a separate piece of hardware. By spreading the pressure, the washer-head screw avoids concentrated stresses that could crack plastics or damage thin wood products.

- Truss-head screws feature an even larger washer surface for improved holding power. Truss heads are excellent for attaching false drawer fronts—the large head hides an oversized hole that permits adjustment. Truss heads also provide excellent holding power when driven through the thin plywood backs of wall-mounted cabinets.

- Finishing washers give a neat appearance and improved holding power when used in

Here are top and side views of many of the screw-head styles you'll encounter. Top row, left to right: flat head, flat head with a separate finishing washer, washer head, and truss head. Bottom row, left to right: round head, oval head, pan head, fillister, and trim head.

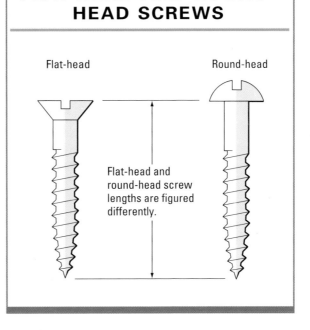

FLAT-HEAD AND ROUND-HEAD SCREWS

Flat-head   Round-head

Flat-head and round-head screw lengths are figured differently.

The thread pattern is an important consideration when selecting screws. From left to right: rolled (deep), cut (tapered wood), wood screw, double lead, and tapping thread.

The rolled-thread screw (left) and cut-thread pattern are two dominant fastener designs used by woodworkers.

conjunction with flat-head screws. Purchase finishing washers that are the same gauge as the screw you're using.

Follow This Thread of Thought

Here are some of the screw-thread patterns that you're likely to encounter, but you also need to be aware that various companies may use different terminology to describe their products. View actual samples, if possible, or study catalog illustrations carefully to make sure that you get the fastener you want:

• Rolled thread (also called deep-thread pattern): This style is manufactured by slimming the screw's shank (in comparison to the cut-thread pattern wood screw). Excellent all-purpose design for solid wood, plywood, medium-density fiberboard (MDF), and other manufactured panels.

• Cut thread (also called tapered wood thread): This is the traditional wood-screw pattern, which mimics the old-fashioned process of cutting the threads into a metal rod. The unthreaded portion of the shank is the same diameter as the major diameter of the threaded portion, and the root diam-

Cut-Thread Screws (Traditional Wood Screws)

Gauge		2	3	4	5	6	7	8	9	10	12	14
Head diameter (in.)		11/64	13/64	15/64	1/4	9/32	5/16	11/32	23/64	25/64	7/16	1/2
Body hole diameter (in.)		3/32	7/64	7/64	1/8	9/64	5/32	5/32	11/64	3/16	7/32	1/4
Pilot hole diameter (in.)	Hardwood	1/16	1/16	5/64	5/64	3/32	7/64	7/64	1/8	1/8	9/64	5/32
	Softwood	1/16	1/16	1/16	1/16	5/64	3/32	3/32	7/64	7/64	1/8	9/64
Phillips-driver size		#1			#2						#3	
Square-driver size		#0			#1			#2			#3	

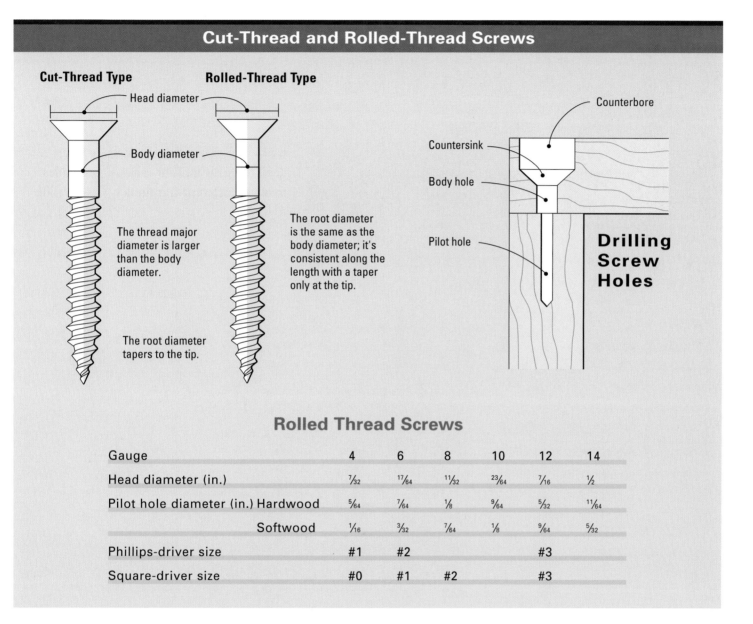

Cut-Thread and Rolled-Thread Screws

Cut-Thread Type

Rolled-Thread Type

Head diameter

Body diameter

The thread major diameter is larger than the body diameter.

The root diameter tapers to the tip.

The root diameter is the same as the body diameter; it's consistent along the length with a taper only at the tip.

Countersink

Counterbore

Body hole

Pilot hole

Drilling Screw Holes

Rolled Thread Screws

Gauge		4	6	8	10	12	14
Head diameter (in.)		7/32	17/64	11/32	23/64	7/16	1/2
Pilot hole diameter (in.)	Hardwood	5/64	7/64	1/8	9/64	5/32	11/64
	Softwood	1/16	3/32	7/64	1/8	9/64	5/32
Phillips-driver size		#1	#2			#3	
Square-driver size		#0	#1	#2		#3	

eter tapers to the tip. The thread depth is consistent along the length of the screw, even in the tapered portion, accentuating the pointed appearance. Good holding power in solid wood.

• Wood-screw thread: The thread design is similar to the deep-thread pattern but formed on a thicker shank. This design is often used on relatively soft materials such as brass or silicon bronze screws. Use this pattern instead of the deep thread when your project requires brass or bronze screws.

• Double lead: This pattern uses two threads around the shank for increased driving speed, is commonly used on drywall screws, and sometimes has a high/low design. Pullout resistance is not as good as the deep-thread design, but you'll gain faster assembly times, especially when you're using long screws.

➤ DAMAGED SCREWS

When everything is working just right, driving screws can be a fast and efficient assembly technique. But when a bit chews a Phillips-drive recess into a powdery mass, you've got trouble. And when a screw refuses to budge from a rocking chair you want to restore, you start to realize why the previous owner put a bargain price tag on it. Here are four techniques that back out stubborn screws and get your project headed forward again.

If the head of the fastener is relatively intact, try adding a drop or two of one of the liquids sold to improve screw-to-driver traction **(A)**. The thick formulation puts a gritty substance between the metal parts, filling gaps and reducing slippage. You can use this technique with any style of head recess. If you can't easily locate a source for one of these specialty products, try valve-grinding compound purchased from an auto parts store.

If you don't use the right clutch setting on your driver, overdriven screw threads can act like the blades of a kitchen blender, quickly turning softwood or MDF into a fluff with nearly zero holding power. But when you put your driver into reverse, you'll also discover that you can't get any bite that will let you back out the screw. When you find yourself in that situation, reach for a spring steel tool **(B)** that will gently pull back on the screw while you run the driver bit in reverse. You'll get enough lift to remove the screw completely or at least grab it with another tool.

If the drive recess is chewed up, try a screw remover. The type shown in photo **C** will work in a hand driver with a ¼-in. hex shank or in a variable-speed driver set in reverse. Run the driver at an extremely slow speed to maximize torque. At first, the remover may throw out tiny chips of metal as its edges bite into the fastener. If the screw is stubborn, apply more downward pressure, and tilt the tool 5 to 10 degrees off vertical.

Grabbing a screw with locking-grip pliers **(D)** may not be an elegant solution, but it's highly effective. Anticipate that the pliers might slip, and keep your knuckles out of harm's way.

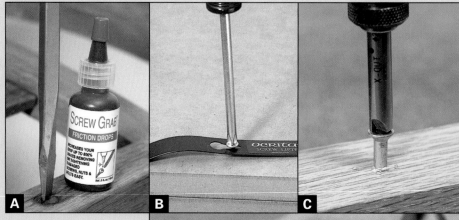

A   B   C

D

• Tapping thread: Although this is sometimes called a "wood-tapping" screw, it is basically a sheet-metal design. Typically the threads extend from tip to head. Sheet-metal screws are generally manufactured to a higher standard than ordinary wood screws. Be sure to drill an adequate body hole in the first board to prevent a jacked joint.

Power Up for Screw Driving

Driving screws with a regular drill, even one with variable-speed control, can be an iffy proposition. You have to get up enough speed to turn the fastener, then shut down and let the screw coast into place. If you shut down too soon, the screw sits proud of the surface; too late, and the driver snaps your wrist or the fastener. A driver/drill with a variable clutch is a much better solution: The clutch stops driving the screw when it reaches a preset torque level. The next step up is the screw gun, a tool engineered exclusively for driving screws with speed, accuracy, and consistency. In addition to the variable clutch, it has a second clutch system that engages when you put pressure against the bit, so you're not constantly cycling the motor on and off. It's a tool that stands up to the rigors of all-day use, even in a trade as fastener intensive as hanging drywall.

When Good Fasteners Go Bad

Here's a quick troubleshooting guide that will help you overcome common problems when driving screws.

• If a screw snaps when you're driving it, drill a larger pilot hole. Sometimes as little as a $1/64$-in. increase in bit size makes a big difference in the ease of driving screws.

The screw gun (top) can drive cabinet-assembly screws all day without complaining, but it's not designed to drive hardware-attachment screws. The variable clutch collar on the cordless drill (bottom) lets you dial the right torque for a wide variety of tasks.

• To keep delicate brass screws from snapping, drill the pilot hole, and drive a steel screw that has the same diameter and thread pattern as your brass fastener. Back out the steel screw, and drive the brass one into the threads you preformed in the wood.
• If your driver chews up the fastener's head, inspect the drive bit. If it shows any signs of wear, junk it. Also try a larger pilot hole.
• A common mistake is driving a fastener too deeply. When you do that, you lose a considerable amount of strength. For example, if you drive a screw halfway through a piece of $3/4$-in. plywood, the holding power at that point is equivalent to a properly driven screw in $3/8$-in. plywood.
• Some people really like using lubricants on screw threads, so if you're in that group, I'd recommend Lloyd's Akempucky. It's easy to use and fun to pronounce. But personally, I've always considered lubricants as a

If you like to use a lubricant on screw threads or nail shanks, slip a tube of Lloyd's Akempucky into the pencil pouch of your tool apron.

Preforming the threads in the wood with a steel screw will prevent damage or breakage to brass screws.

Compare the ordinary screw (left) with the hinge screw (right), and you'll see the distinctive undercut head design that can help ensure better-fitting hinge installations.

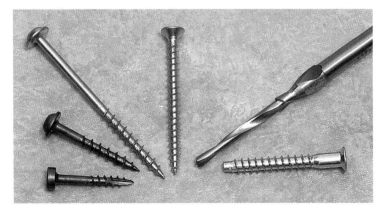

Pocket-hole assembly screws (first three from left) come in a variety of sizes to fasten stock ranging from 1/2 in. to 1½ in. thick. The Spax screw is in the center, and the Confirmat screw and its specialty bit are at right.

time-consuming nuisance. To me, it's easier to simply drill a pilot hole sized for easier driving. If you insist on a lubricant, be aware that it could cause problems when you apply a finish to the wood.

Special Screws

Screws used for pocket-hole assembly are typically a square-drive sheet-metal design with a self-drilling tip. Choose the coarse-thread design for softwoods and manufactured panels, and use the fine-thread pattern in hardwoods. The Spax screw is one brand in a new style of "do everything" screw that is supposed to fasten solid lumber, manufactured panels, drywall, sheet metal, and even anchor masonry. The Confirmat screw, shown in the bottom photo with its special bit, is engineered for improved holding power in plywood, MDF, and other manufactured panels. Precise drilling with the Confirmat bit is mandatory.

I'm sure this has happened to you. You check the fit of a screw into its countersink in the hinge leaf and it looks fine. But when you drive the screw into the pilot hole, the head won't pull down flush with the leaf as it did during the test fit. You try cursing the hinge for a while, but the screw still doesn't fit. The problem occurs under the head of the screw, where you can't see it. As shown in the photo above left, a screw usually raises a curl of wood fibers as the threads enter the wood. The countersunk screw head was supposed to completely fill the recess in the hinge leaf, but the curl got there first. So the screw sits higher than it should. But if you switch to a specialty hinge screw, its undercut head leaves room for the raised wood, so the screw's surface is flush with the hinge.

Drilling Holes

Drilling holes for screws can require a number of bits and setups. You need the pilot hole for the threads, a hole for the body of the screw, a countersink for a flat-head screw, plus a counter-bore if you want to cover the head of the screw with a plug. You can speed and simplify your work by using a bit that's designed to handle all of these operations. One style of bit **(A)** allows you to use a setscrew to adjust the length of the drill to match the screw. If you find that the setscrew loosens during use, get some liquid thread-locking compound at your auto parts store.

The style of bit in the next photo **(B)** is more sophisticated in several ways. The length of the bit adjusts to match the screw, and you can set the lower stop collar to limit the depth of a counter-bore to a specific measurement. In addition, the drill itself is tapered to match the profile of cut-thread wood screws. One additional benefit of this style is that each locking collar has two setscrews for added holding strength and dependability.

Drill collars are made in inch and metric sizes to fit many sizes of bits. Use a light touch as the collar approaches the wood instead of forcing it against the stock **(C)**. Excessive pressure can make the collar slip further upward at each hole until you've lost the accuracy this accessory was designed to provide. The masking tape flag is one of my personal favorites because it's fast, easy to set, incredibly inexpensive, and it even sweeps away the chips when I reach the correct depth.

(Text continues on p. 14.)

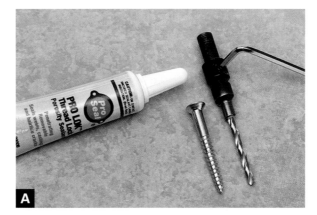

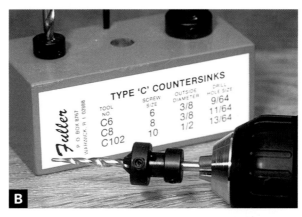

Rapid-change bit holders can be a real convenience if you choose the right one, but to do that you need to understand your options. Some holders work strictly by magnetism, whereas collared varieties are typically designed to hold either ball-detent drivers (top in **D**) or the wire-detent style (bottom). Some drivers combine mechanical holding with magnetic power that holds both the bit and the screw you're driving.

If you put the wrong style of bit into some holders, the bit may either fall out or be trapped almost permanently. To discover which style of bit your driver will handle, look down its shaft. The driver at left in photo **(E)** has a ball that engages ball-detent bits and won't hold the wire style. You can clearly see the retracting wire mechanism in the driver at right. This particular driver will also hold ball-detent bits.

Countersinking

The standard countersink angle for modern wood screws and machine screws is 82 degrees **(A)**, and it's no coincidence that this is the angle you'll find on most countersink bits. So the vast majority of the time you'll never have a problem countersinking a fastener. But every so often you'll encounter a screw that's engineered with a different angle, such as 90 degrees, and if you mismatch a fastener and countersink, you'll have trouble.

You'll find that hardware sometimes needs a bit of modification to improve the fit of the fasteners. For example, if the screws of a hinge stand slightly proud of the leaf, you can use a countersink to remove excess metal **(B)**. The countersink shown in photo **A** has a ⅝-in. diameter and seven cutting flutes for rapid and smooth cutting in wood or metal—the distributor calls it "chatterfree." Each flute is responsible for removing only a tiny bit of material on each rotation, accounting for its steady running.

The next two styles of countersinks can also be used on either wood or metal. The five-flute countersink shown at left in photo **C** will cut a countersink that's up to ¾ in. in diameter: big enough for fasteners that you'd have to lift with both hands. The next two countersinks use a shearing cutting action that's very smooth and easy to control. One edge of the smaller hole in this style of countersink has a honed edge that cuts away the material. Shavings exit through the larger hole.

Using a single tool to drill the pilot, body hole, countersink, and counterbore is a real convenience. The two styles shown in photo **D** are fast and accurate. The bit shown at right utilizes a

(Text continues on p. 16.)

Countersink Angle

82 Degrees

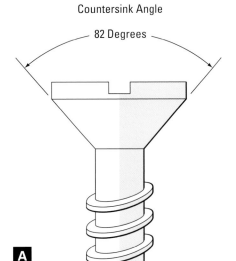

A

C

B

D

E

F

brad-point drill to give you pinpoint accuracy. In addition, it snaps in and out of a ball-detent driver so you can quickly switch from drilling to driving.

If you really want fine control, try a hand countersink. The set shown in photo **E** is inexpensive but rugged. It has a 90-degree angle, so it's not your everyday countersink, but it's handy to have around when you run across a fastener that needs that angle.

Here's a quick way to check whether you've drilled the countersink deeply enough—without driving the screw **(F)**. Drill the body hole and countersink, and invert a screw into the countersink. When the countersink is the correct depth, the rim of the screw head will be flush with the wood, as shown by the screw on the right in the photo.

VARIATION A self-centering bit helps ensure that the pilot hole for a screw is postioned correctly and greatly simplifies the installation of hardware with center-sinked screws.

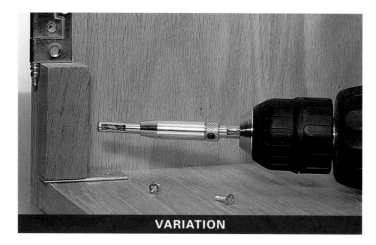

VARIATION

Assembling a Face Frame with Pocket Screws

Begin by ripping your stock to width and cutting all the pieces to length. For the best results, the edges of the stock and the end cuts must be square **(A)**. I usually do most of the sanding prior to assembly to minimize cross-grain sanding scratches. Identify the face of each part with a piece of masking tape, then mark the relationship of the parts to each other on the tape. I like to use the time-tested triangle marking system. As a rule of thumb, always drive the screw through the end grain of one piece and into the long grain of the other piece because long grain holds a screw better than end grain.

Adjust the stop collar on the drill bit to the correct length for the stock you're using, and make certain that the setscrew is snug **(B)**. Clamp a rail into the jig, and drill the pocket holes using a corded drill running at full speed **(C)**. This jig offers the choice of three different hole locations to suit various stock widths. I cover the unused hole with a strip of tape to prevent mistakes. To clear the chips, keep the drill running when you exit the hole. Double-check the stop-collar depth setting by driving a test screw into one hole and gauging its projection against the thickness of the rail **(D)**. There should be a minimum of ⅛ in. between the tip of the screw and the face of the stile.

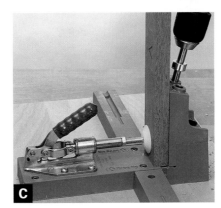

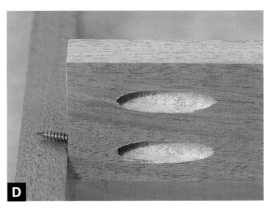

The assembly clamp supplied with the jig helps to keep the faces of the rails flush, even if they are slightly different in thickness **(E)**. Position the large pad on the face of the joint, and align the

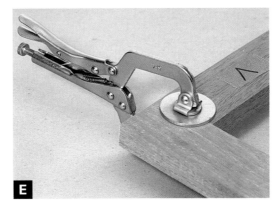

(Text continues on p. 18.)

edge of the rail flush with the end of the stile. Using a driver with an adjustable clutch, drive the assembly screws **(F)**. You should also have a hand driver available for small adjustments. The joint may temporarily separate while you're driving the first screw in each joint but should close completely when that screw fully seats itself. If you add a bar clamp along the joint, you'll prevent the temporary separation during assembly.

When I'm working on a complex face frame, I assemble its perimeter first, then add the intermediate rails and stiles. To ensure precise dimensions, I use a spacer block to set the distance between a fixed part and the piece I'm adding **(G)**. With a little practice, you can make joints that require no additional sanding. But if you do have a slightly misaligned joint, you can quickly erase minor misalignment on the face by using a random-orbit sander **(H)**. You'll find wood plugs in a variety of species and plastic plugs in several colors to fill the pocket holes **(I)**. The tip of the mini jig has a small recess that helps you push a glued plug into place. Let the glue dry for a wood plug, trim it flush, and sand it smooth. If you're using a plastic plug, simply glue it in place after applying the finish to the wood.

VARIATION

VARIATION To use the mini jig on stock that is ¾ in. thick, clamp its end flush with the end of the rail and drill. Adapt it to other stock thicknesses by moving its end forward or back and resetting the stop collar on the drill bit. With the mini jig, the face clamp, and the drill bit, you have a complete pocket-hole system that's small enough to fit into the corner of your toolbox or even into a tool belt for job-site work.

Removing Broken Screws

Trying to dig a broken screw out of a board with a chisel is an extremely efficient way to nick the cutting edge and create a huge scar in the wood. The next time you break a screw, save your chisels and your lumber by using a screw remover.

Create a guide jig from ¾-in.-thick scrap approximately 1½ in. by 4 in. **(A)**.

Position the guide jig over the broken screw so that the guide is approximately centered around the broken screw, and hold the guide firmly or clamp it in place. Chuck the tubular screw extractor into your drill chuck, but be careful not to overtighten because that could crush the tool. If your drill utilizes a chuck key, lightly tighten at all three holes to equalize the pressure. Put the drill into reverse, and drill ¼ in. deep to establish a stable groove, ensuring that the bit does not skate across the surface **(B)**.

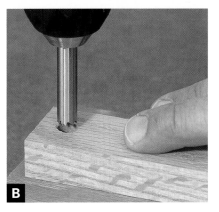

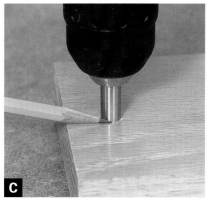

Continue drilling without the drill guide to the full depth of the screw. Withdraw the bit from the hole often to clear away chips that could overheat the tool. When you think you've gone far enough, mark a line on the bit and withdraw it **(C)**. Use the broken screw as a guide to the necessary depth of bit penetration. By subtracting the amount of screw left from the original length, you can determine how deeply to drill.

Use a small, slotted screwdriver to break free the core containing the broken screw **(D)**.

Glue a ⅜-in. dowel into the hole, wipe away excess glue, and trim it flush. If the dowel fits too tightly, crimp it with a pair of pliers **(E)**.

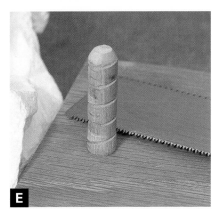

When you drill the pilot hole for the replacement screw, be sure to use a larger bit than you did the first time.

Hinges

Surface-Mounted Hinges

Mortised Hinges

Euro Hinges

Specialty Hinges

I F YOU'RE THE KIND of person who has a tough time deciding at the 31-flavor ice cream store, then a first glance at the number of available hinge choices could send your brain into total overload. But before you despair, consider the fact that most hinges are engineered for very specific applications. So in some ways, hinge selection is a process of elimination. By defining the exact use for your hinge, you can ignore entire categories.

Butt Hinges

The butt hinge is probably the simplest and most familiar type of hinge. But a closer look reveals that even this most basic device holds a surprising number of engineering subtleties.

Referring to the drawing at right on the facing page, you'll see that the hinge consists of two leaves that usually have countersunk holes drilled for flat-head wood screws. Along the center axis, the leaves bulge to form interlocking knuckles. The row of knuckles is called the barrel, and a hole through the barrel accepts the pin. The paint clearance slot keeps the knuckles from rubbing against each other and provides room for a decorative coating or clear protective finish. Pitch refers to the length of a pair of mating knuckles.

End play isn't the result of sloppy manufacturing—modern machinery allows factories to produce even inexpensive hinges with

CENTER OF ROTATION

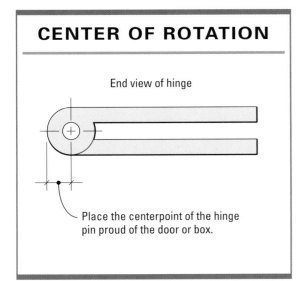

End view of hinge

Place the centerpoint of the hinge pin proud of the door or box.

BUTT HINGE ANATOMY

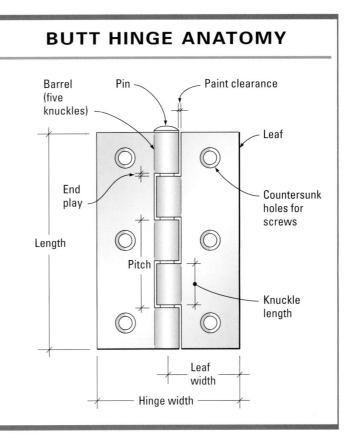

Barrel (five knuckles)

Pin

Paint clearance

Leaf

End play

Length

Countersunk holes for screws

Pitch

Knuckle length

Leaf width

Hinge width

astonishing precision. But generally, you'll find more end play in hinges designed for utility-type applications because this clearance allows a hinge to operate even if the ends of the leaves are not perfectly flush. In addition, end play allows you to easily disassemble and reassemble hinges with loose pins. In high-end hinges designed for jewelry boxes, you'll find absolutely minimal end play.

The first thing you need to know about butt hinge geometry is that its center of rotation is located at the middle of its pin. So it stands to reason that this point must be located beyond the back edge of the box or the face of a door. Anything past the tiniest fraction of an inch will allow the hinge to work, and adding more projection is a matter of aesthetics and controlling the arc of motion (see the drawing above).

Of course, when you mount hinges on the surface of a box or door, you automatically position the hinge pin in a location where it can operate. But when you mortise a hinge, you'll need to make certain that the pin's centerpoint is always out in the open.

BOUND HINGE (SIDE OF BOX)

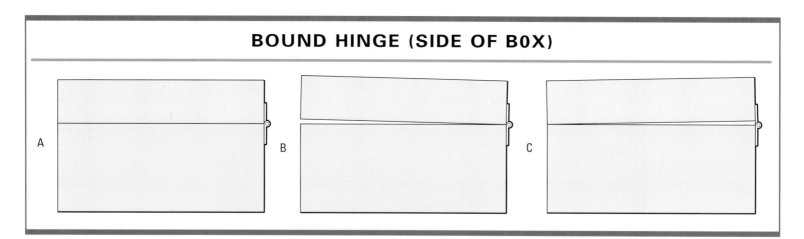

A   B   C

Cutting a full-depth mortise in the box's base made it easy to position and mount the lid.

Cutting matching half-depth mortises in the base and lid is more difficult than the full-depth version, but neat results are the reward of careful workmanship.

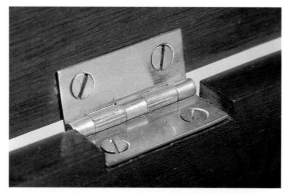

Preventing Bound Hinges

Bound hinges are those that prevent a box lid or door from closing completely. This condition often results from initially hinging a lid so that the base and lid make contact all around. But then the wood expands, and the front edge of the box gapes open in an ugly sneer. The drawing above shows a practical solution. Here it is recognized that the lid may develop a gap, so its location is controlled by concealing it at the rear of the box.

To prevent bound hinges when you use surface-mounted hinges, simply place a spacer between the base and lid at the back of the box before fastening the hinges. You'll get the same result with mortised hinges by making the mortise not quite as deep as the diameter of the hinge's barrel.

Setting the Mortise Depth

Another useful fact about the geometry of a butt hinge is that the depth of the mortise is governed by the diameter of the barrel, not by the thickness of the leaf. This assumes that you're working with hinges that have flat (unswaged) leaves. Swaging alters the relationship between leaf thickness and barrel diameter, and that changes the mortise depth required.

There are two different ways to mortise the hinges—you can cut half-depth mortises in both the base and lid, or a full-depth mortise in the box's base. Checking a test cut for a full-depth mortise is as easy as verifying that it is just short of burying the hinge's knuckle. For half-depth mortises,

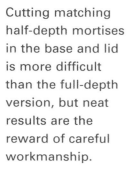

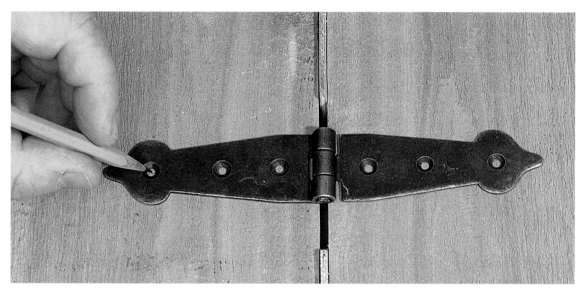

You can quickly and accurately install a surface-mounted strap hinge on a rustic project.

make two test cuts, and hold them face to face with the barrel of the hinge in the middle. If the test boards close completely, the hinges will be bound—the front edge of the lid won't meet the base. Decrease the depth and make another pair of test cuts.

Butt Hinge Variations

The butt hinge has evolved into an extraordinary number of forms to suit a wide range of applications. With the leaves stretched in width, the butt hinge becomes a strap hinge. Stretched in length, it becomes a piano hinge. The leaves can also be flanged—bent around the back of a door, a face frame, or the edge of a box to offer additional strength. If you want a hinge that's as easy to install as a surface mount but hides nearly as well as a mortised version, try a no-mortise hinge. The thickness of the metal automatically sets the reveal between the door and its frame.

For reasons of both aesthetics and function, the shape of a hinge isn't restricted to the familiar rectangular shape. You'll find

Three no-mortise hinge varieties meet special applications. The hinge shown at left is for an inset door; the bent flange of the version in center attaches to the edge and back of a face frame; and the flanged hinge at right is useful for box lids.

hinges with leaves in fanciful shapes, as round as a bullet, or stretched with rounded ends. An elongated double-pinned hinge is often used for a folding card-table top, and the familiar butler's tray hinge has a built-in spring.

The butt hinge shape has changed, but the performance remains. This round hinge hits a bull's eye in both style and function.

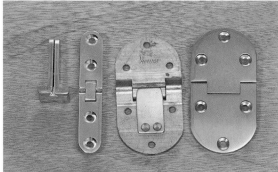

Shown at left are side and front views of a double-pinned hinge that's used for a folding table top, and at right are back and front views of a butler's tray hinge.

Choose a separating hinge that's scaled to fit the size and strength requirements of your project.

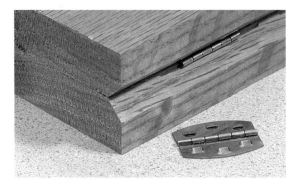

The barbed hinge is small, discreet, and inexpensive. But installation demands careful setup.

➤ See *"Supporting Hinged Lids"* on p. 70.

Separating hinges can be very useful, and they are scaled to handle a wide range of jobs—whether you want to build a sturdy toolbox or a dainty jewelry container. Either way, you can make a removable lid that allows unrestricted access to the contents. The larger sizes can also be used on cabinet doors or clock cases. Plan your project carefully because many of the hinge designs require you to specify right- or left-hand application when you order.

The barbed hinge is nearly an exact opposite of the separating hinge. Once you install a barbed hinge, removal is nearly impossible without destroying the wood. The barbed hinge is inexpensive, but installation requires you to use a specialty sawblade chucked into your drill press. The hinge is widely used for production runs of small boxes.

Hinges That Hold Their Own

Many box hinges require you to add a separate support to hold the lid open for easy access. Other hinges, though, build the support right into the body of the hinge, eliminating the need for additional hardware. The hinge usually holds the lid open at about a

95-degree angle. You'll find stopped piano hinges that you can surface mount or mortise. Or choose from styles of butt hinges that you put into a traditional mortise, let into the back of the box and lid, or surface mount for utility applications. Side rail hinges and quadrant hinges are two other lid-supporting choices. The quadrant hinge requires a mortise in both the back and end of the box's lid and base. In addition, you'll need to excavate a channel into the base for the quarter-circle stop arm that gives this hinge style its name. You'll have a much easier time installing the side rail hinge—simply rout mating mortises in the base and lid.

Specialty Hinges

The barrel hinge is virtually invisible when closed, and it also has the advantage of easy installation because the mortise is simply a hole drilled into each workpiece. But there are a few disadvantages. A slight mismatch in hole locations will make the hinge's operation very difficult, while a larger error will make installation itself downright impossible. But a more serious drawback is the fact that it will not overclose—move past the point where the axis of the lid hole meets the axis of the base hole. As a result, you can't get the lid of a box to close firmly against the base at the front. This drawback is not as serious if you're using the hinge to swing an inset door.

To the right of the barrel hinge in the bottom photo at right is another invisible hinge that nearly everyone refers to by its brand name: Soss. Installation requires a two-level mortise, but a jig and bushing-guided router make its production certain and relatively fast. This hinge does overclose, and it's also self-revealing—a term I use to

Each of these stopped hinges requires a different mounting method. Cut traditional mortises into the base and lid for the hinge at left, mortise the center hinge into the back of the box, and surface mount the hinge at right.

The quadrant hinge (left) and the side-rail hinge (right) are stop-hinge designs that are popular for jewelry boxes and humidors.

The barrel hinge (left) and Soss hinge (right) are both nearly invisible when installed in boxes and doors.

The miniature barrel hinge teams modest price with easy installation, a combination that recommends it for production runs of containers.

The chunky four-way hinge offers the ease of surface mounting and a wide 175-degree opening angle.

refer to hinges that automatically produce a consistent gap between the edge of a door and its frame. You can purchase Soss hinges in several sizes, and the largest one can be used to hang architectural doors with no hardware visible from either side when the door is closed.

The miniature barrel hinge installs into a 5-mm hole drilled into the base and lid of small boxes and pen presentation cases. You then chamfer both pieces so the tip of each cut meets the centerline of the holes. The mating chamfers provide operating clearance as well as a stop mechanism. A drop of

epoxy wiped onto the walls of the holes with a toothpick grips the hinges. It's an inexpensive hinge, a highly desirable virtue for hardware used in producing large batches of boxes.

The four-way hinge gets its name from the number of door-positioning options it offers: inset, half overlay, overlay, and mitered corners. It opens 175 degrees to get the doors well out of the way if you want to operate pullout shelves. It's a solid handful of steel that's suitable for heavy-duty applications.

Euro Hinges

It wasn't that long ago that the overlay hinge was the undisputed king of kitchen and bath cabinets. To order the hinges you needed, you simply counted the number of doors and multiplied by two. But the old hinge king has lost his throne and been replaced by a new group of hinges from Europe. Instead of a single hinge, the new dynasty is actually an extended family of hinges, each one engineered for a specialized purpose. Even a small kitchen may have a half-dozen or more different hinge varieties.

Almost all Euro hinges are completely concealed when the door is closed. That makes a cabinet that's cleaner, both physically and visually. And because the hinges are hidden, their style or finish can't go out of fashion. Most hinges also have three-way adjustability, a feature that transforms door fitting from an exercise in "close enough" to micrometer precision. The hinges have also created new options that let the creative designer unleash his imagination. You can now select between face-frame or frameless construction, inset or overlay doors, and cabinets that angle inward or out.

Despite all of the advantages of Euro hinges, there a few lingering disadvantages. Many home woodworkers fear that the system will require the purchase of several pieces of specialized machinery, each one the size and cost of a car. And even small-shop professionals who recognize the time-and labor-saving potential are overwhelmed by the enormous variety of hinges. But with some knowledge and a few jigs, even a budget-minded weekend woodworker can reap the advantages of the Euro hinge system.

One caution—you can considerably complicate matters for yourself if you choose hinges from several different manufacturers. Installation specifications will vary, and you're unlikely to find interchangeable mounting plates—a fact that will transform the usual nightmare of inventory into a true living hell. Developing brand loyalty with a single manufacturer's line will simplify your life.

Utilize the adjustability designed into Euro hinges to achieve absolute perfection in door alignment. The cross-shaped screw head recesses with the four radiating marks indicate that these are Pozi-drive screws.

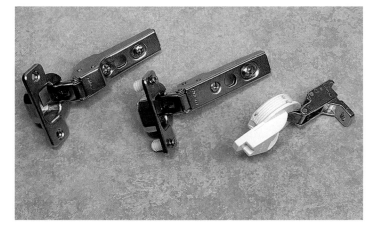

Install the hinge shown at left by drilling pilot holes for two screws; the center hinge requires pressing bushings into holes, then tightening the screws. Press in the ringed plastic hinge cup at right, and then drill a screw pilot hole through the flange at its lip.

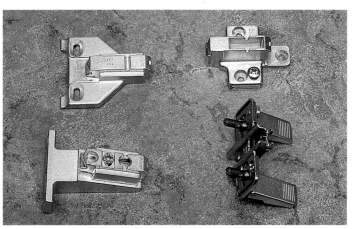

Hinge-mounting plates include (top left) a plate with vertical adjustment slots; a plate (top right) with an integral screw that moves it up and down; a post plate (lower left) that mounts to the rear of a face frame; and a plate (lower right) with pins that expand as you press down levers.

EURO HINGE CHOICES

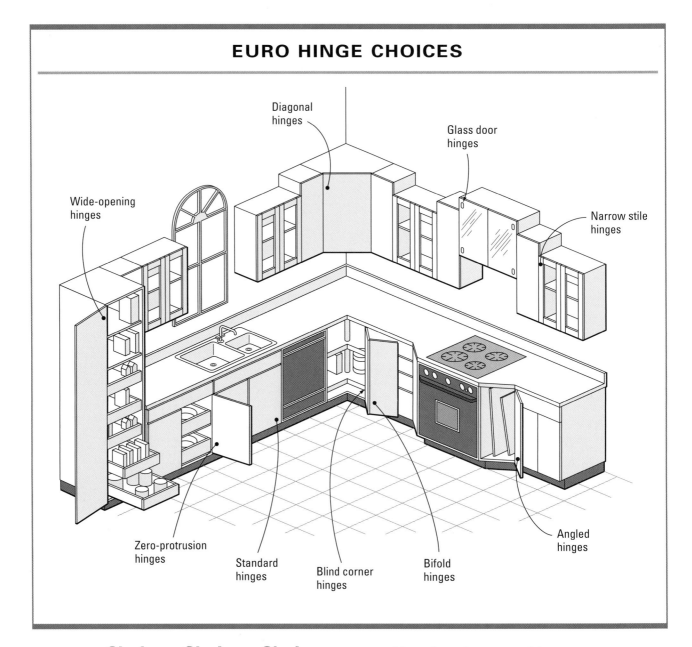

Diagonal hinges

Glass door hinges

Wide-opening hinges

Narrow stile hinges

Zero-protrusion hinges

Standard hinges

Blind corner hinges

Bifold hinges

Angled hinges

Choices, Choices, Choices

If you're accustomed to having only a handful of hinge choices, you may be shocked when you see the options offered by Euro hinges. For example, take a fairly simple hinge, such as a hinge that opens 125 degrees on a frameless cabinet. You can choose whether you want the door to overlay the cabinet's edge, whether two doors are hinged on the same cabinet support, or whether the door is inset. Then you choose between free-swinging or self-closing hinges. Next, you select whether the hinge clips onto the mounting plate or attaches with screws. Then, there are up to four alternate ways of attaching the hinge cup to the door.

Not every hinge has a separate mounting plate and elaborate adjustments. This face-frame hinge has a simple slot in its attached bracket.

But before you feel confused by this ever-widening array of choices, you should realize that every decision you make about building your cabinets rapidly rewinds the process, quickly bringing you to the exact hinge you need. Look at the drawing of the kitchen on the facing page, and you'll begin to see your choices come into focus.

Choosing Hinges and Mounting Plates

One of the first decisions you'll make is whether you want your door to overlay the carcase or face frame, or whether you prefer an inset installation. The drawing at right clarifies your options.

It would be impossible to show every type of system used for attaching hinges and mounting plates. The following examples are

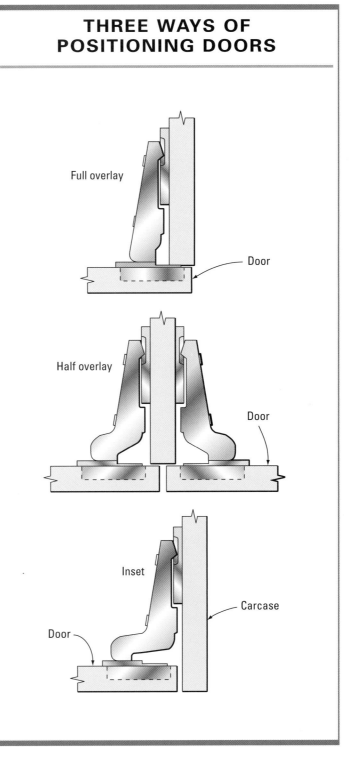

THREE WAYS OF POSITIONING DOORS

Full overlay

Door

Half overlay

Door

Inset

Carcase

Door

HINGE PLACEMENT AND QUANTITY

The design of each hinge sets its boring pattern, but you also need to decide where to place the hinges relative to the top and bottom of the door and how many hinges to use. There are no absolute answers to either question, but you can use the following guidelines:

* Keep the top and bottom hinges close to the ends of the door: no more than 3 in. to the hinge-cup centerpoint.

* Consult the chart at right for suggested additional hinges on large or heavy doors. When you calculate the weight of the door, include attachments such as mirrors or storage racks, plus the weight of any items stored on the door. When in doubt, add another hinge.

CHOOSING THE NUMBER OF HINGES

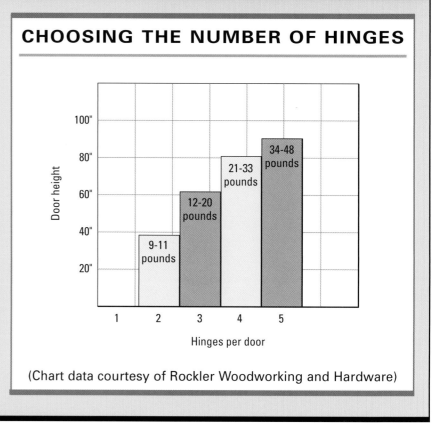

Door height (vertical axis): 20", 40", 60", 80", 100"
Hinges per door (horizontal axis): 1, 2, 3, 4, 5

- 9-11 pounds (at 2 hinges)
- 12-20 pounds (at 3 hinges)
- 21-33 pounds (at 4 hinges)
- 34-48 pounds (at 5 hinges)

(Chart data courtesy of Rockler Woodworking and Hardware)

A flipper door mechanism combines the rotation of a hinge with the motion of a drawer slide. It's widely used in entertainment and media centers.

offered as representatives of the more common styles that you'll encounter—each manufacturer offers variations on these basic themes. The type you'll choose depends on a number of factors, including the tooling you purchase and whether you do all your work in the shop or sometimes build cabinets at the job site. For example, press-in bushings install quickly with a dedicated machine in a production shop but can be an annoyance to tap squarely into place at a construction site.

Simple Box Hinge

If you like the idea of quick and easy hardware installation, you'll love using surface-mounted hinges. There's no complicated routing and chiseling—just great-looking results in a hurry. In this example, I started with a vintage box that's nicely made but suffers from bound hinges so that the front of the box gapes open **(A)**. Whether repairing an old box or hinging a new one, the steps are the same.

➤ See *"Preventing Bound Hinges"* on p. 22.

Put four thicknesses of self-adhesive notepaper (Post-It is one brand) between the base and lid, positioning the spacers near the ends of the box so they won't interfere with hinge placement. Carefully align the edges and ends of the base and lid, and tape them together using package sealing tape or masking tape **(B)**.

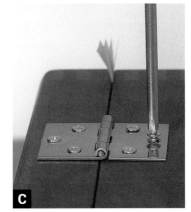

Tip the box onto its front face so you can lay the hinges in position. Move the hinges side to side to let your eyes judge the best location. When you're satisfied with the placement, carefully position one hinge, centering the barrel along the gap at the back of the box **(C)**. If you're uncomfortable visually aligning the hinge, you can position it with a try square. Drill the pilot holes and drive the screws, but keep checking as you work to make certain that the base and lid remain flush. Repeat the process for the other hinge, and remove the tape and the spacers. The slight gap at the back of the box ensures that the front of the box will close tightly even when the box changes size due to changes in moisture content **(D)**.

A

B

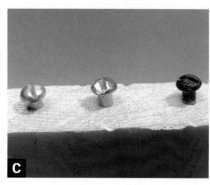

C

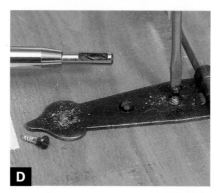

D

E

Strap Hinge

Strap hinges add authentic styling to rustic furniture, and with a few installation tips, you'll get great results fast. I feel that the rustic look is enhanced by relatively large hinge gaps instead of the tight spacing you'd probably use on more tailored furniture, so I put some ⅛-in. plywood spacers between the pieces **(A)**. Make a pencil mark at the centerpoint of the end hole in one leaf. Put a short piece of masking tape about ¼-in. past the tip of each hinge leaf, and remove the hinge.

Place a framing square so that it aligns with the pencil mark, and use a utility knife to scribe a line between the pieces of masking tape **(B)**. This overshot cutline will mimic the mark a country cabinetmaker might have used to align a hinge. Replace the hinge, and use the pencil mark and scribed line to position it.

There were no screws furnished with this hinge, so I had to give some ordinary fasteners the antique treatment. Temporarily drive slotted (not Phillips) screws into the end of the scrap board to hold them for filing and painting. The photo **(C)** shows how an ordinary screw (left) is faceted with a file (center) and then spray-painted flat black (right) for a vintage look. Drill pilot holes for the screws, and drive them to secure the hinge **(D)**. The installed hinge **(E)** is strong, functional, and has the styling appropriate to its use.

No-Mortise Hinge

A no-mortise hinge is a fast and efficient way to hang inset cabinet doors, producing an even reveal between carcase and door on the hinge side. By using the easy jig shown in this demonstration, you'll also help ensure consistent reveals at the top and bottom of the door. As you'll see, the finished height of the door is equal to the opening in the carcase minus the thickness of two mending plates.

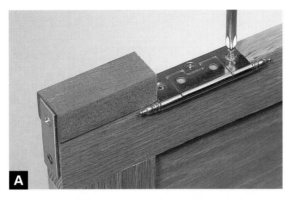

To make the jig, simply cut a block of scrap wood that equals the length of the hinge, and screw a ⅟₁₆-in.-thick mending plate to one end. Of course, you can cut the block any length you wish. Making it equal the length of the hinge merely follows a common rule of thumb for hinge placement **(A).** Make sure that the screw is fully seated in the countersink. Hook the plate over the end of the door, and register the barrel of the hinge against the face of the door. Drill pilot holes, and drive the screws into the holes in the hinge leaf that have the countersinks visible. Move the jig to the carcase, and set a spare hinge atop it and with the barrel against the edge of the carcase **(B).** The hinge will be backward in this position, so drill pilot holes in the leaf that has its countersunk holes toward the side of the carcase. A self-centering bit makes this an easy and accurate job.

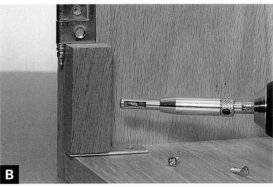

Move the hinged door to the carcase, and drive the screws to complete the installation **(C).**

When the door is closed, you'll enjoy the appearance of even spaces surrounding the door **(D).**

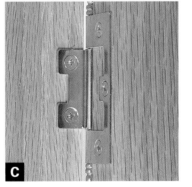

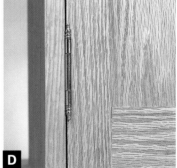

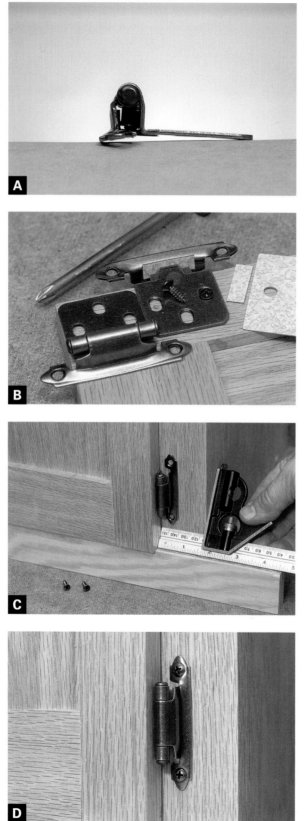

A

B

C

D

Overlay Hinge

When an overlay hinge spring is in an unloaded position (before installation), the leaf that mounts to the frame pulls the door leaf toward it. See the end view in **(A).** So when you screw down the hinge, the spring makes the door move away from the mounting point. Inserting a small piece of plastic laminate near the hinge loads up the hinge enough so that the frame leaf is flat against a reference surface. The installation photo **(B)** indicates where the laminate is placed. It also shows the traditional spacing for overlay hinges: one leaf width from the end of the door. Hold the hinge's leaf against the pencil mark and the knuckles against the edge of the door while you drill pilot holes in two of the slots in the leaf. Use two flat-head screws to attach the hinge leaf.

The usual overlay for kitchen cabinet doors is ⅜ in. The face frame of this cabinet has rails and stiles that are 2 in. wide, so rip a plywood strip 1⅝ in. wide, and place it flush with the bottom rail **(C)**. That way, when you rest the doors atop the strip, their lower ends will overhang the opening by ⅜ in. I also wanted a 1⅝-in. reveal along the vertical edge of the door, but I set my adjustable square about 1/32 in. larger than that to compensate for a bit of springback when the laminate shim was removed from the hinge. Drill pilot holes and drive the pan-head screws to secure the hinge leaf to the stile. If you need to adjust the fit of the door side to side, simply loosen the screws on the backside of the door. When you're satisfied **(D),** drive the third screw into the hinge, positioning it near the end of the slot to ensure that the door won't wiggle out of place.

Mortised Butt Hinge

A box hinged with mortised butts appears tidy and effortless. And like many accomplishments, it looks easy until you try it for yourself. But if you have a basic knowledge of how a hinge's geometry works and then follow a systematic approach, you'll get good results with your first try. Great results come after practice.

This demonstration shows how to hinge a small box, but you can adapt this same approach to hanging a door onto a carcase. In that case, you simply clamp the spacer between the side of the carcase and the door.

To properly position the hinge, you need to make sure that the centerpoint of the hinge pin will be slightly past the rear edge of the box. To do that, close the hinge, and measure the distance from the barrel to the opposite side of the hinge pin **(A)**. Cut a spacer that is that thickness and at least as long as the box.

To help ensure that you position the hinges squarely, measure the distance from the edge of the hinge's leaf to the edge of the pin **(B)**. Use a pencil to transfer this line to masking tape on the base and lid **(C)**. Center the hinges between these lines and they will be square. These lines are for reference only—the spacer determines the actual positioning of the hinges.

Clamp the spacer between the base and the lid **(D)**. You'll probably need to block up the lid to make it level with the base. Lay out the hinges so that you'll install each one identically—one hinge leaf has an even number of knuckles, and the other is odd. It doesn't really matter how you orient them as long as they are the same.

(Text continues on p. 36.)

E

F

G

H

Carefully position a hinge so that the barrel's axis is centered over the spacer, then drill a pilot hole and screw down one leaf with a single screw.

Double-check that the hinge is still square to the box, and secure the other leaf. Secure the other hinge using the same procedure, then finish drilling the remaining pilot holes **(E).** Use a striking knife or crafts knife to score the wood fibers along each hinge's outline **(F).** Start with light pressure for the first cut, then slice deeper in a series of passes.

Lettering the hinges and the lid lets you quickly replace each hinge in its home **(G).**

Remove the hinges and unclamp the parts.

There are two different ways to mortise the hinges—you can cut a full-depth mortise in the box's base, or cut half-depth mortises in both the base and lid, as I did. When you set the router's depth of cut, you'll also want to create a slight clearance gap along the back edge of the lid.

Clamp a scrap board to the box's outer edge to prevent tearout and to increase the bearing surface for the router's baseplate. Rout the mortises in the base and lid **(H).** I used a ⅛-in. bit in a laminate trimmer, a combination that provides adequate power with excellent control. How close you dare to rout to the layout lines depends on your courage, experience, and whether you drink espresso or decaf.

To complete the mortises, begin with a vertical chisel cut at each end **(I).** Next, put the chisel's bevel against the routed bottom of the mortise to

> See *"Preventing Bound Hinges"* and
> *"Setting the Mortise Depth"* on p. 22.

finish removing the waste at the ends. Now you'll change tactics because a vertical chisel cut along the grain could split the delicate wall near the inside of the box. Use a crafts or utility knife to deepen that score line with repeated passes. Finally, remove the waste with the chisel, slicing along the grain with the bevel down. You already drilled the pilot holes for the hinges, so the only thing that remains is screwing the hinges into place (**J**). The completed installation has an unobtrusive look (**K**).

You'll need to install some kind of stop to keep the box lid from falling over backward.

► See *"Slotted-Bar Lid Stop"* on p. 73.

VARIATION If you want to skip the lid support, you can use a hinge with a built-in stop. The geometry of this hinge is a bit different from an ordinary butt hinge because you have to leave the entire hinge barrel proud of the back of the box so that it will operate properly. In addition, you can't lay it flat to utilize the method described above, so you'll have to rely strictly on measuring and marking.

► If the lid doesn't fit perfectly on your first try, see *"Fixing Hinge Mortise Problems"* on p. 43.

VARIATION

A

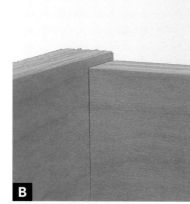

B

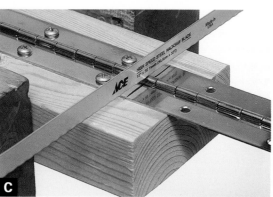

C

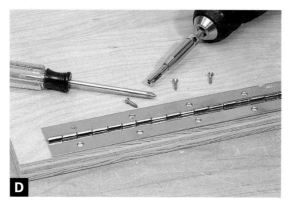

D

Piano Hinge

To create an easy mortise for a piano hinge, simply make the back of the box narrower than the sides and front. To determine how much narrower, measure the diameter of the closed hinge's knuckle, and subtract 1/16 in. **(A)**. That subtraction will help make sure that the front of the box always closes neatly.

➤ See *"Preventing Bound Hinges"* on p. 22.

When you assemble the box, the narrower back makes a full-length mortise **(B)**. In this example, I knocked together a quick plywood carcase to check the proportions of a blanket chest I'm designing.

Mark the cutline on the hinge, and cut it to length by using a hacksaw with a blade that has 32 teeth per inch **(C)**. Cutting the hinge about 1/16 in. shorter than the mortise will help ensure that the hinge will be able to move without scraping against the carcase. Screw the hinge to a scrap block to ensure that it won't flex while you're cutting. File away any cutting burrs.

Keep construction simple by planning the size of the top so that you can mount the hinge flush with the top's rear edge. That way, the only measuring involved is centering the hinge end to end. Drill pilot holes, and drive the screws **(D)**.

Position the other leaf of the hinge on the back of the box—flush with the inner edge is a typical position—and fasten it in place **(E)**. For neatness and maximum strength, use a screw in every hole. A back view of the completed installation shows how the lid is slightly above the back edge of the box **(F)** so that it will always shut completely at the front.

VARIATION For utility applications—where strength is more important than appearance—you can surface mount a piano hinge using the same procedure that you would for individual hinges. Making toolboxes or shop cabinets are two typical applications for surface-mounted piano hinges.

See *"Simple Box Hinge"* on p. 31.

VARIATION Piano hinges available from Rockler, including the specialized flange-leaf type shown here, have slotted screw holes that provide easier positioning and installation. They are available in a variety of sizes for any application.

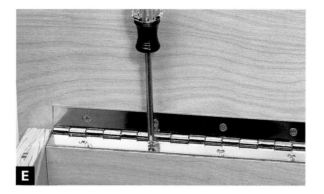

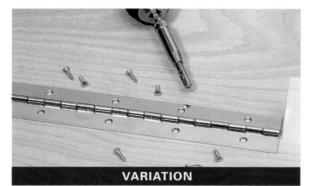

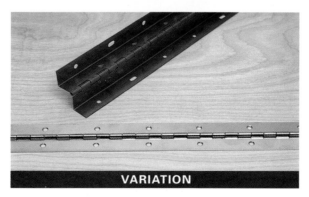

Template for Hinge Mortising

It's always a good idea to test the settings of a jig on scrap stock instead of immediately routing a completed door or carcase. Once you have the adjustments dialed in, you'll be able to move through your project quickly and confidently.

To allow the hinge to fit easily into the adjustable template, unscrew the finials **(A)** or withdraw a removable pin. Clamp the vertical wood fence of the jig to your door, and lightly tighten the knobs. Put the hinge into the opening of the template, slide the bar snugly against it, and tighten the knobs **(B).** To set the width of the mortise, measure the hinge **(C).** With the finials on this hinge, I could bury the hinge only up to the barrel. If your hinge doesn't have finials, you can go further. Transfer this measurement to the edge of the door **(D).**

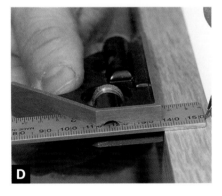

Loosen the knobs under the fence, and move the jig forward or back until its back edge touches the width line you marked on the door. Tighten the knobs, and check for square by measuring the distance from the edge of the jig to the fence **(E).** When the measurements are equal at both ends of the jig, it is square to the fence and therefore square to the door.

Loosen the clamps that hold the fence to the door, and move the edge of the jig's opening where you want to install the first hinge. Use a utility knife to score the wood fibers at each end of the opening **(F).** This will help prevent tearout when you rout the mortise.

Put the piloted bit (supplied with the jig) into your router, place the router atop the jig, and hold the hinge under the jig to set the depth of cut **(G)**. I set the depth of cut at slightly less than half of the hinge knuckle's thickness so that the latch side of the door would close snugly.

▶ See *"Setting the Mortise Depth"* on p. 22.

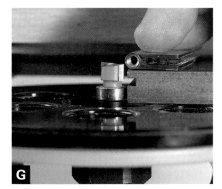

When you rout the mortise, start with a light pass along the edge of the door, rout clockwise around the perimeter of the jig's opening, and finally clear out the waste in the center of the mortise **(H)**. The completed mortise is nearly ready to receive the hinge **(I)**.

▶ To trim the corners of the mortise, see *"Squaring a Routed Hinge Mortise"* on p. 42.

If this test mortise isn't long enough to accept the hinge, you can easily fine-tune the fit. Simply loosen the knobs that hold the sliding bar, and again place the hinge in the opening. But this time, add a piece or two of self-stick notepaper between the end of the hinge and the jig. Try another test mortise until you have the setting perfect.

Routing mortises into a carcase follows the same procedure described above. But bear in mind that the length of the jig may create a clearance problem, requiring you to cut the mortises in the carcase components before assembling them.

VARIATION With this jig from Rockler, you can purchase inserts that match a variety of hinges. The insert shown in the photo matches the butler-tray hinge resting on the jig.

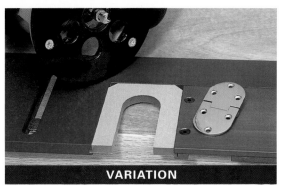

VARIATION

A

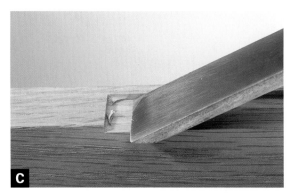

B

C

VARIATION

Squaring a Routed Hinge Mortise

Using a template to rout a mortise can be a great convenience, and if the hinge has radiused corners, you can immediately install it. But if your hinge has square corners, you'll have to do a little bit of chisel work. Interestingly, this is one of the few cases where cutting corners means making them square instead of rounded.

This technique is fast and easy if you have a razor-sharp chisel but slow and difficult with a dull tool. So the first job is to hone your chisel.

With your workpiece securely clamped, register the backside of your chisel against the end of the mortise, rock it to extend the line of the mortise, but don't overshoot the back wall of the mortise **(A)**. As the chisel approaches vertical, gently push downward to deepen the mark. Repeat at the other end of the mortise.

Switch your attention to the back wall of the mortise. Again, use the register and rock motion to extend the line **(B)**. But be careful because too much pressure could make the cut run with the grain instead of in a straight line. Work back and forth between the end of the mortise and the back wall until the lines meet. Hold the chisel vertical at the end of the mortise, and push down to further deepen the line. Now you can turn the chisel bevel down and clean out the waste (**C**).

VARIATION If you need to clear a lot of mortises (or just want a cool tool), consider a corner chisel. You simply register it against the routed mortise, and lightly tap with a hammer to mark a perfectly square corner. Then you use your regular chisel bevel down to clear the waste. Some corner chisels are spring-loaded, but this one from Lee Valley uses rare earth magnets to hold the cutter against the registration block.

Fixing Hinge Mortise Problems

Sometimes, you'll need to fine-tune a hinge mortise to achieve a perfect fit. The lid of the box shown in the photo **(A)** hangs over the base— a dentist would call this an overbite problem. There are two possible cures—either move the hinge in the base backward, or move the hinge in the lid forward. I figured that shimming the back wall of the base mortise might be more visible, so I opted to fix the lid.

The size of the overbite indicates the amount that you'll need to increase the mortise. Measure or mentally note this dimension, and remove the lid from the box.

Set a cutting gauge to score a line indicating the new width of the mortise **(B)** and remove the waste with a chisel. By placing a sharp chisel on its side, you can use it like a miniature cabinet scraper to remove tiny shavings of wood **(C)**. As you work, you can check your progress by sliding the lid onto the hinges that are still attached to the base **(D)**.

You'll have to plug the old screw holes so you can attach the hinges in their new positions **(E)**. Cut or split strips of wood, and glue them into the old holes. Snap the strips sideways, and clean up any splinters above the surface of the mortise with your chisel. Drill new pilot holes, and attach the hinges to complete the installation.

VARIATION Sometimes you'll need to add a shim to change the depth, width, or length of a mortise. The photo shows a wide range of shopmade and purchased shim stock: masking tape, chipboard recycled from a cereal box, index cards, sheet veneer, handplane shavings, veneer edgebanding, aluminum foil, sheet brass from a hobby shop, and metal flashing.

A

B

C

D

E

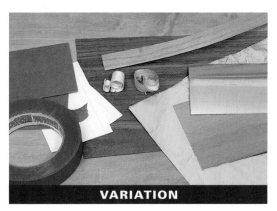
VARIATION

Installing a Passage Door

The idea of hanging a passage door intimidates some people, but it's really not a scary project. By using a mortising jig, you can set the hinges quickly and accurately. The Porter-Cable 59370 jig shown in the photo **(A)** works for hinges that range from 2½ in. to 4½ in. in ½-in. increments. You can use hinges that have square corners or a ⅝-in. radius. Move the spacers to match the size of hinge you'll use, and keep the spacers centered in the opening. For a square-cornered hinge, you'd swap the spacers end for end. To install a 4½-in. hinge, you'd omit the spacers. If you're hanging a batch of doors, you'll save time and possible errors by purchasing three jigs and attaching them to a ¾-in. plywood upright.

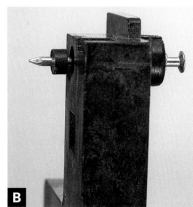

Remove the washerlike plugs from the template, and use them to secure the duplex (double-headed) nails to the body of the template **(B).** Without these plugs, you'd be constantly juggling the nails every time you moved the jig.

The bit supplied with the jig has a ½-in. cutting diameter and a ⅝-in. top bearing. Chuck it into your router, turn it upside down, and place the hinge on the jig atop the baseplate **(C).** Make certain that the bent (swaged) portions of the hinge don't interfere with setting the bit's depth.

Tape a quarter **(D)** to the head jamb of the door and measure downward for the position of the hinge mortises—7 in. from the top, 11 in. from the bottom, and the third centered between those two. Measure all locations from the coin taped to the head jamb. The quarter establishes the reveal at the top of the door because when you transfer the measurements to the door you simply hook the tape over the end of the door. As a result, each location will be automatically offset by the thickness of the quarter.

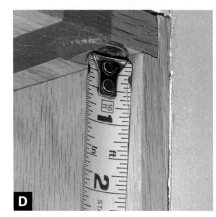

The side-to-side position of the gauge on the jamb is dictated by the thickness of the door **(E)**. Align the ends of the rectangular openings in the gauge with the edge of the hinge jamb. Tap the nails to hold the template to the jamb. Align the top of the hinge opening with the mark on the jamb, then drive the nails. The lower head of the duplex nail secures the template firmly.

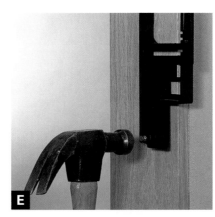

To rout the hinge mortise, first make **(F)** a light cut along the edge of the jamb. Rout clockwise around the perimeter of the template, and clear out the waste in the center. Be sure to hold the router baseplate flat against the template as you rout. When you remove the jig, you'll notice that the end of the mortise doesn't meet the pencil line because the router bit's cutter is a smaller diameter than its guide bearing. This doesn't make any practical difference as long as you always position the jig consistently for each cut. The completed mortise is a very good fit for the radiused hinge. Simply drill the pilot holes and drive the screws **(G)**.

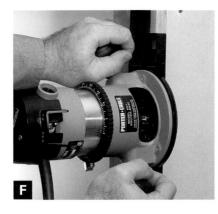

VARIATION To help prevent a door from sagging, replace one of the standard hinge screws with an extra long screw that will reach the stud. This procedure is a must when hanging heavy exterior doors because of their extra weight.

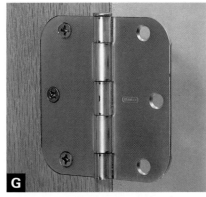

➤ If you are installing a hinge with square corners, see *"Squaring a Routed Hinge Mortise"* on p. 42.

VARIATION

Knife Hinge

A knife hinge consists of two leaves—you install the leaf with the pin to the carcase, and the one with the hole to the door. With the technique I developed, you use the leaf with the hole to lay out the hinge locations in both the door and carcase.

You'll need to rout the hinge's location in the carcase before you assemble it.

This hinge has a pin diameter of ³⁄₁₆ in., and I wanted to place the hinge's center of rotation just past the end of the door. To do that, tape a ⁷⁄₆₄-in.-dia. drill bit to the edge of the door, and place its shank inside the hole of the hinge leaf **(A)**. Hold the leaf approximately centered in the width of the door, and use a crafts knife to scribe its end.

Chuck a ³⁄₈-in. straight bit into your router, and set the height of the bit to match the thickness of a leaf **(B)**. Position your router's edge guide to center the bit in the thickness of the door, and rout the mortise **(C)**. Clamp a piece of scrap wood to the edge of the door to help prevent chipout. Always register the router's edge guide against the front of the door—you'll see why in a moment. Complete the mortise with a chisel **(D)**. Drill pilot holes, and attach the leaf **(E)**.

Following the same layout technique you used on the door, scribe a line on the carcase top and bottom at the end of the leaf **(F)**. You don't need to

be concerned with the front-to-back position of the leaf because the router's edge guide will take care of that. For a door that's flush to the front edge of the carcase, leave the edge guide positioned as it was when you routed the doors. Even if it's not perfectly centered in the door, the same offset will be transferred to the carcase, and you'll get a flush fit. I wanted to set the door back about 1⁄64 in., so that's the amount of distance I added between the router bit and the edge guide. Rout the mortise into the carcase **(G).**

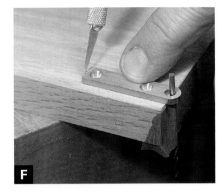

Square the mortise, and screw the pinned hinge leaf to the carcase **(H).** To install the door, screw all of the leaves in place except the top one on the door. Put the hole of the bottom door leaf onto its mating pin, and hold the door in its open position. Gently tilt the top of the door toward you far enough that you can place the last leaf onto its pin. Hold it in place with your finger while you slide the leaf into its mortise.

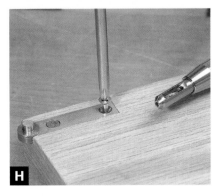

When you've completed the installation **(I),** the hinge is barely visible.

VARIATION To hang an inset cabinet door, use the L-shaped knife hinge to move the center of rotation past the front of the door. The same drill-bit technique you used for the straight hinge will accurately position the hinge on both the door and carcase. Use a piece of plastic laminate to set the distance from the carcase side. Scribe the outlines of the mortises, and chisel them. Once you've installed the hinges, there's no tidy way to change their position.

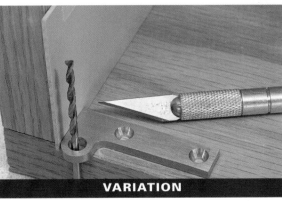

VARIATION

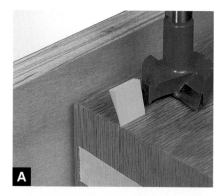

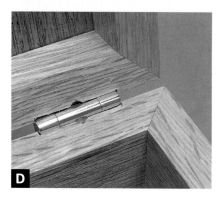

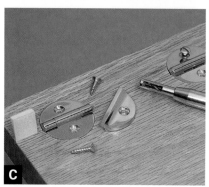

Round Hinge

Installing a round hinge requires a bit of careful setup at the drill press, but once you've done that, the rest of the steps are so fast and easy you may almost feel guilty that you've finished so quickly.

Begin by putting four thicknesses of self-adhesive notepaper near the ends between the base and lid so they won't interfere with hinge placement **(A)**.

> **For the reason behind this gap, see**
> *"Preventing Bound Hinges"* **on p. 22.**

Carefully align the edges and ends of the base and lid, and tape them together, using package-sealing tape or masking tape. Clamp a high fence to your drill-press table so that the base and lid cannot move while you're drilling them. Make certain that the fence is square to the table. Decide on the placement of the hinges, and center the tip of a 35-mm Forstner bit in the middle of the base-lid gap.

Drill the hole 1/32 in. shallower than the thickness of the hinge so it will sit slightly proud of the wood **(B)**. Drop the hinge into the hole, and align its pin with the joint between the base and lid **(C)**. Drilling pilot holes and driving the screws completes the job. You can purchase an optional stop for the hinge (it's shown by itself in the center and installed on both hinges in photo **(E)**. Use the longer screw supplied with the stop to install it atop the bottom half of the hinge. When you untape the box and open it, you'll notice that the tip of the Forstner bit made tiny V-shaped notches in the base and lid **(D)**. This adds an interesting detail, and I mention it only so that you're not surprised by it.

The completed box **(E)** has a clean and sophisticated look.

Installing Euro Hinges

Using a jig is a quick way to locate and drill hinge-cup holes into doors without repetitive measuring. This economical jig from Rockler is also great for job-site work where you don't have access to a drill press. But a drill press is handy for initial setup of the jig. Referring to the installation data supplied by the hinge manufacturer, find the diameter and depth of the hinge-cup hole, and use your drill press to drill a hole of those specifications into a scrap board. In this case, the hole's diameter is 35 mm and its depth is 13 mm. Take the scrap board to your workbench, put the jig plate atop it, and add the drill assembly. Loosen the stop collar on the drill **(A)** and push the bit to the bottom of the hole, fully compressing the spring. Tighten the stop collar, and you're ready to use the jig. Label the hole in the scrap board, and save it for future setup reference.

Mark the hinge positions on the door. Make certain to screw the jig-plate assemblies to the wood mounts so that you'll get the required hole setback from the edge of the door. Assemble the jig by sliding two or more plate assemblies plus an end stop onto the rail. Adjust the plate assemblies to coincide with the hinge locations, and turn the knobs to lock the plates and end stop in position. Use the toggle clamp attached to the wood mount of the plate assembly to lock the jig onto the door. Chuck the drill assembly into your drill and engage its rim onto the plate **(B)**. If you have a substantial number of holes to drill use a corded drill. Remove the jig after you drill all the holes. Insert the hinge into the hole and make certain that its arm is square to the door **(C)**. Drill pilot holes and drive screws to secure the hinge.

[TIP] **To drill hinge-cup holes at the drill press, you can establish the offset by using a drill bit with a diameter equal to the offset. Simply place the bit between the 35-mm drill bit and the fence (D).**

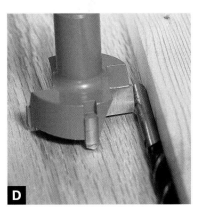

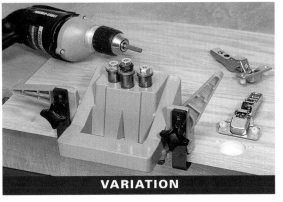

VARIATION

VARIATION **The Ecodrill from Blum drills the 35-mm hinge-cup hole at a variety of offsets. You can simply dial in the offset using the orange cams (visible against the edge of the door). In addition, you can drill 8-mm holes for press-in bushings that expand by driving a system screw. The Ecodrill is particularly well suited to job-site work.**

A

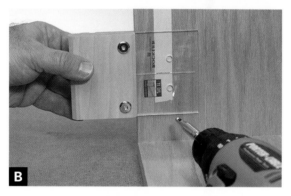

B

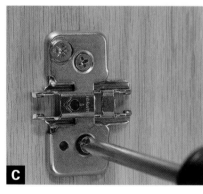

C

D

Euro Hinge Mounting Plates

If you use a jig to help you drill holes for hinge-mounting plates, be sure that the jig absolutely matches the hole pattern in the plate. In addition, you'll need to pay attention to the different positions required for hanging a door in an inset position compared to overlay. For example, the Rockler jig shown in the photo **(A)** has two ways that it can be attached to its wood baseplate, depending on whether you're using the inset or overlay position. Strip the brown protective paper off of the plastic, and position the plastic so that the scored centerline will be against the cabinet when the jig is in use. Insert the bolts, and tighten them.

Mark the centerlines of the hinge locations onto tape on the inside of the carcase, and place the jig so its scored line is over the mark **(B)**. Use a self-centering drill bit to drill pilot holes for the mounting screws. Strip away the masking tape, and screw the hinge-mounting plates into position **(C)**. With this baseplate, an arrow points to the front of the carcase to help avoid mistakes.

Snap the arm of the hinge onto the mounting plate, and adjust the fit of the door. In the photo **(D),** the screwdriver is in the screw that will adjust the amount of overlay.

By moving this screw by different amounts in the upper and lower plates, you'll set the overlay and level the door. Next, adjust the screw at the top of the mounting plate to raise or lower the door's position. Finally, adjust the screw at the rear end of the hinge arm to move the door in or out.

VARIATION 1 The photo at right shows an incredibly well-designed baseplate jig from Blum. After you mark the centerline of the hinge's location in the carcase, you position the jig so that the line meets the apex of the V-shape in the jig. Using a stop collar to prevent the 5-mm bit from drilling too deeply, you drill the first hole. Rotate the jig toward you, and position the metal pin into the first hole. This re-centers the jig and ensures perfect hole-to-hole spacing.

VARIATION 1

VARIATION 2 The Quick Fix is another useful Blum jig. The vertical metal channel holds as many of the orange jigs as you wish to use, and you can easily lock them at any location. The pin at the bottom left of the jig registers against the inside bottom of the carcase, while the flange at bottom right holds the door at any over-lay or inset you wish to set. Tap the point of the supplied metal stylus through the jig's holes, and you can mark hinge and mounting-plate positions in doors, carcases, or even in components before assembly.

VARIATION 2

VARIATION 3 Yet one more Blum jig uses screws to register the position of a postlike mounting plate screwed to the rear face of a face-frame cabinet. Use the holes in the side of the jig to position a mounting plate that's positioned on the edge of the face frame.

VARIATION 3

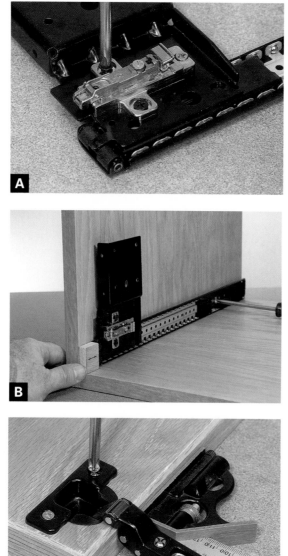

Pocket Door Slides

Combining a Euro hinge with a door slide may seem like a mixed marriage, but the result—a pocket door slide—is one of the key components in many home entertainment centers. The doors swing open, then glide backward into the cabinet to give a nearly unobstructed view of the television as well as clear access to all of the interconnected components. For this use, the slides usually handle vertical doors, but they can also be mounted to the underside of a horizontal carcase member for a retracting door like that used in barrister bookcases. The slide used in this demonstration requires a specific type of Euro hinge for the inlay installation shown, although you could choose a different hinge and achieve an overlay fit. Be absolutely certain that the hinges you select are one of the types recommended by the slide's manufacturer.

The slide has a detent that locks its motion when the door is pulled fully forward. This mechanism is the bent piece of metal engaging the roller in the lower left portion of the photo **(A)**. Use the supplied tapping screws to attach the hinge's mounting plate to the plate of the slide.

Measure the thickness of your door, add ⅛ in., and make a gauge block that length. Hold the block against the detent roller **(B)** of the slide, and drive a screw into a pilot hole drilled into the slot near the back of the slide. (The slide manufacturer supplies black screws, but I temporarily substituted bright ones for photographic clarity.) Slide the plate mechanism backward, and drive another screw into the slot at the front of the slide. Attach the upper slide in the same manner, butting it against the interior top of the carcase.

Rip a piece of stock 2¾ in. wide to serve as the follower strip that unites the two slides. Screw the follower strip to the plates of the upper and lower slides **(C)**. The follower strip ensures that the slides move at the same speed to prevent

the door from racking. I chose edgebanded plywood for this application because it's more dimensionally stable than solid wood.

Drill the hinge-cup holes in the door at the location dictated by the hinge model you selected. Use a square to ensure that the hinge arm is perpendicular to the door **(D)**, and drive the hinge screws into pilot holes in the door. Snap the hinges on their mounting plates **(E)**, and adjust the door in its opening.

> **See *"Euro Hinge Mounting Plates"* on p. 50.**

Install the plastic pivot block at the edge of the door **(F)**. By installing the center screw as shown in the photo, you can slide the block slightly forward and back until you have its location perfect. When properly positioned, the block's edge will touch the door as it moves forward and back and will also just contact the back of the door when it's closed. The pivot block prevents damage to the door by preventing it from rotating before it's fully extended. Install a block to the carcase near the top and bottom of each door. After you have the block's position settled, drive at least one more screw through it to lock it in place. If your slide doesn't come with these blocks, you can buy inexpensive plastic rollers that serve this same function.

Snapping the cover plate onto the hinge arm conceals the adjustment screws, giving the completed installation **(G)** a cleaner look. Drive additional screws into holes in the slide's track to fix it in place. Clean any chips out of the slide track because this debris can cause sluggish operation or damage to the slide's bearings.

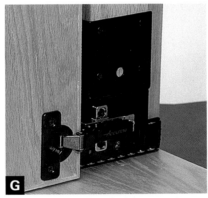

VARIATION

VARIATION Mount the slides onto the interior top of the carcase, and you can make a self-storing horizontal flipper door mechanism. Make a door frame with a glass insert, and you'll have the smoothest-operating barrister bookcase mechanism in town.

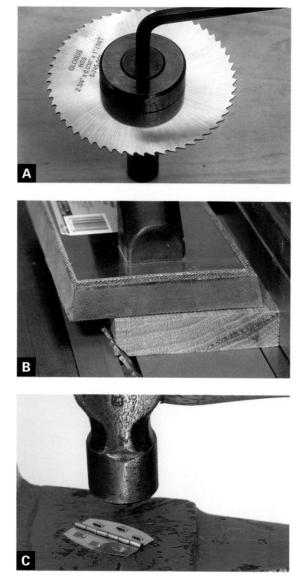

Barbed Hinge

Barbed hinges are a good choice for production work because you can perform the machining steps quickly and accurately. And installation is speedy because there are no pilot holes to drill and no fasteners to drive. In fact, you can complete the installation with your bare hands.

But as with most labor-saving processes, you'll need to invest some time up front if you want to save time later. Building a jig for your drill press is one task, and patiently setting up the height and depth of cut, as well as precisely positioning the stops are other requirements.

Begin by installing the circular blade onto its arbor **(A)**. There are two different sizes of barbed hinges, and you'll need to make sure that you purchase the correct diameter blade for the hinges you've chosen. Make certain that the blade's teeth are pointing in the correct direction to cut when you chuck the arbor into your drill press.

Prepare the back edges of the box's lid and base by cutting or routing a 1/4-in.x 45-degree chamfer **(B)**. The exact size of the chamfer isn't critical— ¼ in. is merely a convenient size that's large enough to function as a stop for the lid. For this demonstration, I used two pieces of ¾-in.-thick stock to make a box with a recess routed in it for a micrometer. This is the same type of construction you would use for making pen presentation boxes. At this point, you should chamfer all of your box parts plus a few extras to use in setting up the location of the kerfs. This is also a good time to apply the finish to all of the box components.

Inserting the hinge into a kerf is a one-way trip because the barbs will grab the wood and rip out chunks of it if you try to remove the hinge. So for the test-fitting, flatten the barbs of a couple of hinges by tapping them flat on a metal surface

(C). Don't get carried away with your hammering, or you could warp the leaves, making the hinge look like a potato chip.

Set the saw at its approximate height in your drill press, and make the fence assembly shown in the drawing at right. Attach only the left fence half to the 2x2 base, leaving the other half loose while you set the saw's depth of cut. On a piece of scrap stock, draw a line ¹⁄₁₆ in. farther from the edge than the width of one of the hinge's leaves (D). Position the fence so that the blade's projection meets the line, then clamp the fence firmly in position. Attach the right half of the fence, covering as much of the blade as possible without touching it.

Put a box component near the blade, and adjust the table so that the blade's lower edge is about ¹⁄₁₆ in. above the tip of the chamfer (E). Clamp a stop block to the left fence to cut the first set of kerfs (F). To make the cut, hold the end of the stock against the stop block, and rotate the box part into the blade running at 250 rpm. After you've made all of the cuts at this setting, rip a kerfed test strip about 1½ in. wide, and place it upside down into the stationary blade so that you can set the stop block at the next position (G). Using the same technique as you used for the first set of cuts, make this second slice into each workpiece (H).

(Text continues on p. 56.)

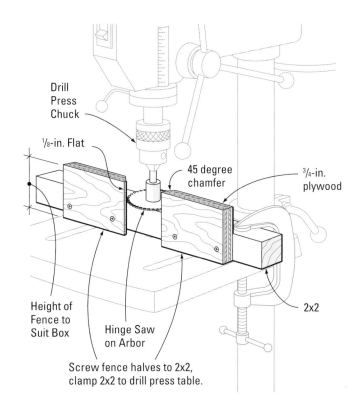

Drill Press Chuck

¹⁄₈-in. Flat

45 degree chamfer

³⁄₄-in. plywood

Height of Fence to Suit Box

Hinge Saw on Arbor

2x2

Screw fence halves to 2x2, clamp 2x2 to drill press table.

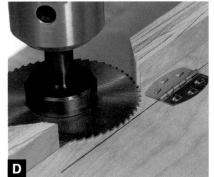

D

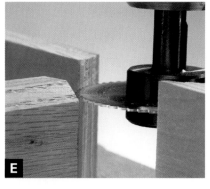

E

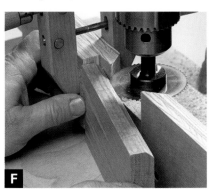

F

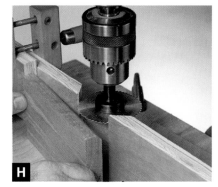

G

H

The blade has very little set, so it's not efficient at ejecting waste from the cut. Therefore you'll need to use compressed air or lung power to blow the fine dust out of each kerf. Press the hinges into the base of the box, using a piece of scrap wood to save your thumb **(I)**. Clamp a wood fence to your workbench, and register the ends of the box against it as you press the hinges home into the box top **(J)**. The halves of the completed box fit together tightly **(K)**. If you want to build some clearance into the box, simply insert a pair of narrow spacers between the base and lid when you press the parts together.

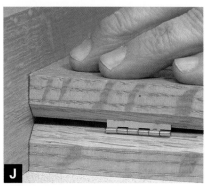

VARIATION Another way of putting a slight space between the base and lid at the back end is by positioning the kerf just below the tip of the chamfer. This places the knuckle of the installed hinge between the base and lid.

➤ See *"Preventing Bound Hinges"* on p. 22.

VARIATION

Barrel Hinge

The barrel hinge demands careful layout and drilling because the only axis on which you can shift the hinges after installation is up or down in their holes. Begin by putting the hinged edges of the box's base and lid next to each other, and block up the lid so it's flush with the base **(A)**. Mark the centerpoints of the hinge locations on strips of masking tape. I centered the holes in the thickness of the box's sides, but moving the holes closer to the outside of the box would have permitted a closer ultimate fit between the lid and base.

Attach a high fence to your drill press, and make sure that it's square to the table. Position the tip of the brad-point bit at the centerpoint, and drill the hole **(B).** Note that you'll position the blocking under the lid so you can use one depth setting for all of the holes. The depth of the hole depends upon the diameter of the hinge you've selected, so consult the hinge's packaging for this data. For some reason, neither of the 14-mm drill bits I have produced a hole large enough to permit insertion of these 14-mm hinges. Even removing the tightening screws from the barrels didn't help. So I resorted to using a small carving gouge and round file to enlarge the holes **(C).**

When you insert the hinges, place the base and lid next to each other, and clamp on a straight

(Text continues on p. 58.)

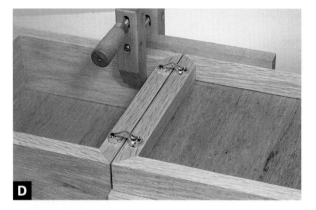

D

E

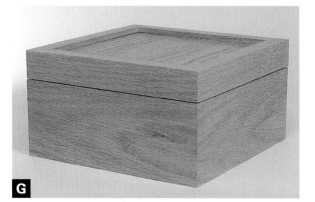

F

edge to keep the two parts aligned **(D)**. Position the end of the hinge barrel flush with the wood, and tighten the screw that slightly expands the barrel to firmly grip the wall of the hole **(E)**. For extra holding power, you can drive a screw alongside each barrel **(F)**. The countersink is partially formed in the barrel, but you'll need to use a countersink bit to extend the recess into the wood.

One drawback of the hinge results from the fact that its design prevents it from overclosing—moving past a zero position when closed. As you can see in the finished box **(G)**, leaving a large enough space at the back of the box so that it can open results in a gap all around the box. While this "levitating lid" look is not what I had planned, it is interesting. I'm considering running chamfers along the mating edges of the base and lid to accentuate the effect.

G

Soss Concealed Hinge

The hinge manufacturer makes a jig that simplifies making the two-level mortise. Having a single jig means that you'll need to install it at each hinge location to rout at one level, then relocate it to rout the second part of the mortise. If you get into production involving these hinges, you'll save big blocks of time by ganging several jigs onto a single fixture and having a router dedicated to each mortise depth setting.

To make the jig work, you'll need a router guide bushing: Porter-Cable No. 42024 (Lock Face Routing) and nut. Depending on the hinge you're installing, you also need a specific diameter router bit—verify the size when you order the jig.

Install the bushing in your router's baseplate, and chuck in the bit **(A).** Put the jig atop the inverted router, and set the height of the bit to match the flange of the hinge **(B).**

Flip down the spacer at the end of the jig, register it against the end of the door, and hold the locating pins against the outside face of the door **(C).** Choose the smaller of the two pairs of nails furnished with the jig, and tap them through the jig into the edge of the door. Referring to the chart supplied with the jig, drill a starter hole approximately centered within the jig's outline. The diameter and depth of the hole will vary depending on the hinge size you've selected. In this case, it was a ⅜-in. hole ²⁷⁄₃₂ in. deep. (Although the chart specifies hole depths to ¹⁄₆₄-in. tolerances, that degree of accuracy is not actually necessary.)

If you use a fixed-base router, tip it on edge atop the jig, start it, then angle the bit into the starter hole. Rout two clockwise passes around the jig's perimeter **(D),** and make sure the router's handles don't hit the nails. Shut off the router, and let the bit stop before you remove it so you won't accidentally damage the jig.

(Text continues on p. 60.)

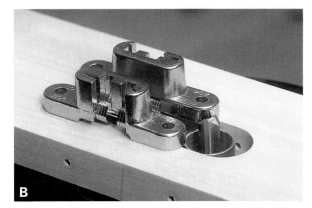

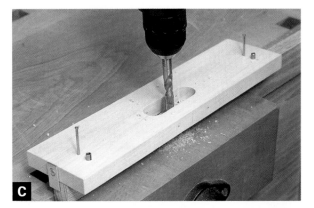

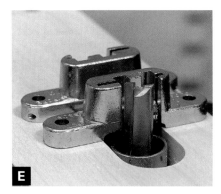

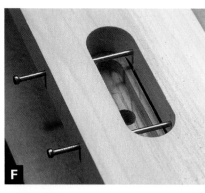

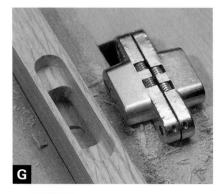

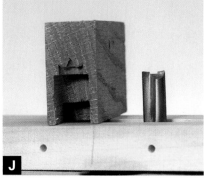

VARIATION

Move the jig to each hinge location, and rout the first mortise in all of them. When you position the jig to rout the mortises in the stiles, turn the tab at the end of the jig so it can rest flush on the wood. The tab automatically sets the reveal at the top and bottom of the door.

Put the jig atop the router again, and advance the bit to set the depth of the second mortise that accommodates the body of the hinge **(E)**. I know I probably should have routed this depth in a series of shallower passes, but then I realized that the surface quality of this cut was inconsequential and that the router simply needed to hog out the waste. Use the remaining set of nails furnished with the jig to confine the router's travel to the central portion of the jig **(F)**. Reinstall the jig on the door by fitting the nails into their original holes and then tapping them slightly deeper. Rout the second level of the mortise.

The next photo **(G)** shows the hinge next to the completed split-level mortise. The hinge fits perfectly if its surface is flush with the door. If the shallow mortise is too deep, you can add shims under the hinge. Drill pilot holes, and drive the screws to secure the hinge **(H)**. The completed installation operates smoothly and is invisible from both sides when the door is closed **(I)**.

To make your router setup easy the next time you install these hinges, cut a successful test mortise in half **(J)**. You can then use this gauge block to quickly set the depth of the starter hole and both levels of the mortise.

VARIATION If you don't want to invest in the jig, bushing, and bit, you can mortise these hinges using a drill and chisel. The instruction sheet packed with the hinge includes templates for the various sizes so make sure you use the template that matches the hinge size you purchased.

Glass Door Hinge

When you shop for glass door hinges, pay attention to the subtleties of design and installation. Some hinges screw to the cabinet, while others utilize bushings you insert into the carcase. You'll also find free-swinging designs and those with a self-closing feature.

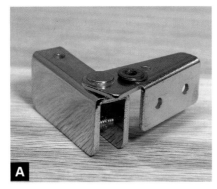

At first glance, this glass door hinge design looked like a real winner—you simply tuck it into the corner of a carcase, drive three screws, and you're finished. But when I turned the hinge over, I discovered a shortcoming. The pivot rivet extends beyond the base flange, so driving the bottom screw would tilt the hinge backward.

Fortunately, there's an easy solution, as shown in the photo **(A)**. By adding a couple of no. 6 brass washers between the flange and the bottom of the carcase, you can keep the hinge level. Thread the attachment screw through the base flange and washers, and drive the screw into a pilot hole in the bottom of the carcase **(B)**. Note that the front of the base flange is flush with the front plane of the carcase. Visually check that the hinge is level, and drive screws through the side flange into the side of the carcase. Install the upper hinge in the same manner.

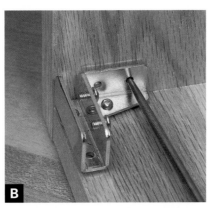

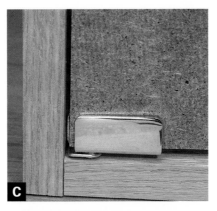

Cut a piece of ¼-in. plywood or hardboard to verify the size of the glass you'll need and to check operating clearances **(C)**. Take the pattern to the glass shop, and order your glass.

When you install the glass, use the metal plates supplied with the hinge between the screws and the glass **(D)**. If you want to stick the plate to the glass, peel the backing off the double-faced tape. The completed installation **(E)** doesn't draw much attention to itself. Instead, it keeps the focus on the contents of your cabinet.

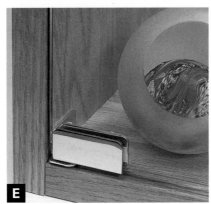

Pivot Hinge

A pivot hinge is the key piece of hardware that puts indoor gliding rocking chairs and porch gliders into motion. The pivot hinge shown here was developed by Rockler and provides a sturdy, weather resistant solution to this heavy-duty application. The nylon sleeve for the pivot hinge is $\frac{7}{16}$ in. long and is designed to sit at the bottom of a 1-in.-dia. counterbore. So the first step is to drill this counterbore to a depth $\frac{7}{16}$ in. less than the thickness of the stock. The easiest way to do this is to use the sleeve as a gauge against the end of a Forstner bit in your drill press as shown in the photo **(A)**. To verify the setup, drill a counterbore near the end of a scrap board **(B)**. Once you establish the setting, it will be accurate regardless of the stock's thickness. Drill the counterbore at the desired location, and change to a ½-in. bit in the drill press. Use this bit to drill through the stock **(C)**, centering the hole in the counterbore.

Drill a ½-in. hole ⁹⁄₁₆ in. deep in the other piece of stock **(D).** Mix up some epoxy and use a nail to wipe a small amount onto the wall of the hole. Align the holes on the flange across the grain **(E),** drill pilot holes, and drive the screws. For extra strength, you may want to substitute longer screws if your stock will accept them. Put the washer with the large hole onto the shaft of the bolt, add the other piece of stock with the nylon sleeve, put the washer into the counterbore, and tighten the nut with a ½-in. socket wrench **(F).** Tighten enough to remove any play in the joint while still allowing free motion.

VARIATION The Roto-Hinge has the virtue of very easy installation—simply drill holes in each piece of stock, and glue in the wood bushings for a virtually invisible pivot joint. On the downside, the shaft is a small-diameter rivet that is adequate for light-duty applications but may not have the shear strength required in large-scale applications.

VARIATION

Rule Joint

If a challenge makes you happy, the rule joint will turn you positively ecstatic. Although none of the individual installation steps are particularly complex, it's difficult to visualize the center of rotation for this joint because it's literally buried within the tabletop. If you've never made this joint before, I'd strongly recommend that you practice on some scrap material until you understand the processes. When you've produced a successful joint, you can then use the practice pieces as gauge blocks to duplicate the machine settings for your good material.

Rip and joint the boards for the tabletop, and check that their mating edges are straight and square. If you don't start with a seamless joint, the following steps will simply make the fit worse. Postpone any shaping of the tabletop's perimeter until after you've successfully made the joint.

Get a matched set of router bits to cut the halves of the rule joint **(A)**. For the ¾-in.-thick material for this tabletop, a set with ½-in. radius roundover and cove is just right. Adjust the fence on your router table so that it is flush with the edge of the roundover bit's bearing, and rout along the edge of the piece that will be the stationary part of the tabletop. The finished side of the top will be against the router table. Of course, you'll advance the bit in steps to ensure a smooth cut. For the final cut, leave just a sliver—¹⁄₁₆ in. or less—along the stock **(B)**. If you removed the entire edge, there wouldn't be enough support along the outfeed portion of the fence, so you'd end up with a cut that wasn't straight. Plane away the sliver by hand, and slightly round this bottom edge of the joint so it won't interfere with the operation of the top.

Chuck the cove bit into your table-mounted router, and place one of the table leaves face up on the router table. Rout along its edge in steps until the depth of the flat matches the fillet that is next to the roundover on the top **(C)**. Check your progress until the two pieces of stock match. Placing two thicknesses of self-adhesive notepaper simulates the clearance that you'll build into the joint. Use a striking knife and square to extend the line of the top's fillet down each end of the board.

Turn the top over, and connect the two end lines by striking a line along the bottom. Cut the notepaper into slim strips, and place them between the fillet on the top and the flat on the leaf. Position the hinge face up (countersinks showing) and with the short hinge leaf on the top **(D)**. Make certain the centerline of the hinge pin coincides with the line scribed on the bottom, and trace the perimeter of the hinge with a striking knife.

Mortising to the thickness of the hinge leaf won't be quite deep enough because you must also allow for the sliver you planed off during the roundover. Refer to the drawing at right to see the geometry of the hinge placement. Set your laminate trimmer's depth setting by gauging against the hinge, then add a little more depth to match the thickness of the sliver **(E).** Rout close to the outlines, then complete the waste removal with a straight chisel.

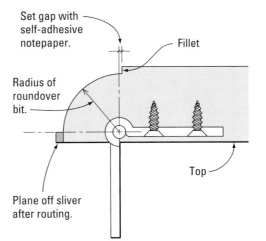

Set gap with self-adhesive notepaper.

Fillet

Radius of roundover bit.

Plane off sliver after routing.

Top

Draw parallel pencil lines indicating the position of the hinge barrel, and use a small carving gouge to excavate the recess. As long as you bury the knuckle, the depth is not critical—just be careful not to break through the top **(F).** Secure

(Text continues on p. 66.)

▶ See *"Squaring a Routed Hinge Mortise"* on p. 42.

Troubleshooting the Rule Joint

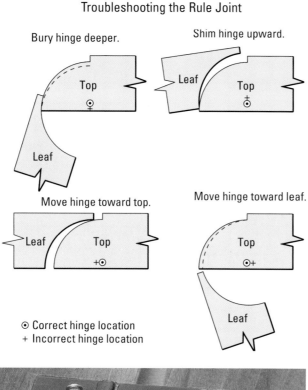

Bury hinge deeper.

Shim hinge upward.

Move hinge toward top.

Move hinge toward leaf.

⊙ Correct hinge location
+ Incorrect hinge location

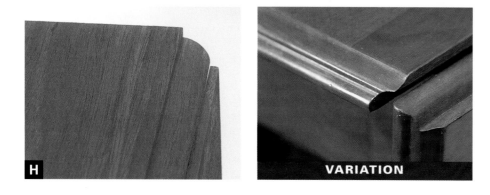

G

H

VARIATION

each hinge leaf with a single screw driven into a pilot hole **(G).** Turn over the tabletop and gently try its action. If the movement isn't perfect, refer to the troubleshooting drawings at left, and correct the position of the hinge.

Resist the urge to simply sand the roundover or cove to correct a poor fit. Instead, get the best action possible by patiently adjusting the position of the hinges. As you shift the hinge, you may want to drill a new pilot hole in one of the unused holes in the hinge leaf. When the joint fits as well as you can make it, you can resort to sanding to deal with any remaining high spots. There should be no wood-to-wood contact as the joint moves, and you should allow a bit of extra clearance for the thickness of the finish.

The completed rule joint **(H)** is the result of perseverance in fitting. Disassemble the components for finishing, and then drive screws into pilot holes to secure the hinges.

VARIATION People say that there's an exception to every rule, and the rule joint is no exception. This vintage gate-leg table shows reversed edge profiles, with the cove in the top and the roundover in the leaf.

Lid Supports and Stays

Lid Supports

➤ Slotted-Bar Lid Stop (p. 73)
➤ Mortised Lid Support (p. 74)
➤ Toy Box Lid Support (p. 76)

Overhead Door Supports

➤ Support for an Overhead Door (p. 77)

IN MANY APPLICATIONS, hinging a cabinet door is only part of the challenge. To finish the job, you must make certain that the door won't swing too widely, damaging a wall or another portion of the cabinet. Although you may be tempted to rely on the hinge to limit the maximum opening angle, doing so will put strain on both the hinge and your cabinet. Sooner or later, one or the other will fail.

You have several choices for hardware that will limit the opening angle of a door. A simple chain stay is easy to install and is effective on cabinet, wardrobe, and armoire doors. Use a pair of wire cutters (also called diagonals) to snip off unneeded links or balls. If you use ball chain for a door, choose the no. 10 size.

Rigid stays may be straight or curved, and both types are easy to install. Simply screw the hinged mounting plate to the back of the door, open it to the desired angle, and screw the small mounting plate to the underside of the cabinet's top. For small to moderately scaled doors, you can use the chains and stays that also serve as lid supports for boxes. For larger-scale applications, choose hardware, such as the wardrobe stay, that's designed to handle the strain. Mounting the wardrobe stay is similar to installing its smaller cousins, and you use the thumbscrew to hold the door open at any desired angle.

► LEFT, RIGHT, LEFT, RIGHT

Knowing left from right is handy for all sorts of tasks: putting on your shoes, following driving directions, marching, and installing drop-front and lid supports. There's nothing complicated about it. For a box, position it so that the hinges are away from you, and the left and right of the box match yours. For a drop-front desk, its left and right match yours when you lower the flap toward you.

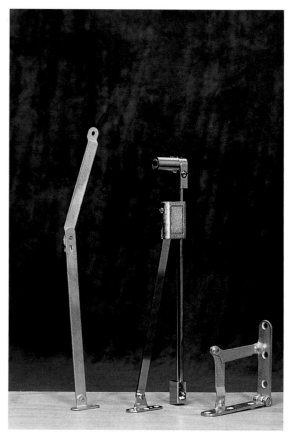

Drop-front hardware includes (left to right): a hinged arm, a vertical rod with an integral magnetic catch, and a stay that's a part of a mortised hinge.

Use door-restraint hardware to prevent damage to the cabinet itself and its surroundings. The chain and downscale stay examples can also be used on small to medium boxes. The wardrobe stay that's screwed to the door and face frame is designed for bigger doors or boxes.

Drop-Front Supports

The drop-front desk is a time-honored classic because of the quiet efficiency of its design. Its writing surface takes up no space when not in use and has the added virtue of instantly hiding clutter when you raise it. But the most fun of a drop-front desk is its self-cleaning feature—when you raise the flap, everything that was on the writing surface tumbles into the desk.

Supports for drop-front desks range from the simple to the sublime. At the low end of the spectrum is a simple hinged arm that's typically reversible for right- or left-handed

You can build a special mechanism into your desk so that moving the drop front activates the support slides. The hardware features low-profile hinges and a low-profile price tag.

applications. The vertical rod is a more sophisticated design, incorporating an adjustment screw that lets you control the speed at which the lid lowers. This type may also include a friction or magnetic catch mechanism that keeps the lid shut.

Another variation uses air pressure within a cylinder to control braking action. Twisting the cylinder rod increases or decreases pressure to meet your needs. A combination hinge and drop-front support eliminates the need for separate hinges, but unlike the other supports that are surface-mounted, it must be mortised.

The most sophisticated piece of hardware in this category automatically pulls out and retracts wood arms that support the writing surface when you move the drop front. In contrast to the surface-mounted alternatives above, you gain an uncluttered work surface. You may be surprised that this hardware kit costs only about $15. Unlike hardware that's applied after a piece is completed, this mechanism becomes an important part of the desk's inner workings.

Supporting Hinged Lids

A length of chain fastened to the lid and side of a box is an easy and economical way to limit the lid's backward travel. For a small box, you can choose no. 3 chain, which is available in the familiar ball variety or in a more decorative ball and bar style. The larger no. 10 chain is more suitable for large boxes or as a door restraint. A variety of end anchors makes it easy to secure the chain to the lid and side of boxes in virtually any design. But chain often has the annoying habit of getting caught between the lid and base and may damage the wood when it does.

You can choose a plain slotted arm support, but if you get one with a friction knob you can lock the lid in an upright position. A slotted arm with a notch is another way to support a lid. Screw the hinged bracket to the box's lid so that the notch points upward when the support arm is level. To install this type, partially drive a screw through the slot

and into the box's side so that the shank engages the notch at the desired lid angle. When a box's limited depth prohibits the use of a straight slot, choose a curved support—the shape provides increased travel while reducing overall length. Another strategy for shallow boxes is a folding lid stay. Some folding stays use a detent mechanism that clicks or snaps to hold the lid upright. To disengage this type, you push at its midpoint.

You'll notice that some supports have a mounting plate that's fastened to the underside of the lid. Other stays are simply flat pieces of metal that you attach to the inner edges of the lid and base.

Of all the lid supports, the one that you mortise into the side of the box is the most difficult to install. But if you invest the work, you'll be rewarded with a very clean look and dependable operation.

Supporting Jumbo Lids

The dainty hardware suitable for jewelry boxes and humidors doesn't have enough muscle to hold the lid of a blanket or cedar

Chain is an economical lid support, but it can get caught between the box's lid and base.

chest, lidded bench, or hamper. Fortunately, several of the supports are available in sizes scaled up to the challenge of these larger projects. One traditional solution is called a cedar-chest hinge and lid support. Actually, it's a set of right- and left-handed hardware that combines the hinge and support into one unit. In its raised position, the surface of the lid is about $^3/_8$ in. inboard of the back of the chest. Another piece of combination hardware moves the lid further backward, up to 1 in. past the rear of the chest.

Although technically not a lid support, there's a piece of specialty hardware that raises the inner tray (also called a till) of a cedar chest as you lift the lid. You'll also find this design in a downscaled version that lifts a till inside a jewelry box. Another choice is a spring-loaded support that prevents the lid from slamming. This item is available in right- or left-handed versions, and either can be center mounted.

Overhead Door Supports

Designers of aircraft interiors have long recognized the enormous storage potential of overhead bins. Now this hardworking style of storage is finding its way into home offices, kitchens, baths, and media rooms. When you close the doors of overhead bins, all of your disorganized belongings are hidden so you appear instantly organized. That's a real improvement over being disorganized *and* looking disorganized.

There's an incredible variety of lid stays on the market, but understanding a few basic types will guide you to one that's right for your project. The first type is a simple mechanism that locks when you raise the door to 75 degrees. Raise it slightly higher

A hinge/support combination (far left) moves the chest's lid farther backward than the traditional cedar chest hinge (second from left). The cedar chest hinge reinforces the rear corner and holds the lid upright. The next mechanism to the right raises a till as you open the lid. Select a self-balancing lid support (second from right) by calculating the torque of the lid. The toy box support (far right) also requires you to figure the lid's torque. See the sidebar on p. 72 for more information on computing torque.

▶ AN EASY TORQUE CALCULATOR

If you've ever done any automotive work, you've encountered the concept of torque as a measure of the turning force applied to a bolt. In a similar way, the hinged lid of a wood box exerts force as it arcs downward to the box's base. When you want to overcome that torque with a self-balancing lid support, you need to calculate the amount of torque in a unit called inch-pounds (IP). To do this, simply multiply one-half of the front-to-back dimension (in inches) of a lid by its weight (in pounds). For example, if a cedar chest lid measures 20 in. and weighs 6 lb., then 10 in. x 6 lb. = 60 IP. If you're using a single support, purchase one that meets the full torque requirement. If you split the work between two supports, divide the total torque in half to get the rating for each support.

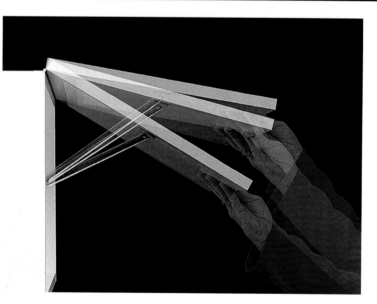

The basic lift-lid support (left) holds at 75 degrees and disengages when you raise the lid slightly higher. Hold onto the lid to lower it to the closed position.

to disengage the mechanism and lower the door. This economical lid support is the kind you'll likely find in woodworking-supply catalogs.

But if you search out specialty hardware suppliers, you'll find more complex (and costlier) mechanisms. These may provide stopping action (holding the door open at any desired angle), braking action (a cushioned descent to prevent slamming), or both stopping and braking action. Seventy-five degrees is a standard support angle, but you can buy some styles of stays that open to 90 or 110 degrees. These greater angles are helpful for eliminating interference with the lid when accessing the cabinet's contents or for bins that are mounted lower on the wall. The third type of lid support uses an adjustable pneumatic (air) cylinder to provide lifting and holding action. If you have a vehicle with a hatchback, you're already familiar with the concept of pneumatic lift cylinders.

Slotted-Bar Lid Stop

There is a wide variety of lid stops: Some attach to the bottom of a slab lid, whereas others are fixed to the inner edge of a box lid. Regardless of the exact setup, the installation basics are the same.

Tilt the lid backward about 5 degrees past vertical, and clamp or brace it into position. Test-fit the hardware, holding it in position against the side and lid, with the slotted bar at an angle of 30 to 45 degrees with the side **(A)**. Mark the position of the lid plate, drill pilot holes, and attach it. Mark the location of the screw in the side of the box, drill a pilot hole, and partially drive the screw. To lower the lid, you'll need to lift the slotted bar to disengage the shank of the screw from the notch **(B)**.

VARIATION Substituting a curved bar gives you the same amount of travel with reduced overall length. That means you don't need as much depth in the box for the stop to operate.

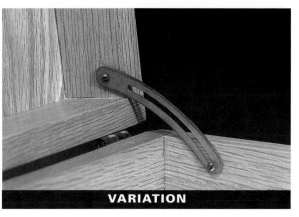

VARIATION

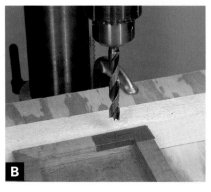

Mortised Lid Support

When you mortise the lid support into the side of the box, you virtually eliminate the possibility of snagging the box's contents and you also create an unobstructed interior. You can then fill the clear interior space with trays that slide or lift to maximize the storage capacity. But those advantages come with several disadvantages. First, the support is pricey. Second, the installation procedure is as unforgiving as an army drill sergeant. Third, you'll do the installation into a box that's already been assembled and finished, so a mistake transforms your project into kindling.

This style of lid support is manufactured by Brusso in two sizes: with a body that is ¼ in. wide by 2⅞ in. long or ⅜ in. wide by 4⁵⁄₁₆ in. long. Choosing between them is more a matter of the scale of the box and aesthetics than holding power. The supports are unhanded, meaning that they can be installed into either side of a box. The photos show the larger size being installed.

Hinge the lid onto the box, and prop up the lid so that it's level with the base. Apply a strip of masking tape along the lid and end of the base so you can make your layout marks **(A)**. First, draw on the tape the key reference line, the centerline of the hinge pin. Measure 1½ in. from that centerline onto the lid, and mark the centerpoint of the hanger stud. Turn your attention to the end of the box, measuring ¾ in. from the hinge pin's centerline, and mark one end of the mortise. From that point, measure and mark the other end of the mortise 4⁵⁄₁₆ in. toward the front of the box. Draw a centerline along the thickness of the box's side and lid. Remove the lid, take it to your drill press to drill the ⁷⁄₁₆-in. hole ⁷⁄₁₆ in. deep **(B),** and strip off the tape. Take the base of the box to

your drill press, chuck in a ⅜-in. Forstner bit, and drill a hole at each end of the mortise **(C)**.

Remember that the layout marks you made indicate the end of the mortise, so the centerpoint of your drill bit goes ³⁄₁₆ in. toward the center of the mortise. With a Forstner bit, you can drill a line of overlapping holes to remove the bulk of the mortise's waste to its ¾-in. depth. Remove the remaining waste using a chisel **(D)**. Test-fit the support body into the mortise, aiming for a fit that's perfectly flush with the upper edge of the box. Shim the mortise if it is too deep; continue chiseling if it's too shallow.

Tap the support body into place with a deadblow mallet **(E)** and screw it into the mortise. Reattach the lid, put a few drops of epoxy onto the lid stud, and push it into the hole in the lid **(F)**. The stud flares slightly, so resistance will increase as you push it into the hole. Make certain that the box closes easily: The pin on the end of the stud should drop neatly into the hole of the support body without binding. Add a lining to the interior of the box, and you're finished **(G)**.

VARIATION After drilling the end holes of the mortise, you may want to plunge-rout the mortise in three passes, advancing the bit in steps ¼ in. deep, until you reach the completed depth. Photo H shows using an edge guide and a ⅜-in. bit, but it would be safer to use a ¼-in. bit to remove most of the waste, and then use a chisel to complete the mortise to its full ⅜-in. width.

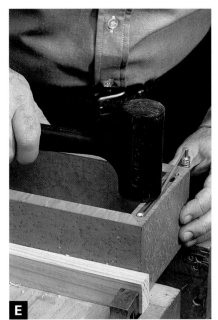

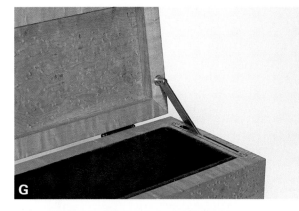

VARIATION

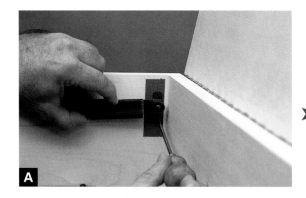

A

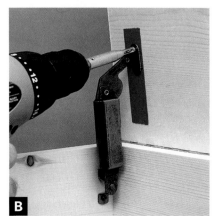

B

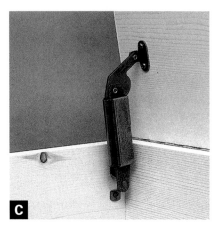

C

> ⚠ **WARNING** Safe installation and operation require that the mounting screws have a solid target that's at least ¾ in. thick. Use the largest diameter of screw in the greatest length that your project will hold.

Toy Box Lid Support

Before purchasing a toy box lid support, you need to figure the torque requirement for your lid.

> ➤ See *"An Easy Torque Calculator"* on p. 72.

Next, you have to choose the mounting location: left, center, or right. If you're using a single support, positioning it in the center is the best choice. Using a pair of right- and left-handed supports is another good strategy, especially for a long or heavy lid. No matter what mounting position you choose, the installation procedure is similar. The following demonstration will install a left-handed support.

Hinge the top of the toy box to the base.

> ➤ See *"Piano Hinges"* on p. 38.

The directions supplied with the support gave the location of the upper hole in the side mounting bracket at 1 in. from the centerpoint of the hinge pin and 1¼ in. from the rear face of the back (½ in. inboard from the ¾-in.-thick back). Mark this centerpoint on a strip of masking tape, position the support, and use a scratch awl to mark the centerpoint of the lower mounting hole **(A)**. Drill pilot holes, strip off the tape, and screw the bracket to the side of the toy box's base. Put a strip of masking tape on the toy box lid, and mark the centerpoint of the lower mounting hole for that bracket, positioning it 3 in. above the hinge pin's centerpoint. Swing the support against the lid, and mark the centerpoint of the other mounting hole. Drill pilot holes **(B),** strip off the tape, and screw the bracket in place. The support holds the lid open at an 85-degree angle **(C).**

Support for an Overhead Door

Even if your hardware comes with an instruction sheet, I'd strongly suggest that you do the trial installation suggested here to make sure that the support will function without banging into the bottom or back of your bin. The easiest time to install a support on an overhead bin is before you put it overhead and before adding the back. By placing the hinged bin on its side on your work-bench **(A),** you can position the fully extended support without being concerned that the door will smack your head or pinch your fingers. Rip a 4-in.-wide strip of plywood, and use your miter saw to cut a 15-degree angle on one end to gauge the 75-degree open angle of the lid. Nip off the corner of the gauge so the tip doesn't interfere with the piano hinge that joins the lid to the bin.

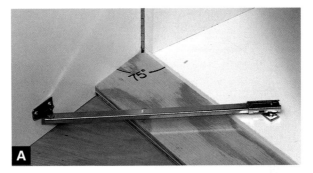

> ▶ See *"Piano Hinges"* on p. 38.

See *"Piano Hinges"* on p. 38.

Position the support's baseplate about 1¼ in. back of the front edge of the bin and about 1 in. below the vertical midpoint of the box. Extend the support until it locks, and place that baseplate against the lid. To hold the hardware in place while running it through its cycle, add small pieces of double-faced tape to each baseplate **(B).** The support should never touch the back or bottom of the bin. You can easily verify this by looking through the open back of the box **(C).** (In the photo, the bottom of the box is at the left.) If there is any interference, you merely reposition the baseplates and test again. You can leave the tape on the baseplates when you drill the pilot holes and drive the screws to secure them. Add the back to the bin, and hang it on the wall **(D).**

Catches, Latches, and Locks

Catches & Bolts

➤ Elbow Catch (p. 89)
➤ Hook Catch (p. 90)
➤ Magnetic Catch (p. 91)
➤ Bullet Catch (p. 92)
➤ Double-Ball Catch (p. 94)
➤ Flush Bolt (p. 95)

Locks

➤ Cam Lock (p. 97)
➤ Full-Mortise Lock (p. 99)

Escutcheons

➤ Surface Mounted Escutcheon (p. 101)
➤ Flush Escutcheon (p. 102)

S OMEWHERE THERE MAY BE a clever student of word origins who could explain the subtle differences in meaning among the words clasp, catch, and latch. But wherever that person is, you can be sure that he doesn't work for a hardware manufacturer or supplier because those sources use those words almost interchangeably. So this section will follow the same approach, using the terms you're most likely to encounter in hardware catalogs and retail outlets.

Latching Methods

Some latches are surface mounted and can be a bold accent on your project or a barely noticeable detail. Other catches are completely concealed when a cabinet's doors are closed. And locks range from traditional elegance to no-nonsense security. But all of the hardware in this section relies on three basic technologies:

• Mechanical latching/locking is the most basic system, and it is used with a wide range of hasps, hooks, and latches.
• Spring pressure is the basis for ball catches, bullet catches, and many other latches.
• Magnetism is a popular holding technology for many inexpensive catches. Move up the price line to the more powerful rare-earth magnets, and you gain impressive holding power.

Some latches combine two technologies. Touch latches, for example, usually employ a magnet at the end of a spring-loaded rod.

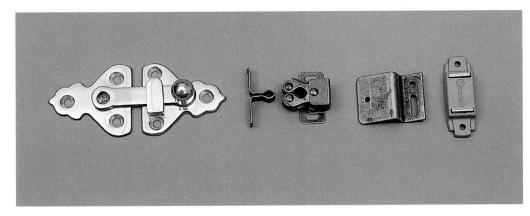

Here are examples of the three basic latching technologies (from left): mechanical, spring, and magnetic. Some other latches combine two of these holding methods.

Catches and Latches for a Single Door

The mechanical latches shown in the photo at right represent only a few of the many styles that are used for inset doors, those in which the surface of the door is flush with the cabinet's carcase or face frame. All of the latches shown are reversible, meaning that they can be used for either right- or left-handed doors. You can also use these types of latches to secure one door of a pair, but you'll have to add a separate piece of hardware to anchor the other door to the carcase.

▶ See *"Double-Door Catches and Latches"* on p. 82.

Surface-mounted cabinet latches have three dominant mechanisms: you can lift a bar, press or slide a spring-loaded handle, or twist a knob. Browse through hardware catalogs and you'll find a wide range of available shapes, metals, and finishes. Latches with a narrow baseplate permit mounting on a cabinet stile.

Mention surface-mounted bolts, and many woodworkers will think of the locking mechanism employed on old-fashioned screen doors. But this common mechanism

Surface-mounted mechanical latches are a no-nonsense way to keep a door closed. Catalogs offer a wide range of styles.

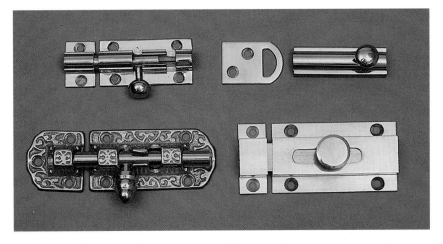

Surface bolts are a time-tested positive latching mechanism that can add a decorative accent to your project.

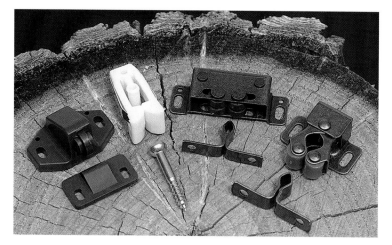

Single-door spring catches are available in a range of shapes and materials. You'll find spring pressures that range from mild to extra-strong.

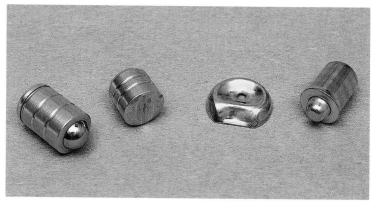

Bullet catches can be pricey for the machined version (left) or inexpensive for the hardware-store variety (right).

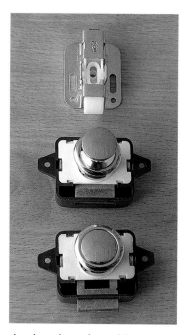

In the closed position at bottom, the push knob is nearly flush with the door's surface. Push the button once, and the knob springs outward (middle) so you can grab it.

is also available in upgraded materials and surface treatments: ornate work reminiscent of the Victorian age, highly polished brass, and sleekly contemporary. The quartet of surface bolts shown in the bottom photo on p. 79 only hints at the many styles that are available. The two bolts on the left have an almost identical action but completely different styling. The bolt at the upper right could also be used on the upper back of a left door to secure it to the carcase. The bolt at lower right has a distinctly contemporary look.

The push-button catch shown in the photo at left is a highly interactive piece of hardware. Push the button once, and the strike retracts as the button moves forward, revealing a knob for easy gripping. Close the door and push the button again to retract it and engage the strike. Its nearly flush mounting gives it a sleek look and also makes it ideal for use in tight walk-through areas. For all those reasons, it's a style that's often used in boat and recreational vehicle cabinets.

Catches Mount Inside a Single Door

Another category of catch mounts inside the cabinet and uses spring pressure or magnetism to grab and hold the door. When a cabinet door fits well, you can count on the light force exerted by a small catch mounted near the handle to hold it shut. But when you're faced with a door that twists, you'll appreciate the extra holding power of larger-scale catches. For example, if you have a kitchen cabinet door that gapes open at the top, installing a spring or roller catch can pull the door flat against the face frame.

The group of spring catches shown in the top photo at left offers a wide range of methods to hold a door. You may see some spring catches described as "friction catches." The plastic spring that captures the head of a bulb-head screw is an inexpensive choice: A package of 10 retails for a few dollars. The next two items are spring catches. The spear-shaped projection mounts on the door, and you need to plan its location carefully to minimize the risk of snagging clothing or ripping flesh. The one with the larger spear has a baseplate with heavier springs for increased holding power.

Magnetic latches include the familiar standby at left, the small alternative in the center, and the powerful rare-earth variety at right.

You'll find touch latches in many styles, shapes, and sizes. The one at top mounts on the surface, whereas the other requires you to drill a mounting hole for the press-in insert. You then screw the threaded latch body into the insert.

Bullet catches (sometimes called ball catches) are a popular and unobtrusive piece of hardware. But you'll have to tailor the gap of the door to meet the geometry of the catch or risk wearing a rut into the door's surround every time you open or shut the door.

The photo above displays three styles of magnetic catches. The type at left is widely available at many hardware stores. Slots in the plastic mounting plate allow you to adjust its location fore and aft. You install the magnetic catch at center by drilling the body into the door, giving this style a more discreet appearance. It's a catalog item useful for small doors that fit well. The powerful rare-earth magnet at right gains even more strength when installed in the optional and very inexpensive mounting cup. Simply drill a hole for the mounting cup, and secure it with a screw driven through the hole in the bottom. There's no need to glue the magnet in place—when you move it close to the cup, the magnet will literally jump into position.

Of all the items covered in this book, this one represents the only piece of self-installing hardware. You can purchase a steel washer to use as a target for the rare-earth magnet, but you may find that you'll get enough holding strength by simply counter-sinking the head of a steel screw flush with the wood.

A word of caution about magnets in general and the rare-earth variety in particular: It's a prudent idea to keep them away from computers, cathode-ray tube monitors and televisions, as well as magnetic data-storage media such as diskettes and tapes. The magnets could cause picture distortion and cor-ruption or loss of data. Maybe you'll be lucky and not have a problem, but there are so many latching choices that it's easy to pick another type to use near these sensitive applications.

Touch latches shown in the photo above offer good holding power and can completely eliminate the necessity for knobs. These latches are available in several different styles

➤ SHOPMADE DOOR STOPS

Stops prevent inset doors from swinging too far inside the cabinet. You can mount stops at the bottom of the door, the top, or at both locations. Here are several strategies for shopmade doorstops. In a face-frame cabinet, simply glue or screw a block to the top inner frame **(A)**.

At the top or bottom of the carcase, a ½-in. by ½-in. by ¾-in. block made from wood that matches the cabinet is a discreet but effective stop that's large enough for a pair of doors **(B)**. Drilling a ¼-in. hole for the #8 x 1¼-in. washer-head screw permits adjustment fore and aft as well as side to side. Adding tiny bumper dots muffles the sound when the door closes.

You can use self-adhesive felt dots, but I like the look of ⅜-in. shopmade leather dots. Buy a punch at the hardware store or from a leatherwork supplier, and within minutes you can hammer dozens of dots from a piece of scrap leather or even an old belt. Use yellow woodworker's glue to bond the leather to the wood.

You can easily make a stop for a single door by slicing a ⅜-in. length from a ½-in.-dia. dowel **(C)**. By offsetting the hole from the center, you create a cam action that allows you to fine-tune the fit of the door to absolute perfection. A quick production tip: Drill the mounting hole into a length of dowel immobilized in a hand-screw clamp, and cut a batch of stops to length.

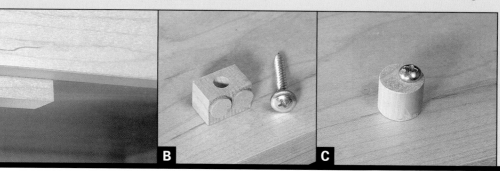

A   B   C

(some employ a magnetic latch, whereas others use a mechanical latch), but they all work on the same principle: As you press inward on the face of the door, the latch releases, and a spring-loaded mechanism pushes the door open far enough for you to grasp the edge of the door. To close the door, you gently press the face of the door until the latch engages. Touch latches can give your cabinet project a clean look, but at the same time, not-so-clean hands will be touching your carefully crafted doors. For that reason, touch latches are better suited to an occasionally used buffet cabinet than to a busy baking center in the kitchen.

Double-Door Catches and Latches

Whenever two doors meet without a cabinet stile between them, the traditional approach is to secure the left door to the cabinet or a fixed interior shelf using an elbow catch or sliding bolt. Then you can install a surface-mounted latch that secures the right door to the left one. The elbow catch is a surface-mount item, but some sliding bolts require careful mortising into the rear face and top of the door stile.

If you want to eliminate fumbling with a piece of hardware every time you open the

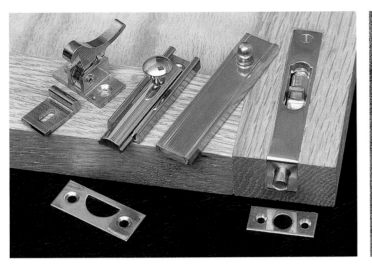

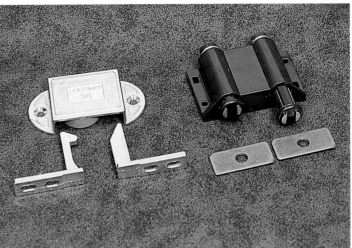

You can immobilize one door of a pair by surface mounting an elbow catch or sliding bolt. The sliding bolt at far right requires careful fitting into a mortise.

Secure a pair of doors with a mechanical catch (left) or touch latches in a double-wide baseplate.

left door, choose a library catch. This ingenious mechanism forces a spring bolt into the end of the left door when you close the right one. You can mortise the library catch into the carcase at the top or bottom of the doors' opening or at both locations for extra security. As a bonus for left-handers, you can even install the library catch so that the left door opens first.

If you don't need the security of rigidly latching both doors of the pair, you can choose among a number of latching solutions that combine two mechanisms into a single housing. You'll save space, money, and installation time. In addition, you'll be able to open and shut the doors in any sequence you wish.

Inventive minds have devised still other ways to secure a pair of doors. The latch shown at left in the top photo at right secures one door when you close the other. Like the library catch, you still need a lock or latch for the second door but you can decide which door you want to open first. On the negative side, you need to attach a 1-in.-long weapon-shaped projection to each door: One is a spear and the other is a hook. For safety, install these only where there is virtually no chance of metal-to-flesh contact. The more benign alternative shown at right is a pair of magnetic touch latches twinned into a single baseplate. Surprisingly, this double mechanism costs only slightly more than an individual latch.

Catches, Hooks, and Hasps

Look through this grouping, and you'll discover hardware that will secure lids from a dainty trinket box all the way to a job site-tough toolbox. The top photo at left shows catches that hook, snap, and latch. As a general rule, you fasten the smaller ones with escutcheon pins (usually supplied) and the larger ones with screws (sometimes you must purchase the screws separately). The draw latch, familiar from its use on toolboxes, provides a more secure lid-to-base connection than the models that simply snap shut.

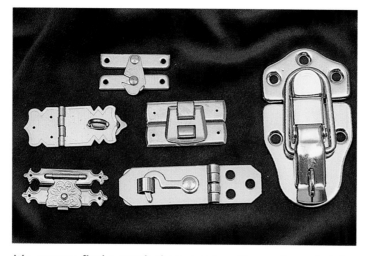

It's easy to find a catch that matches the scale and style of the boxes you build. Some hasps have an attached hook, whereas others permit you to add a small lock.

Mini padlocks make even ordinary boxes seem more important. Get a few extra locks to help childproof power tools.

Locks

Locks on small boxes and briefcases serve more of a psychological role rather than a practical purpose, but even a tiny lock makes a big statement—the contents are valuable. Although a briefcase may protect a peanut butter and jelly sandwich instead of top-secret documents, a pair of combination locks is absolutely essential.

Other locks serve a more practical role, securing the contents of desks, chests, and file cabinets.

Miniature padlocks are an inexpensive accessory for small boxes and can also prevent unauthorized use of power tools. Simply put the lock's shackle through a hole in the tool's plug as shown in the photo at left.

For larger-scale lock applications, consider a new padlock that has the styling of an antique. Nothing would ruin the look of a vintage trunk faster than sealing it with the combination lock you saved from your high school gym locker. The examples shown in the top photo on the facing page weigh in at about 1 lb. each and offer serious security. The lock with the square body is considered a trick lock because the visible keyhole is a ruse—you have to know the secret to reveal the true entrance to the six-lever lock. The lock with the ice shield that swings over the keyhole offers no deceptions, but it more than compensates by featuring an eight-lever mechanism, complex enough to frustrate most lock pickers less skilled than Harry Houdini.

While Houdini richly deserved his reputation as an escape artist who could get out of nearly anything, the average toddler has an equal ability to get into things. One way to protect youngsters from their own curiosity is the remarkably clever magnetic latch (bottom right). The latch and its strike are completely concealed by the door. When you bring the knob up to the door, its super-strong magnet retracts the latch and also attaches itself to the door, allowing you to swing it open. The magnet is powerful enough to work through doors $\frac{3}{4}$ in. thick, and you can recess the latch into thicker doors. In addition to child-proofing cabinet doors, you can also use this latch to create secret compartments that are safe from nosy adults.

Selecting a Lock

Selecting a lock is a three-step process:
• Define the use of the lock. For example, do you need a lock for a hinged door or one that slides, a cedar chest, or a drawer?
• Choose the installation method you prefer: surface mount, half mortise, or full mortise.
• Make certain that the lock and escutcheon are compatible with the style of furniture or cabinet you're building.

Getting down to specifics, you'll find two broad categories of locking mechanisms. One is a bolt that moves in and out of the lock's body, and the other is a cam that rotates. Let's start by looking at the bolt-action locks.

The use of the lock determines the shape of the bolt. For cabinets, clock cases, cup-boards, drawers, and doors, all you need is a straight-sided bolt that extends into a slot in the carcase or into a strike plate (sometimes simply called a "strike"). You'll notice that some locks have dual keyways, permitting them to be used horizontally as a drawer lock or vertically on a door. In almost all double-door applications, the lock body installs on the left stile of a right-hand door.

These padlocks have an old-fashioned look but are tough enough to defeat modern thieves.

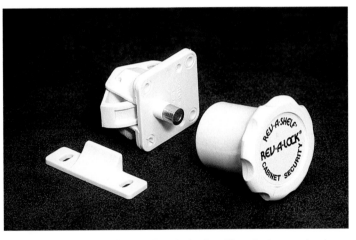

A magnet hidden in the knob is the "key" that unlocks this childproof lock.

The lock shown at left is designed for full-mortise installation into a right-hand door. The half-mortise lock shown at right has dual keyways so you can use it vertically or horizontally for a door or drawer.

For chests, sliding doors, overhead bins, and tambours such as a rolltop desk, you need a bolt that has hook-shaped latches that extend past the edges of the strike plate's opening to lock it. There are several variations on this theme. One style of lock has spring-actuated latches on the bolt. The full-mortise model shown at far left in the photo at left is particularly suited to installation on a tambour (rolltop) desk because it has a spring-loaded strike that maintains a smooth surface on the desktop and also keeps debris out of the strike. The full-mortise model (second from left) has a hook that moves up and to the side. The next lock has a bolt with a pair of hooks that move sideways into the strike. The half-mortise chest lock (far right) uses another variation, putting the hooks onto the strike plate.

The cedar chest lock and latch is in its own subcategory. This surface-mounted lock is sized for sides that are $7/8$ in. thick. You unlock the chest by turning the key and pushing the button. The model shown in the right photo below has a safety feature to reduce the chance of self-entrapment: You must also push the button to latch the chest.

Mortised and Surface-Mounted Locks

There is a wide range of locks that can be grouped into the three installation categories shown in the drawing at right: full mortise,

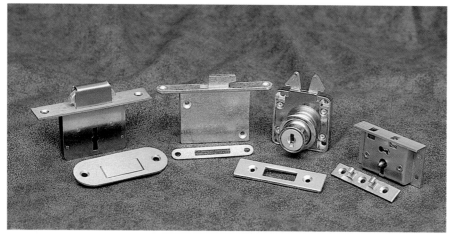

Locks suitable for chests, rolltop desks, and sliding doors have hooked latches that expand inside the strike plate for a firm grip.

A product of hardware evolution, this lock meets the specialized requirements of securing a blanket or cedar chest.

half mortise, and surface mounted. That sequence also describes the degree of difficulty involved in installation. Full-mortise locks can be a bit finicky, and surface-mounted locks are the easiest. On the other hand, a full-mortise lock can be a bit less expensive because it has less exposed metal that requires polishing at the factory.

From the outside of a solid cabinet, you can't tell the difference among these three types because all you see is the keyhole or escutcheon. However, if you're building a curio cabinet with glass sides, a half-mortise or surface-mounted housing will be visible, so you'll want to be sure that its metal and finish are compatible with the rest of your hardware.

Escutcheons

Escutcheons serve both functional and decorative roles. They protect the wood surrounding the keyhole from accidental key scratches and also provide a metallic contrast to the wood. As you can see in the photo at right, escutcheons range from starkly plain to wildly extravagant. Installation of a flush-fitting extruded escutcheon is an exacting task, but plate escutcheons can involve nothing more complicated than a couple of screws or some tiny nails called, appropriately enough, escutcheon pins.

Cam Locks

Cam locks get their name from the tailpiece that rotates to secure a door or drawer. Many locks come with both a straight and an offset cam (sometimes called a "tail") that can be mounted with the bend toward the front or back of the lock's housing. These arrangements create a choice of three offsets.

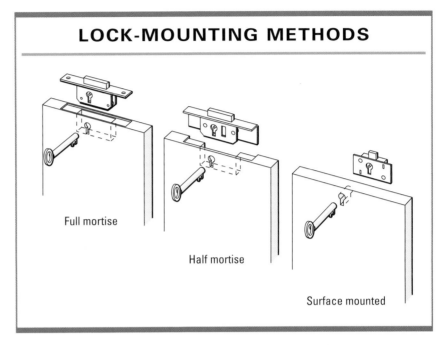

LOCK-MOUNTING METHODS

Full mortise

Half mortise

Surface mounted

Patina or polished, discreet or bold, plain or scrolled, this small sampling of escutcheons only hints at the vast variety available.

►LOCK-BUYING TIPS

- If you choose a full-mortise lock, carefully note the mortise size listed in the catalog description to make certain that your stock is thick enough to house it.

- Pay close attention to what's included with the lock you purchase. Some locks include a strike and escutcheon; others require that you purchase the items à la carte.

(Offset is the distance from the back of the housing to the cam's surface.) These options allow you to suit the lock to a variety of applications, whether your door is lipped, flush, or overlay. A square hole on the cam engages with a matching projection on the lock, so you can mount the cam in four positions: 12, 3, 6, and 9 o'clock.

When you order a cam lock, pay attention to the thickness of stock in which you can mount it. Hardware catalogs typically have locks sized for ³/₄-in. and 1¹/₂-in. stock. But some catalogs and nearly any local lock shop can supply cam locks for thin material, such as ¹/₄-in. plywood or acrylic or even sheet metal.

Hardware catalogs sometimes refer to cam locks as "cylinder locks" because of the shape of the housing. But to a locksmith, the cylinder or plug is the key-actuated mechanism that's inside the housing.

From thick to thin, you can find cam locks that secure a variety of doors and drawers. The lock shown at left has a mounting bracket that adjusts for panels that range from ¾ in. up to 1⅜ in. thick.

Elbow Catch

The elbow catch consists of two parts: the plate that attaches to the cabinet's carcase or a fixed shelf, and the spring-loaded hook that attaches to the door. If you're able to turn the cabinet upside down, you won't be fighting gravity during the installation process. Cut a piece of cloth double-faced tape, and attach it to the hook's baseplate **(A).** Engage the hook with the plate, and position them inside the carcase and against the closed door **(B).** Note that the hook doesn't bottom out into the carcase-mounted plate— hooking about two-thirds of the plate provides plenty of holding power while still allowing the door to close easily. Mark the centerpoint of the plate's mounting hole with a pencil. Drill a pilot hole, and screw the plate into position **(C).** Swing the door open, drill pilot holes, and screw the hook to the door **(D).** If you need to adjust the catch, loosen the plate's screw so you can move it forward or back. The completed installation **(E)** has a clean appearance and provides dependable performance.

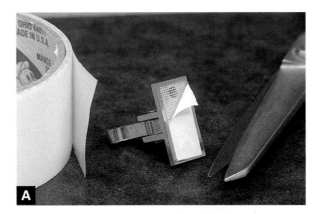

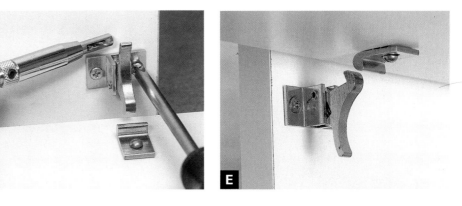

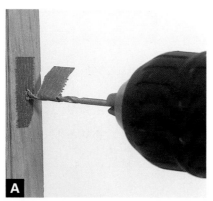

Hook Catch

A hook catch is uncomplicated, but knowing a few tricks will help you achieve rattle-free doors. Begin by holding the hook against the side of the carcase and the edge of the door, positioning it so that the hole in the hook is centered on the door's edge. Use a scratch awl to mark the center of the hook **(A)**. Drill a pilot hole, and partially drive a screw at this point **(B)**. Select a screw with a body diameter that matches the hook's slot. You'll notice in this photo that I like to have the door overhang the carcase about ¹⁄₁₆ in. at the latch side because it creates a shadow line on the carcase when viewed from the side. Engage the hook onto the screw, and mark the center-point of the pivot screw **(C)**.

Drill the pilot hole, and place a pair of brass washers onto the screw before screwing it in place **(D)**. The washers provide clearance to keep the hook from rubbing the finish off of your project. The properly fitted hook doesn't touch any wood—at the carcase or on the door **(E)**. If the hook doesn't seat fully, use a needle file to slightly reduce the diameter of the screw on the carcase **(F)**. Masking tape protects the carcase from scratches while you file. The completed hook installation **(G)** is neat, attractive, and absolutely efficient.

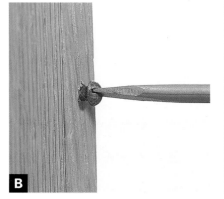

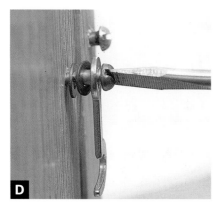

Magnetic Catch

To install a magnetic catch, put the flat plate onto the magnet, positioning its edge about ⅟₁₆ in. above the lower end of the base. Hold the assembly inside the carcase, with the base against a fixed carcase member, usually the underside of the top or a fixed shelf **(A)**. Incidentally, positioning the carcase upside down during this installation procedure puts gravity on your side. Use a scratch awl to mark the position of the mounting screws, centering them in the length of the base's grooves. Drill pilot holes and mount the base about ⅛ in. forward of its centered position.

With the plate still adhered to the base, firmly close the door to make an impression of the dimple in the plate into the door **(B).** Open the door, remove the plate from the magnet, and slide the plate lightly on the door until you feel the dimple fit into the hole it made in the door. Drill a pilot hole, and screw the plate into position **(C).** Turn the cabinet right side up. Loosen the mounting screws in the base, and adjust it until you're satisfied with the closed position of the door and the amount of magnetic pull **(D).**

VARIATION A touch latch, which has a spring-loaded catch in its base, is an evolutionary development of the basic magnetic catch, and installation is virtually identical until you get to the adjustment step. You'll have to do a little trial and error fussing with the position of the base until you achieve a good balance between easy opening action and good holding power.

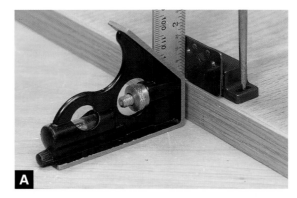

A

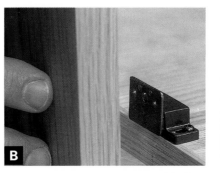

B

C

D

VARIATION

Bullet catch installation—cutaway view

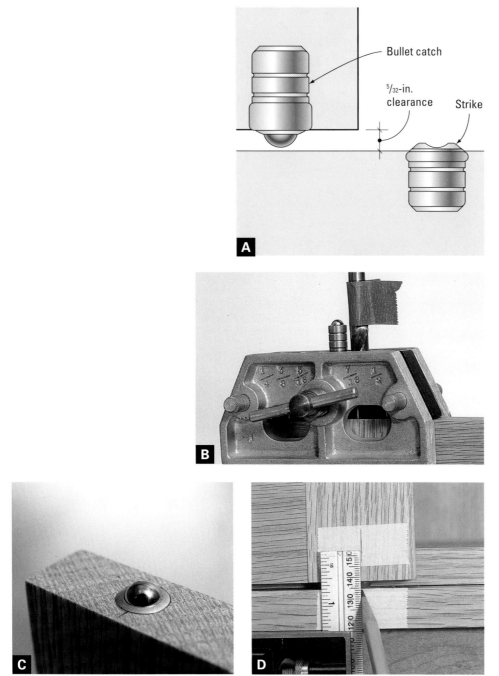

Bullet catch

$^5/_{32}$-in. clearance

Strike

A

B

C

D

Bullet Catch

At first glance, the bullet catch looks like a simple piece of hardware: It appears that you would simply drill a couple of holes, drop in the parts, and walk away. But anything named after ammunition can't be entirely innocent. The catch actually requires quite careful installation because it's virtually impossible to adjust after you insert the components. And installation is usually a one-way trip—removal involves damage to the surrounding wood. In addition, the design of the catch dictates the clearance from the bottom of the door to the carcase. For the catch I installed, the ball extends about 0.15 in. (slightly more than $^9/_{64}$ in.) from the shoulder of the cylinder **(A)**. That means you need to provide at least $^5/_{32}$ in. of clearance between the bottom of the door and the carcase or the ball will drag across the wood and wear a rut into it. But you can't increase the clearance by much, or the ball won't engage the strike. When you use a bullet catch, you'll need to utilize a cabinet design with a built-in door stop or add a separate stop to limit the inward swing of the door.

I installed the catch into the bottom of the door, but you can locate it at the top or at both locations. Hang the door onto the carcase, and adjust the clearance to $^5/_{32}$ in. where you'll install the catch. Remove the door, apply finish to it and the carcase, and put the door in your vise. Measure the barrel of the catch with a caliper and drill an exactly matching hole ($^7/_{16}$ in. for this particular catch) centered in the width and thickness of the door's stile **(B)**. A doweling jig will help you drill straight. Insert a brad-point bit into the jig, and lightly tap its end with a hammer to set the tip into the wood. You can then use masking tape to fairly accurately gauge the depth of the hole directly from the cylinder of the bullet.

As you near the marked depth, double-check the hole with an accurate depth gauge, such as the end of a vernier caliper. If the bullet is a snug fit, you can simply press it into the hole, but for extra security, use glue. I chose yellow woodworking glue (aliphatic resin) instead of messing with epoxy, although epoxy would certainly give a much stronger wood-to-metal bond. The shoulder of the installed cylinder should be flush with the end of the stile **(C)**. Rehang the door onto the carcase and swing it shut. Mark the center of the stile's width onto tape applied to its front, and transfer that centerline onto tape on the carcase **(D)**.

Open the door and transfer the line again, this time onto the base that is the target location for the strike. By measurement, mark the centerline of the door's thickness. At the crossmark you've created, drill a 7⁄16-in. hole to bury the strike up to its shoulder **(E)**. If the construction of your cabinet permits it, switch to a 1⁄4-in. bit to continue the hole through the carcase. This access hole will permit you to use a hammer and punch to drive out the strike if it ever needs to be replaced **(F)**. If you drill the hole for the bullet or strike too deeply, you can drop a washer into the hole before gluing the hardware into place **(G)**. The completed installation is barely visible but holds the door securely **(H)**.

A

B

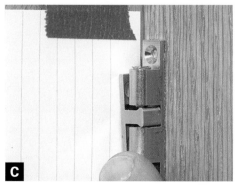

C

D

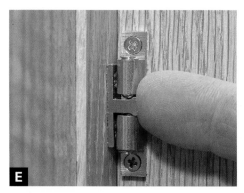

E

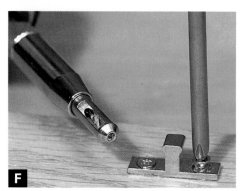

F

G

H

Double-Ball Catch

This little catch is one of my personal favorites for a number of reasons: It's small, inexpensive, easy to install, can be used horizontally or vertically, and also acts as its own stop. But the best feature is that it's so easy to adjust the latching pressure. You can get a firm grip for a stubborn door or light holding power for a clock case door.

Back off the adjustment screws on the female half of the base to minimize latching pressure (A). Attach double-faced tape to the base of the female half of the catch, trimming it to size with a crafts knife (B). Join both halves of the catch, and slide it into position until the tape on the base grabs the carcase (C). Taping a piece of index card to the inner face of the door positions the female baseplate so there will be a slight amount of tension between it and the male portion of the catch. Separate the catch, drill pilot holes, and screw the female half to the carcase (D).

Apply double-faced tape to the base of the male portion, join it to the female half, and close the door. Push on the male portion to adhere it to the door (E). If you can't reach inside the cabinet, reduce the catch's pressure by completely removing the upper ball and backing off the adjustment as far as possible on the lower ball. Screw the male baseplate to the door (F). Advance the adjustment screws until you get the amount of holding power you want (G). You can roughly judge for equal pressure at the top and bottom by noting the position of the setscrews relative to the housing. The completed installation is neat, functional, and adjustable (H).

Flush Bolt

Installing a flush bolt into the edge or back side of a cabinet door is not an easy task because there's nowhere to hide any imperfections in the wood-to-metal fit. To make it even more difficult, you also need to cut a mortise into the end grain of the door's stile. And if you go through all the steps to achieve a great fit, you then hide your careful craftsmanship—literally behind a locked door. Whenever possible, I'll choose another method of securing a door. But sometimes, you simply have to install a flush bolt, so here's how to do it.

Before you order a flush bolt, check its dimensions carefully. The bolt in this demonstration has a maximum thickness of ¾ in. at the top mortise, so that part would have poked through the front of a ¾-in.-thick door. Fortunately, I was working with a 1-in.-thick door **(A).** Place the bolt on its side on the stile. Using a square, ensure that the end of the bolt is flush with the end of the stile, and mark the lower end of the bolt. Looking at the bolt from the side **(B),** you'll see that when I set the router bit deep enough for the groove to house the spring, the mounting post for the screw would lose contact with the bottom of the mortise. To make up the difference, I figured that I'd have to add several no. 8 washers below the post.

Set the fence on your router, and cut the mortise to final depth by making several shallow passes **(C).** Use a chisel to square the end of the mortise **(D).** Test-fit the bolt into the mortise, chiseling the mortise wider, if necessary, until the surface of the bolt is flush with the rear face of the door. At this point, the end of the bolt can't reach the lower end of the mortise because you need to

(Text continues on p. 96.)

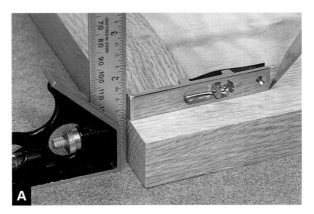

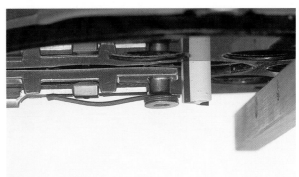

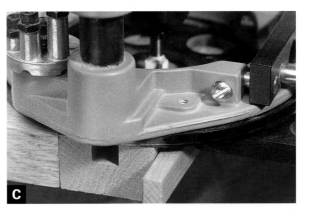

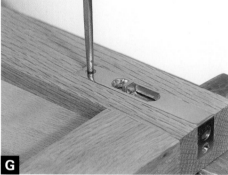

cut the mortise into the top of the door. Use a sharp crafts or utility knife to scribe the end of the bolt into the top of the door **(E)**. Chisel the mortise to fit the top end of the bolt **(F)**. You'll need an extremely sharp chisel to make smooth cuts into the end grain.

Place the bolt into position, mark the center-points of the attachment screws **(G),** and drill pilot holes. Remove the bolt, add washers under the screw post if necessary, and fasten it **(H).** After hanging the door, mark the end of the bolt with correction fluid **(I)** and press the bolt against the carcase to transfer the hole location to the cabinet **(J).** Drill a hole that's about $\frac{1}{16}$ in. larger than the diameter of the bolt. Position the strike plate around the hole, drill pilot holes for the screws, and drive them. Trace the perimeter of the strike plate with a crafts knife to scribe its location onto the carcase. Using a chisel, mortise the strike plate flush with the wood.

Cam Lock

When you buy a cam lock, make certain that its body length suits the thickness of the door stock you're using. The lock in this installation is adjustable for panels ¾ in. through 1⅜ in. thick, so the first step is to screw the flange in or out to match the thickness of your door **(A).** The spring-loaded black detents ride up and over the threaded part of the barrel as you rotate the flange. Make sure that the detents rest on the flats of the barrel when you've completed the adjustment. For the ¾-in.-thick door I used, I had to move the flange to the full forward position. I chose to use the straight cam (also called the tail) for this installation instead of the cranked cam that the factory attached to the lock.

Use a nutdriver **(B)** to swap the cams. At this point, don't worry about which of the four possible cam-mounting positions to use—lightly snug the nut with the cam seated in any position. To determine the mounting position on the door, measure the distance from the center of the mounting bolt to the tip of the cam **(C).** With this measurement, you can finalize the design of your door. The drawing at right shows how I positioned the lock in relation to the side of the carcase.

To accommodate the lock body plus the escutcheon for this lock, use your drill press and a Forstner bit to drill a ¾-in. hole into the stile of your door **(D).** Remove the cam so it won't be in your way as you center the lock body in the hole. I like to position the lock so the teeth on the key point downward as the key goes into the lock, but it will function just as well if inverted. Partially insert the press-fit escutcheon, and use a

(Text continues on p. 98.)

Cam Lock Installation

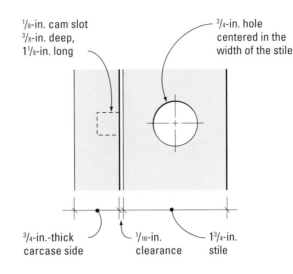

⅛-in. cam slot
⅜-in. deep,
1⅛-in. long

¾-in. hole centered in the width of the stile

¾-in.-thick carcase side

1/16-in. clearance

1¾-in. stile

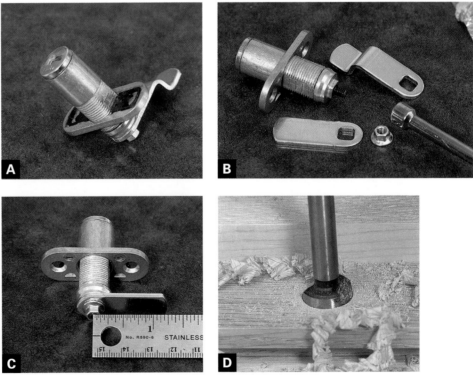

A

B

C

D

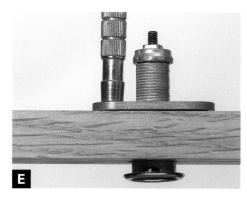

self-centering punch to mark the centerpoints of the mounting holes **(E).** Drill pilot holes and drive screws into the rear face of the stile to fasten the flange to the stile. Positioning the lock over the open vise on your workbench is an easy way to provide clearance for the lock and escutcheon while you drive the screws **(F).**

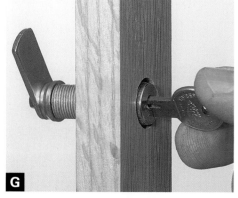

As a rule of thumb, you want to position the cam so that turning the key counterclockwise engages the cam **(G).** I wanted a carcase-to-stile gap of approximately ¹⁄₁₆ in., so I taped samples of plastic laminate to the carcase to establish this spacing. If you can access the interior of the cabinet with the door in place, you can directly mark the position where the upper end of the cam contacts the carcase **(H).** If you can't mark directly, paint the tip of the cam with correction fluid purchased from an office-supply store. Also make a mark on the carcase to indicate the lower end of the cam.

Using a router or laminate trimmer, rout a ⅛-in. slot ⅜ in. deep into the side of the carcase **(I).** I like to rout about ¹⁄₁₆ in. past each end mark to ensure that there is adequate clearance for the cam. There's no need to square the ends of the slot. Check the action of the lock to ensure that the cam easily engages the slot **(J).** Finger pressure is enough to press the escutcheon onto the lock's body **(K).** The finished lock installation provides good security while retaining an unobtrusive appearance for your cabinet **(L).**

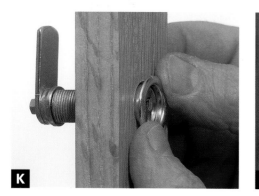

Full-Mortise Lock

To make it easy to center your router bit across the thickness of the chest's upper front edge, draw the centerline onto a piece of white masking tape. Chuck a centering tool into your router and adjust the router's edge guide until the tool's tip perfectly matches the centerline **(A).** Remove the tape, and mark the ends of the lock's selvage onto the chest's edge. (Selvage is the edge of the lock that's visible after installation.) Change to a bit that equals the width of the selvage (⅜ in. in this case), and rout the mortise **(B).** Clamping a piece of scrap wood to the rear edge of the chest's front stabilizes the router's base by giving it a larger bearing surface. (The next photo gives you a clearer view of this scrap wood support.) Turn the lock upside down, and test-fit it to check the length and depth of the mortise **(C).**

Carefully measure to the centerpoint of the lock's keyhole **(D),** and transfer that point to the front of the chest. Drill a hole (⁵⁄₁₆ in. for this lock) halfway through the chest's front **(E).** Put a piece of masking tape onto the lock, and use a crafts knife with a new blade to cut the outline of the keyway **(F).** Carefully transfer the masking tape to the front of the chest, aligning the cutout with the hole you already drilled and making sure that the taped shape is vertical. Drill a hole (⁹⁄₃₂ in. for this lock) at the lower end of the keyway to remove the majority of the waste, then chisel away the remainder and discard the tape **(G).**

(Text continues on p. 100.)

A

B

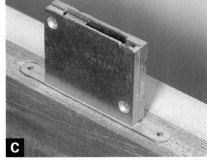

C

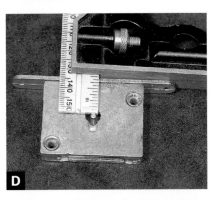

D

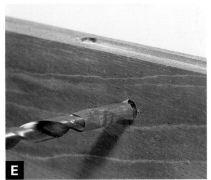

E

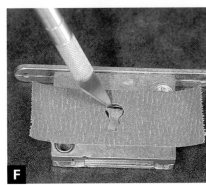

F

G

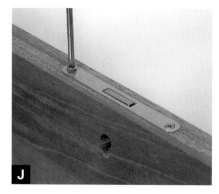

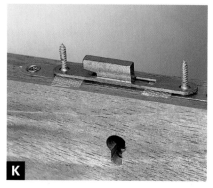

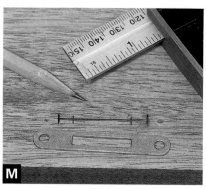

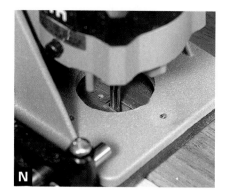

Drilling out the mortise for the lock's body is easy when you use a self-centering doweling jig (this one is manufactured by Dowl-It) **(H)**. The jig helps you drill overlapping holes that are vertical and a consistent depth. Drill holes (⁵⁄₁₆ in. for this lock) at the ends of the mortise first, then work toward the center. Clear out the remaining waste with a chisel **(I),** and test-fit the lock body into the mortise. Aim for an easy sliding entry without any binding. Drill pilot holes, and screw the lock body into position **(J)**. Use the key to move the bolt into the locked position, and put small pieces of double-faced tape onto the selvage to hold the strike plate and its screws in position. Make certain that the strike plate is centered front to back and fully engaged under the bolt's hook **(K)**. Lower the chest's lid until the tips of the screws mark their location on the underside of the lid **(L)**.

Remove the lid from the chest, and put it onto your workbench. Draw a centerline between the two screw tip marks, put the strike into position, and mark the ends of its opening. To create clearance for the bolt's hook, make secondary marks ¼ in. beyond the strike plate's opening **(M)**. Technically speaking, you need clearance only at one end of the strike for this lock, but it's faster to mark both ends than to figure out the correct one. Attach an edge guide to your laminate trimmer or router to cut the ¼-in. slot ³⁄₈ in. deep for the strike **(N)**. Drill pilot holes, and fasten the strike in place. For a chest, I prefer not to mortise the strike because the metal's thickness creates a single contact area between the strike in the lid and the body of the lock. This helps ensure secure locking action even if the lid slightly changes shape over time. But if you're using this type of lock to secure doors, you'll need to mortise the strike plate into the cabinet's carcase.

Surface-Mounted Escutcheon

Driving a couple of escutcheon pins sounds like no big deal until you realize that these delicate small-gauge fasteners are no match for many hardwoods. Get around this problem by installing softwood plugs to accept the escutcheon pins.

The first important step is to make gravity your working partner by placing a chest onto its back when you install an escutcheon. Put the key through the escutcheon and into the lock **(A)**. Carefully center the escutcheon around the key's shaft, and make sure that the keyway's centerline is perpendicular to the edge of the chest's front. Use a scratch awl through the escutcheon's holes to mark the chest, and use a pencil to mark the area of the wood that's visible through the keyway. Blacken inside the penciled outline with a fine-tipped permanent marker (Sanford's Sharpie is one brand) to give the escutcheon a neater appearance **(B)**.

Drill holes at the centerpoints you marked, and glue in ¼-in. lengths of a wood kitchen matchstick **(C)**. A ⁷⁄₆₄-in. bit produced a snug fit for the match I used, a toothpick was the right scale as a glue applicator, and a tack hammer drove in the plugs. Use a scratch awl to mark the centerpoints of the softwood plugs **(D)**. Put the escutcheon back into position. You'll be able to feel when the tip of the escutcheon mates with the dimpled centerpoint. Holding the pin with miniature long-nose pliers saves your fingers from taps of the tack hammer **(E)**. The completed escutcheon protects the front of the chest from key damage **(F)**. Compare this photo to photo A and you'll see how blackening the wood behind the keyway gives the escutcheon a sharper look.

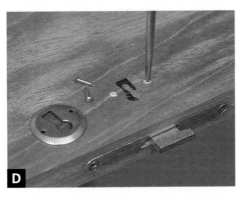

A

Flush Escutcheon

Inlaying a flush escutcheon is an exercise in careful workmanship that will reward the patient woodworker with a precise wood-to-metal fit. This demonstration will show how to install an escutcheon into a drawer front that later receives a surface-mounted lock behind it. Whether working on drawers or doors, I like to cut all of the joints and test-fit the assembly, then inlay the escutcheon before glue-up. It's much easier to work with an individual component rather than to struggle with the bulk of a completed assembly.

B

To make the layout marks easy to see, put a piece of white masking tape at the installation site. I pack the interior of the escutcheon with Plasti-Tak to keep it from slipping while marking the outline with a fine mechanical pencil **(A)**. Plasti-Tak is the brand name of a rubbery low-tack plastic adhesive sold in office-supply stores and crafts shops. It's generally used for no-mark mounting of posters onto walls and similar holding tasks.

C

Drill a pilot hole through your workpiece, and insert a scrollsaw or fretsaw blade through the opening **(B)**. I used a no. 9 scrollsaw blade and cut about one blade width to the waste side of the pencil line. To check your progress as you fit the metal, position the escutcheon and hold the wood up to a light **(C)**. Use a file to remove wood where the light *doesn't* show. A round and triangular file will let you follow the keyhole shape **(D)**. Keep the walls of the cutout vertical if possible, or undercut only a couple of degrees. When the cutout matches the escutcheon, file a 1/16-in. chamfer along the rear perimeter of the escutcheon to ease its entry into the wood. Remove the masking tape so it doesn't get caught between the escutcheon and the wood.

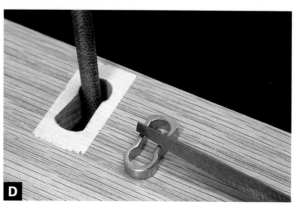

D

Start the escutcheon by hand squarely into its opening, and press it flush with a handscrew clamp or wood-faced vise **(E)**. If there are any gaps between the wood and metal, mix up a slurry of sawdust and glue (or epoxy), and pack it firmly into the gaps with a plastic putty knife **(F)**. Let the glue dry before moving to the next step. Using 100-grit sandpaper in a block, sand the wood and brass escutcheon until they are flush. Repeat with 220- and 400-grit sandpaper to minimize the appearance of scratches **(G)**. Thoroughly dust or vacuum the drawer front to remove all dust. Apply finish to the metal and wood after assembling the drawer, being careful that liquid doesn't pool in the keyway. The completed installation is a seamless wood-to-metal fit **(H)**.

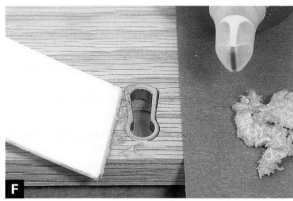

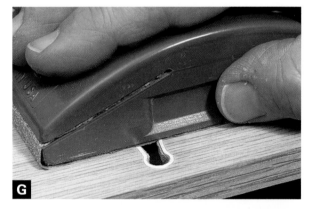

Table, Chair, and Leg Hardware

Leg-Mounting Hardware

Casters & Glides

Tabletop Hardware

Table-Extension Slides

Pop-Up Table Hardware

THE SIGHT OF A COLLAPSING table and chairs with arms, legs, and food going in every direction is an absolutely hilarious gag—in the movies. But replay the scene in your home in the middle of Thanksgiving dinner, and the humor drains out of it very quickly.

Safety and strength are only two of the reasons you need to know about the wide range of choices in table, chair, and leg hardware. With the innovative hardware on the market today, you can build function and versatility into your furniture: tables that rise, expand, or level themselves. Or you can make chairs that swivel, rock, or simply stand rock-steady. In addition, choosing the right hardware can save you time and money.

For example, shopmade wood "buttons" are a traditional way of holding a tabletop firmly to the apron while still permitting seasonal expansion and contraction of the top across the grain. Even though these buttons look quite simple, making them involves two setups at the table saw, one at the miter saw, and another at the drill press. Unless you like to impress your customers or yourself with how little metal you put into your projects, you could better use your time by crafting a detail that's visible without crawling under the table with a flashlight in hand. The photo at left on the facing page shows wood buttons and inexpensive metal alternatives that also permit movement in solid-wood tops.

Manufactured panels such as plywood and MDF have such excellent dimensional stability that you don't really need the figure-8 fasteners or Z-clips for their ability to adapt to movement. In tabletop sizes, these materials move such a small amount that you can ignore it. But you can still use tabletop fasteners with these materials and enjoy the benefits of speed, economy, and convenience.

Folding-Leg Hardware

Legs that fold are handy for a wide variety of tables. Folding tubular-leg assemblies are easy to install and let you quickly build a banquet/utility table and matching benches from plywood or solid stock. If you prefer the look of folding individual legs, you can choose tubular steel or brackets that accommodate square wood legs that you make. The bracket shown at right below handles wood legs that range from 1¼ in. to 1¾ in. square.

Expanding-Table Hardware

Making a table is a good idea. Making a table that can get bigger is an even better idea. One familiar mechanism is made for a four-legged table, and its operation typically

involves a person at each end of the table, dragging the legs across the floor as the center of the table opens to accept a leaf or two. But when you have a pedestal table, you need an equalizer slide. One person can operate this type because pulling on one end of the table pushes the opposite side open so that the table doesn't tip. But beyond these two familiar types of slides, you'll find a number of other extension devices. Buy a geared aluminum table slide, and you can expand a four-legged table without dragging the feet. The apron of the table also stays intact as the equalizer mechanism simultaneously pulls and pushes to divide the tabletop.

There are two more extensions that are little known but highly useful. Instead of splitting the table in the center, both of these mechanisms add space at the ends of the table. The parson's table extension stores a leaf below each end. Simply pull on the leaf and it extends, then moves upward, flush

You can attach a tabletop with (from left) shopmade wood buttons, figure-8 fasteners, or tabletop Z-clips.

Whether you need a table or bench indoors or outside, folding-leg assemblies keep construction quick and easy.

Whether you prefer steel legs from the factory or a wood leg that you add to the hardware, you can build tables that fold the way you want.

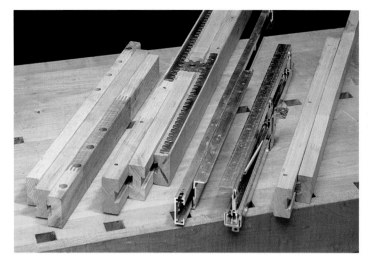

Expand your table by selecting one of these mechanisms (from left to right): four-legged table extension, equalizer pedestal slide, geared aluminum slide, parson's table extension, and trestle table slide. (Only one of each slide is shown; you'll install a pair.)

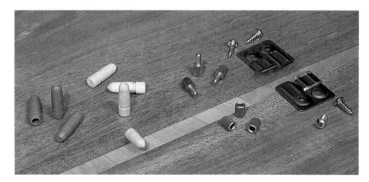

Keep table sections and leaves aligned with table pins in plastic, wood, or brass, or select the eveners shown at far right.

with the rest of the tabletop. Depending on the model you choose, you'll gain 11 in. or 16 in. at each end. The final slide is generally used with trestle tables that have false breadboard ends connected to the main table surface by the slides. You then insert a leaf between the breadboard end and the table.

You can solve most expanding-table problems with off-the-shelf solutions, but if you run into the need for special extensions, you can have them custom manufactured, saving

you the time and uncertainty of engineering and making your own slides. Walter of Wabash is one company that offers custom extensions.

▶ See *"Manufacturers and Suppliers"* on p. 214.

If you build an extension table, you'll also need hardware to keep the halves aligned and locked when closed as well as pins that join the leaves to the top. You can choose table pins in plastic, wood, and brass, and that sequence also describes the upward price progression. Tabletop eveners are another product that can be used instead of pins or in addition to them. Personally, I prefer table pins, especially for removable leaves because the metal edges of the eveners could cause cuts. But the eveners are handy as a corrective measure to help cure alignment of a sagging leaf.

Most people install a lock to keep the table latched in the closed position, but you can also attach locks to the leaf so that the top is also secured in the open position. When you shop for a table lock, the most important question you need to ask is how easy it is to operate strictly by feel. The fork design with the U-shaped keeper is promoted as extremely traditional and very British. But I wonder how long you're supposed to fumble around trying to insert the loose piece into both catches before you give up and crawl under the table.

Drop-Leaf Supports

Drop leaves are another popular way to expand the size of a tabletop. But to be certain that the leaf doesn't drop unexpectedly, choose a pair of sturdy supports for each leaf. If there's no apron, you can choose a pullout support that has great strength and reliability. Purchase an all-metal pullout, or a bracket that lets you add your own wood support. You can also purchase folding supports for a table with or without an apron. The supports come in a variety of sizes, with extended lengths of 6 in. to 12 in.

Tables That Tilt and Rise

If you're one of the millions of people who hunch over the coffee table to eat dinner in front of the television, there's a product that can quickly improve your table manners. You can build a mechanism into a coffee table to raise its top 6½ in. and also shift it 17 in. closer to you. Then you can eat without banging your knees or bending over.

Tilt-top tables have always been a favorite among draftsmen, artists, and architects. The traditional support features a rod that's locked by turning a knurled knob. The usual mounting spot is one-third of the distance from the back of the tabletop. Moving it further forward increases the maximum lift angle. The lift-up ratchet support allows you the advantages of a tilting top without the hassle of running back and forth between the ends of the table to adjust the hardware. Simply lift and release the top to select any of 13 positions. To close the top, lift slightly to disengage the mechanism. Choose the range of motion you want by moving the support toward or away from the pivot point. Other uses for the ratcheting support include adjustable bookstands and backs for reclining chairs. If you build a chaise lounge for outdoor use, be sure to secure the support with galvanized or stainless steel screws.

The latch shown at top has a built-in alignment feature; the lock at center is another no-look fastener. The forked design shown at bottom is long on tradition but short on user-friendliness.

You can use the first three supports shown for a table without an apron. If your table has an apron, choose the support shown at far right.

With a pop-up table, couch potatoes can eat more neatly and comfortably. (Photos courtesy Rockler Woodworking and Hardware)

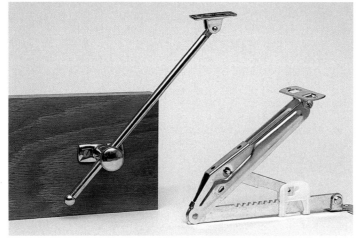

To make a tilt-top table, select either the traditional drafting table support (left) or the ratcheting mechanism.

Corner Leg Braces

Corner braces do an amazing job of strengthening apron-to-leg joints in both tables and chairs. The 3-in.-wide kerf-mount variety is primarily used in new construction, and the $2\frac{1}{2}$-in. surface-mounted type is easier to use for retrofits and repairs. Corner braces are often shown in catalogs with wing nuts, but I prefer to use standard hex nuts unless I'm building a piece with removable legs. You'll also find corner braces that are $1\frac{7}{16}$ in. wide, a handy size for building or reinforcing chairs.

Leg Tips

Before you can truly say that you've completed a table, chair, or other furniture project, you need to attach a tip, glide, or cushion to the legs. These little pieces serve two principal purposes: protecting your furniture from the floor and the floor from your furniture. Use a soft tip, typically thick felt, on hard floor surfaces such as wood, ceramic tile, and sheet vinyl. But when you place furniture on carpet or rugs, use a hard tip such

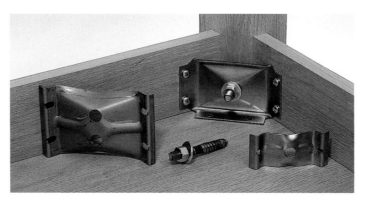

Corner braces are inexpensive, easy to install, and strengthen new projects or old work.

as metal or nylon. Some people advocate slippery Teflon glides for use on both hard and soft surfaces, but I feel more confident about the guideline of hard-on-soft and soft-on-hard.

Putting nylon glides on outdoor furniture serves another important purpose: By keeping the end grain of legs out of standing water, you help prevent water from wicking into the wood to cause premature decay.

Leveling Tips

Physicists merely theorize about the curvature of space and time, but some of the floors in my house serve as absolute proof. That's why leveling furniture tips are such useful products. One choice is a simple leveler that threads into a teenut or insert in the bottom of the leg. To use these, you get down on the floor and manually advance or retract each leveler until all of them touch the floor and the table is level. A more elaborate adaptation is the somewhat misnamed self-leveling table glide. Its spring-loaded mechanism automatically maintains contact with the floor, while you keep your hands and knees off the floor. Although this may keep the table from rocking, these "levelers" don't actually level the table.

Complete a table leg by screwing in a Teflon glide, sticking on a heavy felt cushion, or nailing in a nylon glide.

Glides screw on or thread into the bottom of the leg. The self-leveling glide installed on the leg is furnished with teenuts; with the other glides you purchase the teenuts separately.

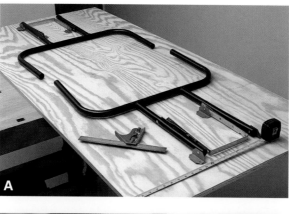

A

B

C

VARIATION

Utility Table Legs

Attaching fold-up legs for a utility table is an extremely easy process. The following demonstration shows the construction of a plywood-topped table that can be used for a variety of tasks: as an assembly bench in the shop, as a picnic table or potting bench in the backyard, or as a fabric-cutting center or game table in a hobby room. Add a tablecloth, and you instantly have a buffet or dining table. Of course, you don't have to limit yourself to ordinary fir plywood. With hardwood plywood or plastic laminate, you can add durability and good looks.

Begin by laying the plywood top face down on your work surface, and center the folded-leg assemblies side to side and 4 in. from each end **(A)**. To provide knee room for a person to sit at the end of the table, you'll need to make a table that's 8 ft. long, and position each leg bracket 16 in. from the plywood's end.

Drill pilot holes, and drive the supplied #10 x ⅝-in. screws through the brackets into the top **(B)**. Raise the legs to check that they work smoothly, then lower them. Complete the ends of the legs by adding the supplied plastic tips. Alternatively, you can purchase plastic inserts and stem casters to make your table mobile **(C)**. You can use a hacksaw to easily shorten the tubular metal legs to compensate for the height added by the casters.

VARIATION If you want even more strength than screws can provide, drill and countersink to attach the leg brackets with 10 to 24 flat-head machine screws, washers, and nuts. The nylon-insert nut shown in the photo resists loosening due to vibration.

Corner Braces

Place the tabletop face down on your work-bench. After attaching the table aprons to the legs, turn the assembly upside down on the tabletop. Fold a 3-in. by 5-in. index card in half, and place it between the brace and tabletop. When you remove the card later, it creates a small amount of clearance that ensures that screws driven through the brace into the table-top will pull the assembly together tightly. Mark the centerpoints of the mounting holes on the aprons, drill pilot holes, and drive screws to fasten the brace **(A)**.

Place one of the hanger bolts next to the drill bit you'll use to drill its pilot hole. Use masking tape to make a depth-gauge flag on the bit **(B)**. Put the bit through the hole in the brace, and stop drilling when the flag touches the brace **(C)**. Next, put two nuts onto the machine-threaded portion of the hanger bolt, jamming them against each other. Using a wrench on the uppermost nut, drive the hanger bolt into the leg **(D)**. When you've finished driving the hanger bolt, remove the top nut and tighten the remaining one against the brace. Don't overdo the torque or you'll simply create unnecessary strain in the joint. This step completes a joint that will keep your table solid for generations **(E)**. If you used a plywood top, you can drive screws through the brace into the tabletop to add one more element of strength to the assembly.

VARIATION If you build a table with a plywood top, you can screw the aprons and corner brace to it and make the legs completely removable. Using wing nuts on the hanger bolts speeds knockdown.

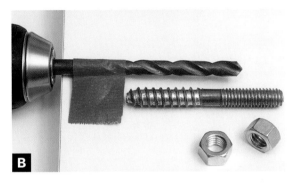

A

B

C

D

Furniture Glides

Drill a ¾-in. counterbore ⅟₁₆ in. deep into the end of a table leg **(A)**. In the center of that counterbore, drill a ⅝₁₆-in. hole 1¼ in. deep for the ¼-in. pronged teenut and install it by using a sharp hammer blow **(B)**. This puts the surface of the installed teenut flush with the end of the leg **(C)**.

▶ See *"Teenuts"* on p. 137.

Complete the installation by screwing in the leveler **(D)**.

VARIATION **Putting a self-leveling glide into the end of a chair leg or the bottom of case goods is very easy. The glides shown here were supplied with ⅝₁₆-in. teenuts that require a ⅜-in. hole. The glides excel at eliminating chair wobble and are tough enough to use on outdoor furniture.**

[TIP] **Be sure to gauge the depth of the hole from the length of the glide's shank, not merely from the body of the teenut.**

VARIATION

Stem-Mounted Casters

It's easiest to install the housings for stem casters before you assemble the piece of furniture. Draw diagonal lines on the end of your leg stock to locate the centerpoint. Using a self-centering doweling jig will help ensure that the hole is centered and vertical **(A)**. Drill the hole ¼ in. deeper than the caster's stem, not merely the insert. The cutaway view **(B)** shows how the bulge on the caster's stem goes beyond the end of the insert. Insert the housing into the hole, and bury the prongs into the end of the leg with a sharp hammer blow **(C)**. Put masking tape over the end of the insert to keep out chips, sawdust, and finish that could affect the fit and function of the caster **(D)**. After you've assembled the furniture and applied the finish, push on the caster to snap it into place **(E)**.

VARIATION Some people mount a roller ball as if it were a caster, with all of the workings visible. Other woodworkers like to partially conceal it in a counterbore. I prefer to bury virtually the entire piece of hardware into an extremely deep counterbore in the end of the leg. That way, the table or cart seems to mysteriously glide over the floor without any visible means of support. To do this, drill a counterbore deep enough to enclose all but ¼ in. of the length of the ball's housing, then drill the hole for the shaft.

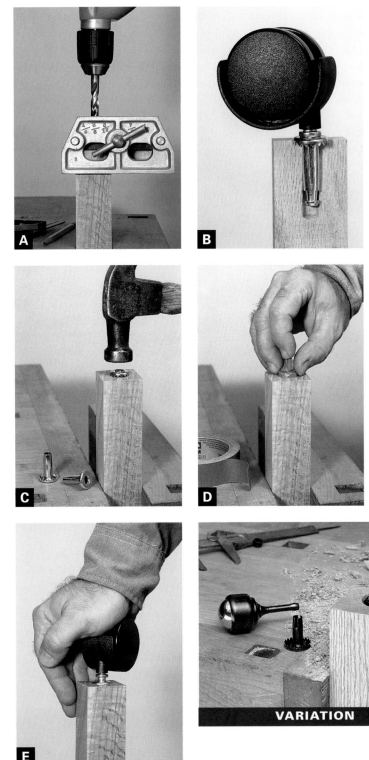

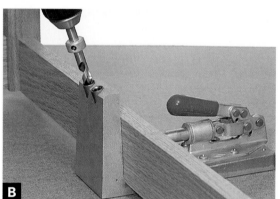

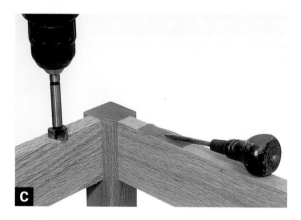

Figure-8 Tabletop Fasteners

Depending on the hardware catalog you're using, you'll find that this piece of hardware uses a number of aliases: desktop fasteners, figure-8 fasteners, or tabletop fasteners. But no matter what they're named, you'll call them extremely handy. You'll attach one end of the fastener to the top and the other end to the rail. Anchored at these two points, the figure 8 can rotate to accommodate the changing width of a solid-wood top as it expands and contracts in response to changes in humidity.

Most of the time, you'll use hardware straight out of the package. But every so often you'll run into items, like this batch of tabletop fasteners, that you need to modify. In this case, the countersink was poorly formed, and that would have affected the function of the fastener. Rather than waste the time returning the figure-8 fasteners, you can complete the machining the factory should have done **(A)**.

Mark the inside center of the table's end aprons, and use a pocket-hole jig to drill an angled hole and counterbore at each centerpoint **(B)**. When you drive these screws later, they will help to keep the tabletop flat, firmly attached, and they also equalize the expansion of a solid-wood top on both sides of its centerline. With a top made from a manufactured panel, such as plywood or MDF, you can skip the pocket-hole step.

Before you can drive the pocket-hole screws, you need to create counterbores for the tabletop fasteners. Stand the base assembly on its feet, and mark the location for the fasteners on the upper edge of the aprons. For a top the size of a kitchen table, you'll use 10 fasteners. Mark for two on each end apron, 2 in. from the inner corner of the leg, and three on each side apron, again 2 in. from the leg and one centered on the apron's length. You'll need to drill some test counterbores in scrap stock to determine the distance of the centerpoint from the inner edge of the apron stock that gives the figure-8 fastener a wide range of rotation. Using a Forstner bit, drill a counterbore at each location on the apron, drilling ½₂ in. deeper than the thickness of the fastener **(C)**. This slight bit of extra depth will help pull the tabletop down snugly. By the way, if your table has extremely thin aprons, you can counterbore the smaller portion of the figure-8 fastener and still get the same range of motion.

[TIP] Before you install the figure-8 fasteners, give them and the counterbores a quick coat of paste wax. This will help the fasteners move freely as the top expands and contracts.

Drill pilot holes for the mounting screws centered in the counterbores, and screw the figure-8 fasteners in place **(D).** You need to torque the flathead screws very carefully: snug enough that the fastener doesn't rattle up and down but loose enough so that it can rotate freely. Put the tabletop face down on your workbench, center the table's base on it, and drive the pocket-hole screws **(E).** Align the fasteners perpendicular to the end apron and at a 45-degree angle to the side aprons **(F).** The fasteners on the side apron should make a V-shape with the fasteners on the opposite apron. Drill pilot holes into the top, and drive the round-head screws, but do not overtighten them.

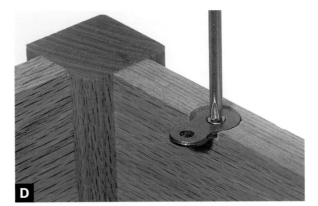

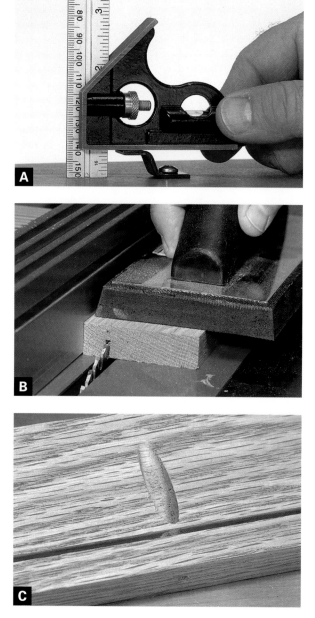

Z-Clip Tabletop Fasteners

This little piece of hardware does a better job of accommodating wood movement than figure-8 fasteners and requires only half as many pilot holes and screws, so it's also a time and money saver. The fastener, also called a Z-clip because of its shape, fits into a ⅛-in. groove that's ⅜ in. deep along the top inner edge of the aprons. To locate the groove on the apron, temporarily screw a clip to a piece of scrap wood and measure the distance to the top of the fastener **(A)**. Set your rip fence at this distance from the inner edge of the blade and cut the groove **(B)**. This procedure positions the groove slightly lower (by the thickness of the metal) than the offset of the fastener, and that creates a bit of tension to pull the tabletop flush against the apron when you drive the screws later.

After assembling the table's aprons and base, mark the inside center of the table's end aprons, and use a pocket-hole jig to drill an angled hole and counterbore at each centerpoint. Pocket-hole screws at these points help to keep the tabletop flat and firmly attached, and their placement equalizes the expansion of a solid-wood top on both sides of its centerline. If you have a top made from a manufactured panel, such as plywood or MDF, you can skip the pocket-hole step.

The standard setup of a pocket-hole jig can make the angled counterbore break through the groove in the apron **(C)**. That could mean that the tip of your pocket-hole screw would reach through the tabletop. Avoid that problem by drilling a shallower counterbore. Holding a strip of ¼-in. hardboard between the drill's depth collar and the jig's body is a fast fix that raises the counterbore **(D).** Put the tabletop face down on your workbench, center the table's base on it, and drive the pocket-hole screws **(E).** On the end aprons, position a fastener about 2 in. from the inner edge of each leg. Slide the fastener into the groove in the apron, mark and drill the pilot hole, then drive the round-head screw **(F).** Don't overdo the torque on the screw or the fastener won't slide easily from side to side.

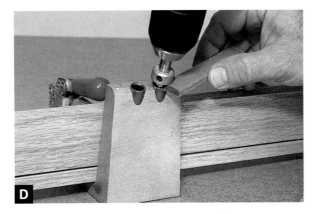

For the side aprons, position a fastener 2 in. from each leg and in the center. The fasteners in the side aprons work on a completely different basis: Instead of gliding from side to side, they move in and out of the groove. Based on that knowledge, position these fasteners so that they will have space to move in the groove. If the moisture content of the wood is high, as in spring and summer in the northern hemisphere, place the fastener so that it grips two-thirds of the depth of the groove. As the wood contracts, the fastener will still have a grip in the groove. Reverse your thinking if the wood is drier, which usually occurs in heated shops during the fall and winter. In that case, screw in the fastener so that it grips only one-third the depth of the groove. Again, don't apply too much muscle when you tighten the round-head screw—just enough to hold the fastener in the groove.

Wood Extension Slides

There's no absolute rule that governs how far you should place the slide from the edge of the tabletop, but 4 in. to 6 in. is a reasonable range. Wood extension slides are typically shipped from the factory already lubricated with tallow. You'll want to be sure to keep this greasy stuff away from unfinished wood to avoid potential finishing problems. And because there's no need to apply finish to wood extension slides anyway, you'll avoid difficulties by installing the slides after you've applied the finish to the top.

You can install extension slides before or after joining the leg structures to the tabletop halves. To make things easier for you to see, this demonstration will show installation before adding the legs. If you follow a similar path for your table, draw the outline of the aprons and pedestals or legs on the underside of the tabletop **(A)**. By following this simple precaution, you'll eliminate guesswork and potential mistakes.

Another potential error you'll want to avoid is using the wrong screw size to fasten the extensions: too short, and you'll sacrifice strength; too long, and you'll have to make a new tabletop. The slides I used are drilled and counterbored to use #10 x 1½-in. screws for proper penetration into a ¾-in.-thick top **(B)**. In the photo, you'll notice in the end view of the slide that the manufacturer cut a shallow groove along the edge of the slide that meets the underside of the top. This is called a back-out groove, and it provides clearance for wood fibers raised from the top when you drive the screws. Otherwise, the fibers would lift the slide, creating a jacked joint.

Begin by butting together the two halves of your tabletop face down on your workbench. To make sure that they don't move, use wood handscrew clamps to hold the edges flush. Use a framing square to position the slide at a right angle to the joint line. Drive the screw in the hole nearest the joint first, then skip to the hole at the far end of that same strip **(C)**. You'll drive screws in the remaining holes later, after you've checked that the slide works perfectly. Fully close this first slide, then open it about ½ in. That will ensure that the slide won't bottom out before it is fully closed. Drive two screws through this strip of the slide into the opposite half of the tabletop **(D)**.

To ensure that the second slide is parallel to the first, roughly position it by measurement, then rip a plywood spacer to fit between the slides **(E)**. By butting the second slide against the spacer, you eliminate tedious measuring and ensure that the slides are parallel to each other. After you've installed two screws into each of the two mounting strips of the second slide, check the action of the top. When you're satisfied with the motion, drive the remaining screws. Although you could consider the job complete at this point, makers of better-quality tables reinforce the slides with rub blocks that you can make from 3-in. lengths of ¾-in. quarter-round molding **(F)**. They're called rub blocks because you coat their edges with glue, then rub them back and forth until the glue grabs, eliminating the need for clamping. Using a self-centering doweling jig and dowel centers simplifies the process of installing table pins into the top halves and the leaf **(G)**.

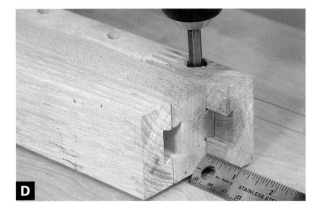

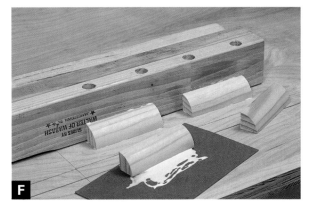

Pop-Up Table Mechanism

The manufacturer states that the spring-counterbalanced mechanism is designed for a top with an optimum weight of 20 lb. To choose between a top of birch plywood or MDF, I weighed a 1-ft. square of each material and calculated the weight of the top **(A)**. At 3 pounds per square foot (psf), the MDF would have been considerably over-weight. The birch plywood, weighing about 1.75 psf, would make a top about 5 lb. too light, but I figured that I could add an MDF square under the birch to increase the total weight if necessary.

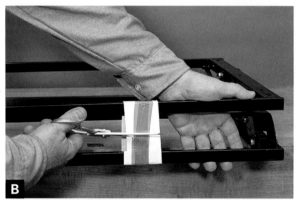

> ⚠ **CAUTION** Get a firm grip on the mechanism before you cut the shipping strap holding it closed **(B)**. Otherwise, the spring tension will make it jump open.

The mechanism is reversible, so you can screw either side to the top, centering it side to side and end to end **(C)**. Calculate the size of any additional weight needed, and screw it to the top within the perimeter of the mechanism. Drive two screws through the mechanism into the base, and test the action of the hardware **(D)**. You'll notice in the photo that I mounted the mechanism onto riser strips. The extra storage room in my base design made the strips necessary because its depth exceeded the 3¾ in. needed by the mechanism. If you don't use riser strips in your design, you may want to anchor the mechanism by driving machine screws into teenuts inserted in the base. If the top descends so rapidly that it slams, cut down the size of the counterweight. If the top doesn't want to stay fully closed, add weight to the top.

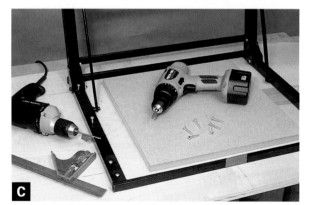

➤ See *"Teenuts"* on p. 137.

Assembly, Knockdown, and Mounting Hardware

Knockdown Cabinets

➤ Knockdown Corner Fitting (p. 128)
➤ Cross Dowels (p. 130)
➤ Minifix Fittings (p. 132)

Countertop Connectors

➤ Coountertop Joint Connector (p. 134)

Threaded Inserts & Teenuts

➤ Threaded Inserts (p. 136)
➤ Teenuts (p. 137)

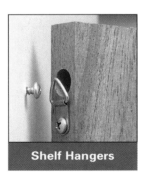

Shelf Hangers

➤ Invisible Shelf Hangers (p. 138)

SOME WOODWORKING CATALOGS will have a section devoted to knockdown (KD) fittings, while other catalogs will call identical hardware ready to assemble (RTA). In reality, there seems to be less real difference between these categories than in the debate over whether the glass is half empty or half full. If there is a subtle distinction, "ready to assemble" gives a slightly more positive marketing connotation to a box of boards.

On a more practical side, the furniture designer and builder should base hardware decisions on the structural requirements of the project, the tooling required to make and assemble the joints, and whether the hardware will be used for one-time construction or repeated setup and dismantling. In addition, some hardware is completely concealed within the carcase, whereas fittings that are visible from the outside can be—depending on your viewpoint—either decorative or distracting.

Threaded Inserts and Teenuts

When you put metal threads into wood, you create a firm anchor point for hardware or provide an easy way to quickly assemble a project and take it apart. You can select from a wide range of threaded inserts and teenuts, and each style comes in a variety of internal thread sizes. Install barbed inserts by pressing with a clamp or tapping with a hammer. The standard style is installed flush with the

It's easy to put metal threads into wood with this lineup of threaded inserts and teenuts. The size designation for these fasteners refers to the internal thread.

When you need a strong panel-to-shelf connection, choose a cross bolt (left) for a joint that relies on threads to secure it, or knockdown fasteners (center and right) that tighten as you turn a cam.

surface, whereas the collared variety, which offers additional pull-through resistance, will stand proud of the surface unless you drill a counterbore. You'll find threaded inserts in both steel and brass. Although brass is softer, it's a must to prevent rust in outdoor projects and also helps prevent fastener stains due to chemical reaction with the wood in both interior and exterior projects.

The barbed teenut is easy to install, although you may need to drill pilots for the barbs in hardwoods. Again, you can counter-bore for a flush installation. The screw-on teenut provides a solid anchoring point for a leveling glide in the bottom of a leg.

When you shop for threaded inserts, you'll discover that they are designated by the size of the internal machine screw thread. That tells you what size fastener you can attach to it. But you also need to know the hole size to drill into the wood. Refer to the chart on p. 127 for that information.

The recommended hole sizes are the engineering ideal to provide maximum pull-out resistance. However, you may find that cheating up $1/64$ in. to the next larger drill size may make installation considerably easier, especially in end-grain applications.

Cross Bolts, Chicago Bolts, and Knockdown Panel Connectors

Installing a cross bolt is an easy way to make a knockdown joint with excellent shear strength. Ask an engineer, and he'll define shear as the force that is parallel to the plane of connection of two parts. For example, if the connections between the ends of a shelf and the sides of a bookcase have inadequate shear strength, the fasteners will bend or break (literally shear apart) and the loaded shelf will crash to the bottom of the case.

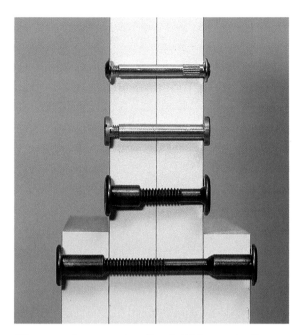

This tough plastic panel connector provides a knockdown joint that's concealed inside the cabinet.

The panel connector (top), Chicago bolt (second from top), and connector bolts (the two fasteners at bottom) may look similar at first glance, but not all knockdown fasteners are created equal.

You'll also find knockdown fittings that are variations of the cross-dowel concept, using a connector with an internal cam to capture the head of a bolt and pull it snug.

A panel connector is specifically made for joining bookcases and cabinets with ³⁄₄-in.-thick sides. A hammer tap seats the knurled end of the shaft to resist rotation as you tighten the screw. Chicago bolts, sometimes known as threaded bolts, also provide excellent shear strength for face-joined panels and come in a variety of lengths. The bolts fit in ¹⁄₄-in. holes and are available in six length increments to handle connection chores from ¹³⁄₁₆ in. to 2⁹⁄₁₆ in. Each bolt has a range of adjustment of 6 mm (about ¹⁄₄ in.). Both the Chicago bolt and the panel connectors have a large-diameter unthreaded shaft spanning the joint, and that's what provides outstanding shear strength.

Connector bolts are available in a variety of metric lengths from approximately 1³⁄₁₆ in. to slightly more than 3¹⁄₂ in., all of which work with a cap nut.

A knockdown panel connector is an extremely useful piece of hardware for making joints that hold securely but come apart easily by removing a screw. An additional advantage over many other knockdown fasteners is that this piece of hardware discreetly hides inside the cabinet. Both parts are surface mounted, so installation is quick and easy. If you need one more reason to try this tough plastic fastener, you can also use a pair of them as rustproof pivots or hinges.

Cabinet-Hanging Hardware

Hanging cabinets onto a wall can be an experience that makes you wish you knew how to grow another hand or two. But if your walls are reasonably straight and plumb, there are a couple of pieces of hardware that can make the process very easy. One solution is a pair of interlocking steel cleats—screw one level on the wall, and bolt the other

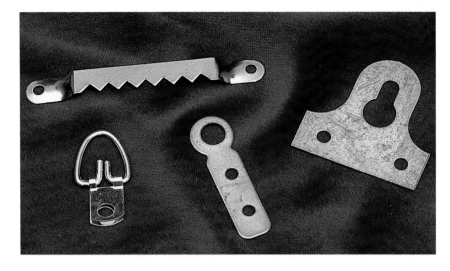

The triangle-shaped wire hanger is strong and versatile. Use the sawtooth hanger for small picture frames and the larger hangers for wall-mounted clocks, shelves, and curio cabinets.

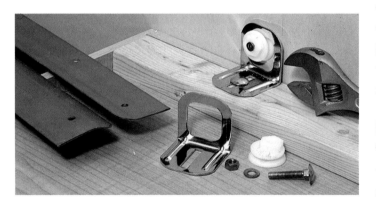

Two helpers for wall-cabinet installation are shown. One type uses a metal bracket and plastic cam to provide three-axis adjustment, and the other uses interlocking cleats to make cabinet hanging as easy as putting a picture on the wall.

through the cabinet back, which should be recessed ³⁄₈ in. to provide clearance for the hardware. Then you simply lift the cabinet, lower it onto the cleat, and let gravity take over from there. This system is very useful for an individual cabinet, but the irregularities in most walls would make it difficult for

you to align the faces of a series of cabinets. The second type of cabinet hanger mounts to the top of the cabinet and provides an impressive amount of adjustment in three axes: ¹⁄₂ in. side to side, ¹⁄₄ in. up and down, and 1 in. toward or away from the wall.

More Wall-Mounting Choices

After you've invested time into the construction of a wall-mounted project, you want to make certain that it doesn't crash to the floor. For light-duty applications, such as a small picture frame, you can select a sawtooth hanger that gives you lateral adjustment on a nail in the wall. Upholstery tacks are a fast way to attach these hangers. But to gain more security for larger frames as well as shelves and cabinets, choose a hanger that will let you drive a screw or two deeply into the carcase. Whenever possible, attach the hangers to the rear edge of the sides and not merely to the top.

Interlocking Connectors

There's a group of interlocking connectors that relies on wedging action to join cabinet components to each other or to mount them onto a wall. Attach a keyhole fitting to one piece, and it will capture a screw that slightly projects from the other part. Taper connectors are strong enough to hang a cabinet on a wall or to interlock parts, such as a rail-to-post connection for a bed frame. The more weight you apply to a taper connector, the tighter it becomes. Another style of interlocking connector utilizes pieces of sheet metal that mate together to invisibly and securely hang curio cabinets, speakers, mirrors, and many other items. A right-angle

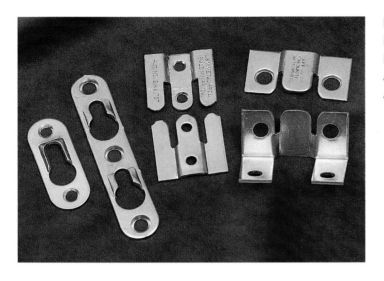

Interlocking connectors are inexpensive but strong. This lineup includes keyhole fittings and flush mounts in straight and right-angle varieties.

version of this style can be used for light-duty shelves.

See *"Rail Fasteners"* on p. 185.

Hanger Bolts and Dowel Screws

Hanger bolts and dowel screws appear similar at first glance, but a closer look shows you that a dowel screw has wood threads on both ends, whereas the hanger bolt has wood threads on one end and machine screw threading on the other. Some typical uses for the dowel screw include creating a large column, such as a bedpost, from a number of shorter pieces or adding a wood finial to the top of an assembly.

You'll use a hanger bolt for applications where you need a machine thread connection to add a nut or other threaded fastener. One typical application is a corner block that's used to reinforce table and chair construction. You can drive hanger bolts with a wrench and two nuts jammed against each other, but a hanger bolt driver that fits your drill is much faster. A specialized knob hanger bolt has 8 to

32 threads on one end to match most cabinet knobs. Locking-grip pliers enable you to drive a dowel screw into the first piece of your assembly, and you can then screw the first piece into the second part by hand.

You'll need to drill pilot holes for the wood threaded portions of both types of fastener. Referring to the drawing below, select a pilot drill bit that equals or is slightly larger than the fastener's root diameter.

See *"Corner Braces"* on p. 111.

ROOT DIAMETER

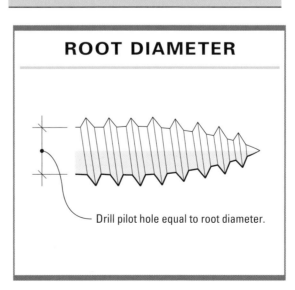

Drill pilot hole equal to root diameter.

Klick knockdown fasteners allow you to simply snap moldings into place, giving knockdown furniture an additional element of style without visible fasteners.

Knockdown Molding Connectors

Sometimes you'd like to be able to add infill strips or moldings to a knockdown assembly, but you'd also prefer that these pieces not require on-site carpentry. If you use Klick knockdown fasteners, you'll be able to add moldings with your bare hands. A dovetail slot routed into the back of the molding securely clips onto the fasteners mounted on the carcase. One type of fitting is simply screwed to the surface of the carcase, whereas the other mounts in a groove routed into the carcase. This dovetail groove may be continuous or individual stopped slots.

The hanger bolt driver in the drill speeds installation of hanger bolts. Machine screw threads on these fasteners enable you to use a hex, square, or wing nut. The tiny fastener shown in the center is a knob hanger bolt. The dowel screws shown at right excel at wood-to-wood joinery.

Countertop Seam Connectors

Sometimes it's actually true that an item isn't really heavy; it's simply awkward to handle. But in the case of plastic-laminate countertops, the pieces have an extra helping of both heavy and awkward. Traditional clamping techniques aren't much help when it comes to joining runs of countertops, especially along a miter joint. So several specialty connectors evolved to fit this need. One type requires you to drill holes into both the edges and bottom face of the countertop. At assembly, you must then thread the bolts as you align the countertop sections. As a matter of personal preference, I choose a different style: one that fits into recesses milled in the bottom surface by the countertop fabricator. It saves the hassle of drilling the holes and there are also fewer individual hardware components to juggle.

Hole-Drilling Sizes For Teenuts	
Inch size of internal thread	Installation hole diameter (in.)
4-40	11/64
6-62	11/64
8-32	13/64
10-24	15/64
10-32	15/64
1/4	5/16
5/16-18	3/8
3/8-16	15/32

The countertop fastener shown at top fits into recesses routed by the countertop fabricator. The other connector requires you to drill holes using the inexpensive bit shown or your own 7/8-in. Forstner bit and a 7/16-in. bit. The jig shown at lower right guides the drilling of both holes.

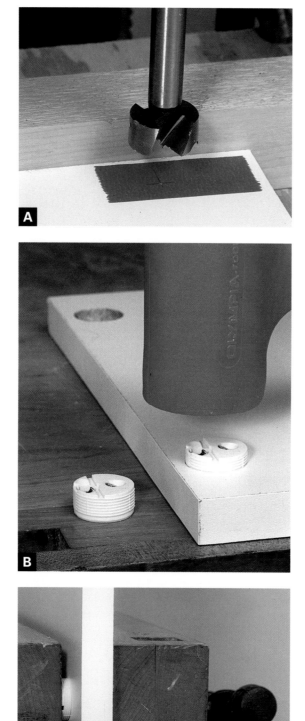

Knockdown Corner Fitting

Blum manufactures this style of knockdown fitting in two sizes, for installation into panels that have a thickness of 16 mm (⅝ in.) or 19 mm (¾ in.). Installing both sizes involves the same steps but slightly different dimensions. This demonstration will show you how to use the 19-mm size to make a simple carcase.

At the top and bottom inner edges of the vertical carcase members, strike a layout line 1½ in. from the front and back edges **(A).** Putting these marks onto masking tape eliminates the chore of erasing stray lines later. When you strip off the tape after drilling, the marks disappear. Set up a fence on your drill press, and drill 25 mm holes that are13 mm (½ in.) deep and located 17.5 mm (¹¹⁄₁₆ in.) from the end at each layout line. Start the nylon press-in fitting into each hole by hand, making sure that the line on it is parallel to the end of the panel **(B).** Put the panel into your bench vise, and tighten the screw until the insert is flush with the surface of the panel **(C).**

Next, install the screws into the ends of the horizontal panels. Make the simple jig shown in the drawing at right to help you drill ³⁄₁₆-in. holes that are centered in the end and 1½ in. from the front and back edges. To get a perfectly flush corner, do a test installation on a scrap piece of panel. If your first test fitting isn't perfect, simply advance or withdraw the adjustment screws to fine-tune the fit with micrometer precision. When you're satisfied with the position of the holes in the horizontal panels, use the jig to drill all of them **(D).** Drive the connector screws into the panels until its shoulder just touches the end of the panel **(E).** Fit the head of the connector screw into the hole in the insert, and turn the screw on the insert to lock the joint **(F).**

Knockdown Fitting Jig

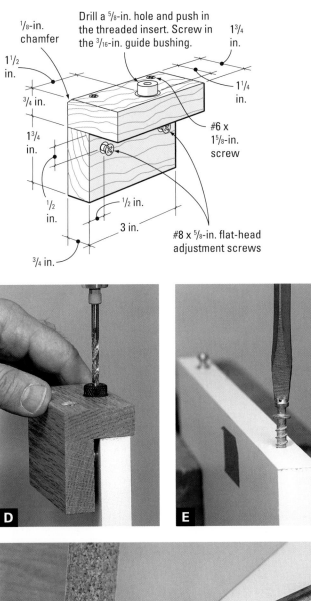

Drill a ⅝-in. hole and push in the threaded insert. Screw in the ³⁄₁₆-in. guide bushing.

⅛-in. chamfer

1½ in.

¾ in.

1¾ in.

½ in.

½ in.

3 in.

¾ in.

1¾ in.

1¼ in.

#6 x 1⅝-in. screw

#8 x ⅝-in. flat-head adjustment screws

Clamping Jig

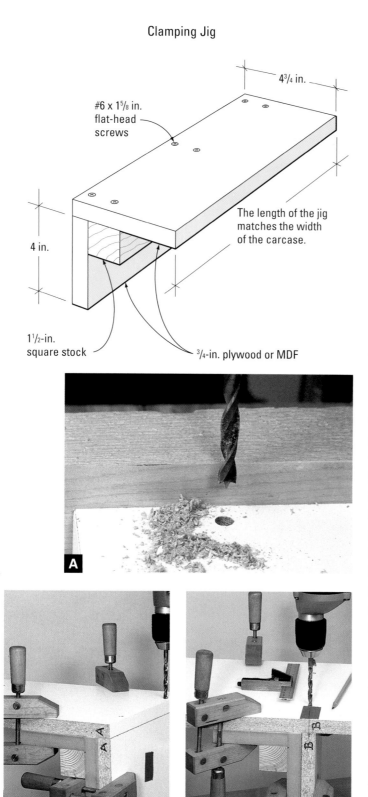

4³/₄ in.

#6 x 1⁵/₈ in.
flat-head
screws

4 in.

The length of the jig
matches the width
of the carcase.

1¹/₂-in.
square stock

³/₄-in. plywood or MDF

A

B

C

Cross Dowels

The cross-dowel installation method shown here is accurate and fast because it eliminates tedious measurements and the errors that can creep in when transferring dimensions from one part to another. I'll make a small carcase to illustrate both corner and T-joints.

Begin by cutting all of the carcase pieces to size, making certain that the parts are identical in width and have square ends. Onto the outside faces of the sides mark the centerlines of the top, bottom, and shelves. Mark a centerpoint 2 in. from the front and back edges, plus at any intermediate points you want to add, and drill the ⁷/₃₂-in. (or 6-mm) holes **(A).** Use your drill press to ensure that the holes are perpendicular to the face of the sides. Make the clamping jig shown in the drawing at left.

Using the jig, clamp one side and the bottom together **(B),** making certain that the ends and edges are flush and square. Using the holes in the sides as guides, drill a ⁷/₃₂-in. (or 6-mm) hole into the edge of the bottom for the 5.4-mm-dia. bolt. Be sure to drill at least ⅛ in. deeper than the length of the bolt you'll use so that the fastener doesn't bottom out in the hole before the joint is tight. For the 50-mm bolt length used here, drill a hole 2⅛ in. deep. Before unclamping the pieces, mark the lower face of the bottom with a piece of masking tape. In addition, identify the parts so that you'll reassemble them in the same position.

For an assembly that will always be against a wall, simply write the part name or make your identifying marks on the back edge of the parts with a permanent marker. This identification is necessary because you don't have the huge industrial machinery to crank out absolutely inter-changeable pieces. As an advantage of this system, though, your project is likely to fit together much better than a piece of commercial knock-down furniture. That's because you are able to custom-fit each part into its exact assembled position when you mark and drill for the fasteners, and you don't have to hope that all of the manufacturing tolerances will balance each other to permit a perfect fit. Draw the centerline of the stock's thickness on the edges of fixed shelves, and extend the centerlines of the shelves' locations that you earlier marked on the carcase sides to their edges. Match up these centerlines when you use the clamping jig **(C).**

Transferring the cross-dowel location to the face of the shelf board is quick and accurate when you use the easy jig shown in the drawing at right. To use the jig, simply insert the projecting bolt into the hole in the end of the top, bottom, or shelf, and use a scratch awl to mark the cross dowel's centerpoint **(D).** Set up a fence on your drill press, and drill these 10-mm holes ⅝ in. deep **(E).** As a note of caution, drill a test hole first because you're drilling most of the way through when using ¾-in. stock. Press the cross dowels into their holes and reassemble the parts, threading the bolt into the cross dowel. The line on the cross dowel is parallel to the hole through it. Use a hex key to tighten the fasteners **(F).** A T-handle hex driver is easier on the hands than an L-shaped key, but for real speed, you can chuck a hex driver into your variable-speed drill. Using a drill with adjustable clutch settings prevents excessive torque and also is much easier on your wrist.

➤ See *"Bed Bolts"* on p. 190.

You'll find cross dowels in a variety of sizes, some large enough to securely hold a bed frame.

Cross Dowel Jig

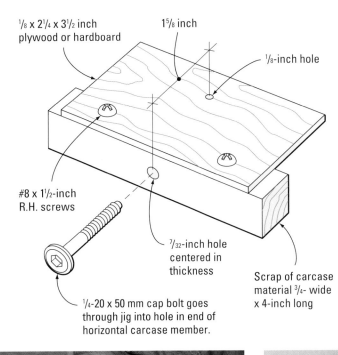

⅛ x 2¼ x 3½ inch plywood or hardboard

1⅝ inch

⅛-inch hole

#8 x 1½-inch R.H. screws

⁷⁄₃₂-inch hole centered in thickness

Scrap of carcase material ¾- wide x 4-inch long

¼-20 x 50 mm cap bolt goes through jig into hole in end of horizontal carcase member.

D

F

E

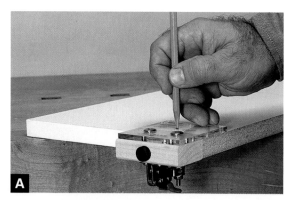

A

B

C

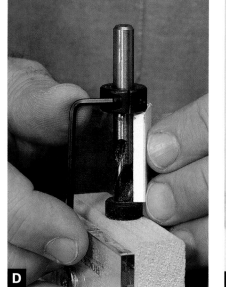

D

E

Minifix Fittings

One of the advantages of Minifix fittings is the absence of any visible hardware on the exterior of the carcase. And with a jig you can purchase from Rockler, installing the fittings into ¾-in.-thick stock is a quick and accurate process.

After you assemble the jig, hold it against the top end of the side, positioning the edge of the jig with the edge of the side **(A)**. Use a pencil to make a mark through the hole in the jig identified "for 8-mm hole." Repeat at each corner of the sides. For a T-joint, such as for a fixed shelf, mark the centerline of the shelf location on the inner face of the side. Align the edge of the jig with the centerline, and make a mark by putting your pencil into the notch in the jig **(B)**.

Adjust the jig's clamp to the thickness of your carcase components, and clamp it to the end of the carcase's bottom, with the edge of the jig flush with the bottom's edge. Make a pencil mark through the hole in the jig identified "for 15-mm hole" **(C)**. The face with the mark on it is the lower surface. To prevent mistakes as you mark the horizontal members, identify this face with a piece of masking tape. Put an 8-mm bit into the bushing in the jig, and give it a few turns with your drill so that the brad point enters the carcase stock. Remove the drill and add a stop collar to the bit so that the hole will be 1½₂ in. deep. Instead of juggling the collar and a rule at the same time, I cut a spacer and put it between the bushing and collar while I tightened the setscrew **(D)**. Drill the holes into the ends of the top, bottom, and fixed shelves **(E)**.

Chuck the 8-mm bit into your drill press, and set the fence against the edge of the side so that the bit is centered over one of the hole centerpoints. Drill all of the holes for the bolts **(F)**. Without changing the position of the fence or drill-press table, remove the 8-mm bit and chuck in the 15-mm bit. Drill holes for the cams at the marked centerpoints in the top, bottom, and fixed shelves **(G)**. Lightly tap the bolts into the sides so that the plastic collar is flush with the side **(H)**. This step engages plastic barbs against the walls of the hole for a firm grip. Don't drive the bolt past the collar, or its bulb head may not engage the cam at assembly. Push the cams into their holes, and use a no. 3 Phillips screwdriver to turn the cam so that the arrowhead on it points to the end of the carcase member. (I highlighted the arrowhead in the photo with white paint so you can see it more clearly.) Insert the bolts into the end of the board, and turn the cam to lock it against the head of the bolt **(I)**. As an optional finishing touch, you can snap a plastic cap into the drive slot to conceal the cam **(J)**.

F

G

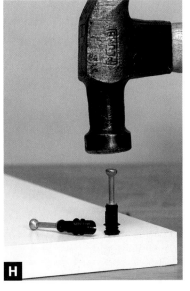

H

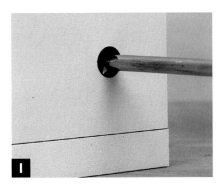

I

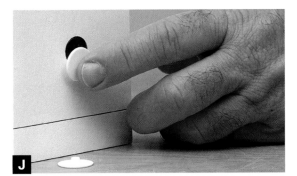

J

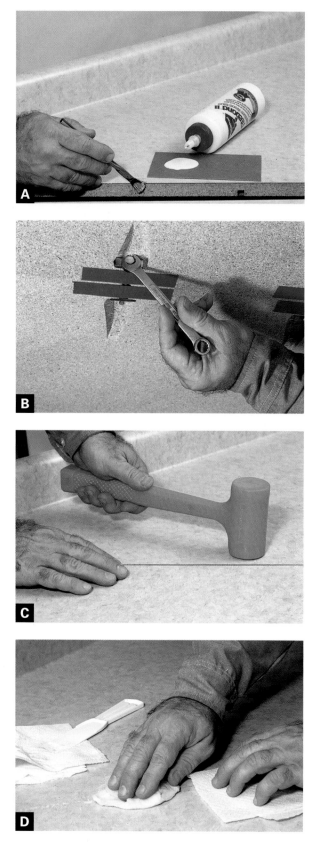

Countertop Joint Connector

The countertop sections in this demonstration were purchased at a home center with the miters already cut and the substrate machined for the joint connectors. Transport the sections carefully to avoid damage. Begin by test-fitting your countertop sections to make certain that there are no gaps along the joint line and that the surfaces of the pieces are reasonably flush. If necessary, place shims under your countertop to correct the alignment and give your countertop a firm foundation. The assembly of this joint works best with a two-person team: one working topside to keep the pieces aligned and flush, and the other person working below to tighten the connectors.

Use a ½-in. acid brush to brush water-resistant glue (Franklin's Titebond II is one brand) onto both sides of the joint **(A),** and push them together by hand, carefully aligning the ends. You're using the glue primarily for its ability to protect the substrate from swelling due to water penetration. Although the glue provides some holding power, you're really counting on the fasteners to provide mechanical strength to the joint. The person working from below snugs each of the fasteners a little at a time **(B).** The strips of masking tape prevent the connectors from falling until they get a good grip into the recesses in the countertop. The person working below can't necessarily judge the alignment of the pieces by the match of the recesses machined into the substrate. The person working topside is responsible for front-to-back alignment and a flush fit, and can tap near the seam line with a deadblow mallet to gently urge the pieces into perfect adjustment **(C).**

As the joint tightens, glue will begin to squeeze out. Simply scrape it away with a plastic putty knife. Clean up any residue with a paper towel that's barely damp, then follow with a dry paper towel **(D).** Use the connectors to bring the sections firmly together, but resist the urge to overtighten. That could produce a weak, glue-starved joint. Moving your fingertips gently along the seam will reveal irregularities that are difficult to see. Strange as it may seem, wearing a lightweight cotton glove (from a photo-supply shop) actually increases your sensitivity **(E).** Inspectors at automobile factories use this glove technique to check sheet metal before painting.

Even after you've tightened the connectors, the joint can slide out of position slightly due to a phenomenon known as "glue creep." Avoid this problem by bridging the seam with mending plates **(F).** The thicker the plates, the better: I use ones made from ⅛-in.-thick steel. But even with the mending plates, check the joint frequently during the first hour after assembly to make certain that it stays in place. After the glue dries, you can add seam filler to the joint to make it less noticeable **(G).** Purchasing seam filler made by the laminate manufacturer ensures a close color match. Be sure to knead the tube before opening it to make certain that the ingredients are thoroughly mixed. Squeeze a small bead of filler along the seam, and gently scrape away the excess with a plastic putty knife.

If you want to use this style of hardware with your own shopmade countertops—with either mitered or butt joints—you'll need to make a template to help you rout the recesses for the fasteners. To design your template, take a pencil, paper, and tape measure to a home center to record the dimensions of the recess in a factory-made countertop, and buy the fasteners. Your recess doesn't require the sloped end of the factory version, but you should make a test joint in scrap stock before routing your countertop.

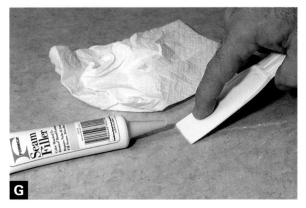

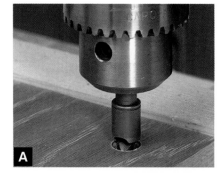

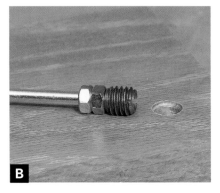

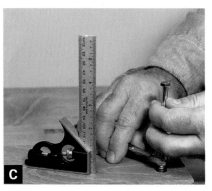

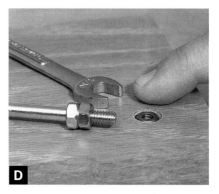

VARIATION 1

VARIATION 2

Threaded Inserts

Although threaded inserts have a screwdriver slot across one end, that slot would be more useful for removal than installation. In fact, you should install the slot upward only in softwoods. In that application, the insert is thread forming. In most wood applications, you'll get better results by installing the insert slot first into the wood. The slightly reduced thread diameter at the slot end produces a cutting action to make installation easier and also to reduce radial stresses that could cause the wood to split.

Drill the hole for the threaded fastener, and use a countersink tool to create a slight chamfer along the edge of the hole **(A)**. This chamfer will prevent wood from erupting as you drive the insert. Make an installation tool by jamming two nuts together near the end of a 4-in. bolt **(B)**. Hold the insertion tool perpendicular to the hole **(C),** using a small square to help you judge the vertical positioning. Use a wrench to drive the insert until it is ½₂ in. below the surface of the wood. Simply turn the tool counterclockwise to release it. Lightly rubbing your finger over the insert will tell you if you need to drive it further **(D)**.

VARIATION 1 You can purchase a driver that uses the power of your variable-speed drill to speed the process of installing threaded inserts. The only drawback is that the tool relies on the slot in the insert, so you can't use it to install the fastener's slot first into the wood. But this tool is still very helpful for installations into softwood or plywood.

VARIATION 2 Install hex-drive threaded inserts with the inexpensive L-shaped wrench shown or use a T-handled version. As an alternative, you can get a power assist by chucking a hex driver into your drill. In this case, a variable-speed drill with adjustable clutch settings helps prevent overdriving the insert.

Teenuts

To install a teenut flush to the surface of your wood, begin by drilling a counterbore slightly larger than the overall diameter of the fastener. For this ⅜-16 teenut, drill a 1-in. counterbore ¹⁄₃₂ in. deeper than the thickness of the top plate of the teenut **(A)**. Check the diameter and depth by placing the teenut upside down in the counterbore. Centered in the counterbore, drill a hole that's the diameter of the teenut's shank: ¹⁵⁄₃₂ in. in this case **(B)**. Position the teenut, and drive the barbs into the wood with a sharp rap or two with your hammer. Using a socket wrench as a driver will minimize the risk of hammer tracks on your wood **(C)**. In extremely hard woods, you may need to tap the teenut lightly to transfer the barbs' location to the wood, then drill small pilot holes to ease their entry **(D)**.

VARIATION 1 The screw-on teenut is very useful for applications where the threaded fastener wouldn't pull the barbs of a teenut into the wood. One typical installation is in the bottom of a table leg to provide a mounting point for a leveling glide. Simply drill for the shank of the teenut, and drill pilot holes for the screws.

VARIATION 2 The riveting teenut eliminates the problem of teenuts that push out or fall out. It's available with ¼-20 internal threads in three shank lengths: for stock that's ½ in., ⅝ in., or ¾ in. thick, without the necessity of counterboring. Insert the teenut in the conventional manner, and turn the stock over. Chuck the inserting tool into your drill, and you'll quickly and neatly spin the projecting metal downward into a finished collar that locks the teenut in place.

VARIATION 1

VARIATION 2

Invisible Shelf Hangers

When you need to hang a curio shelf or other small project on your wall, you often must choose between the security of hardware that's bulky and visible, or hidden hardware that's flimsy and insecure. I like to combine an inexpensive triangular-shaped hanger with an easy and secure mounting method. The following demonstration shows you how to mount a shelf with typical ¾-in.-thick sides.

Drill a ⁷⁄₆₄-in. pilot hole centered in the width of the rear edge of the side near the top, and drive a #8 x ¾-in. pan-head screw to secure the hanger to the shelf (A). Use your scratch awl to make a mark at the inner tip of the triangle (B). Flip the triangle out of the way, and drill a ½-in. hole ½ in. deep at that centerpoint (C). This hole creates clearance for the head of the hanging screw. Repeat the process on the other side. Attach a self-adhesive cork pad near the bottom of each side of the shelf to match the thickness of the hanger and to prevent the shelf from rubbing against the wall (D). When you flip the triangles back, you're ready to hang the shelf onto flat-head screws secured to the wall (E).

Drawer Slides

Drawer Slides

➤ Center-Mount Slide in a Face-Frame Cabinet (p. 147)

➤ Utility Slides in a Frameless Cabinet (p. 149)

➤ Utility Slides in a Face-Frame Cabinet (p. 150)

Tray Slides

➤ Pullout Tray (p. 151)

WHILE PRICE IS CERTAINLY one of the factors to consider when choosing drawer slides, it's not the only one. In fact, there's such an interdependent relationship among the carcase, slide, and drawer that successful drawer-slide selection begins in the design phase of a project. As you make certain design decisions, you'll eliminate some types of slides—or you may like a particular slide's features so well that you'll find yourself designing your cabinet around its specifications. If you're doing a kitchen, remember that there's no rule that says all of the drawer slides must be identical. Some drawers may work fine with 3/4 extension slides, while you may prefer to use full-extension or even overextension slides in other drawers or install pullout trays to maximize accessibility.

If you're replacing slides as part of a renovation project, you're not obligated to use the same type of slides the original cabinetmaker did. But you do need to understand how the construction of the carcase and drawer limits your options. The first step in that direction is becoming reasonably fluent in the design language of drawers and slides.

The Vocabulary of Drawers

Drawers and slides have their own specialized jargon, so take a look at the two "Drawer Anatomy" drawings on p. 140 to familiarize yourself with the terminology.

The top drawer is an *overextension* style, and you can see that the drawer's back extends past the front plane of the carcase, making it easy to reach items in the back,

DRAWER ANATOMY
(SIDE SECTION VIEW)

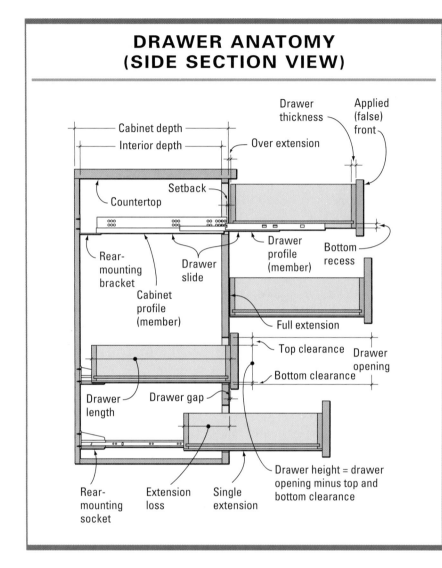

Cabinet depth

Interior depth

Over extension

Drawer thickness

Applied (false) front

Setback

Countertop

Rear-mounting bracket

Drawer slide

Cabinet profile (member)

Drawer profile (member)

Bottom recess

Full extension

Top clearance

Drawer opening

Bottom clearance

Drawer length

Drawer gap

Rear-mounting socket

Extension loss

Single extension

Drawer height = drawer opening minus top and bottom clearance

DRAWER ANATOMY
(FRONT VIEW)

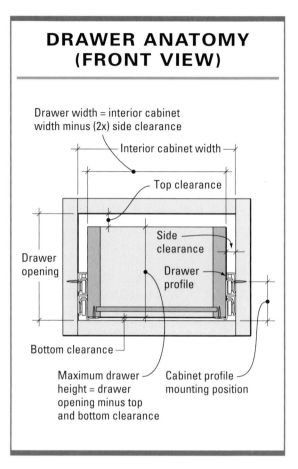

Drawer width = interior cabinet width minus (2x) side clearance

Interior cabinet width

Top clearance

Side clearance

Drawer opening

Drawer profile

Bottom clearance

Maximum drawer height = drawer opening minus top and bottom clearance

Cabinet profile mounting position

The *bottom recess* is the distance from the underside of the *drawer bottom* to the lower edge of the drawer side. This dimension can be critical for the installation of bottom-mounted or center-mounted slides.

A *drawer slide* consists of two parts that usually separate from each other for installation. The *cabinet profile*, also called the *cabinet member*, is the portion that you screw to the carcase, and the *drawer profile*, or *drawer member*, is the one you fasten to the drawer box. *Setback* is the distance from the front plane of the carcase to the forward end of the cabinet member. The manufacturer's installation specification sheet will tell you the correct amount of setback to utilize for each style of slide. There also may be a setback from the front plane of the drawer to

even when there's an overhanging countertop. The design of the slide and the method of installation influence the amount of overextension.

The *drawer thickness* refers to the thickness of the stock used to make the sides, back, and front of the drawer box. This excludes the thickness of an *applied (false) front*. Most wood drawers have sides that are ½ in. thick, but this is somewhat arbitrary because it usually doesn't affect the operation of the drawer or the attachment of the slides.

the forward end of the drawer member, but many drawer members simply mount flush with the front of the drawer box.

A *rear-mounting bracket* or *rear-mounting socket* may be a plastic or metal piece that attaches the rear end of the cabinet profile to the back of the carcase.

A *full-extension* drawer slide is designed to bring the rear of the drawer back flush with the front plane of the carcase.

The specification sheet for a drawer slide will state the minimum dimensions for the *bottom clearance* and the *top clearance*. You can usually make these clearances (especially the top one) larger than the specified minimums but never smaller. The *drawer height* refers to the height of the drawer box, not to the applied front.

The *drawer length* is the overall front-to-back measurement of the drawer box.

The *drawer opening* is a crucial dimension in a face-frame cabinet. For a given vertical drawer opening, subtract the top and bottom clearances to obtain the maximum drawer height. The drawer you make for that opening can have a shorter drawer height than this maximum dimension.

The *drawer gap* is the distance from the front plane of the carcase to the rear plane of the applied drawer front. You may want to establish this gap to keep the applied front from slapping the carcase every time you close a drawer. Another reason for the gap is so you can apply bumpers to silence the closing action.

A *single-extension* drawer slide brings only a portion of the drawer's total length past the front plane of the carcase; the remainder is the *extension loss*. A single-extension slide is usually specified by the proportion of extension to the drawer's length. For exam-

A kitchen scale will weigh small drawers and their contents, but you'll need the bathroom scale to figure load ratings for file drawers.

ple, a 3/4 single-extension slide that's 12 in. long will have a forward motion of 9 in. Two common single-extension ratios are 2/3 and 3/4. The amount of extension is sometimes called *travel*.

Referring to the front view drawing on the facing page, you'll see the *side clearance*, a critical dimension for side-mounted drawer slides. The *cabinet profile mounting position* is another important measurement. One usual method of specifying this location is from a fixed reference, such as the top of a face-frame rail, to the centerpoint of the mounting screws.

The Weight and Measure of Drawer Design

Catalogs often list the load rating for slides of a particular design. To determine the weight rating that's appropriate for a cabinet you're designing, knock together a drawer box of the size you have in mind, load it up with the contents you expect to put into it,

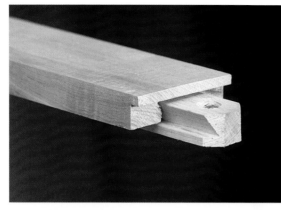

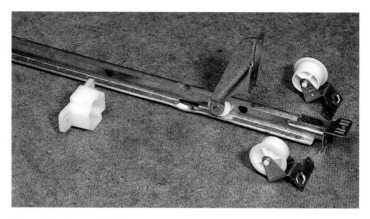

A manufactured center-mount slide in wood is a classic style that's easy to install and can give years of dependable service.

The single-track drawer slide utilizes a three-point suspension—two nylon rollers attach to the face frame, and the center roller rides the rail.

Choose a center-mount slide with ball-bearing action, and you'll have a quiet drawer with hidden hardware.

and put it on a scale. As a rule of thumb, I'd suggest adding a 50 percent overload factor.

Catalogs will sometimes list only the length of the slide, which is the closed length of the two members when assembled. As a general rule, you want to use the longest slide that will fit on the drawer box to maximize its range of motion.

The overall depth required by the slide is another essential dimension you need when designing cabinets, especially when you're considering slides that attach to the back

wall of the cabinet with sockets. The sockets usually provide a certain range of motion for you to fine-tune the fit, but you must make certain that your design works around the specifications of the slides.

Center-Mounted Slides

Your choice of the basic construction method for the cabinet's carcase influences the range of available drawer slides. For example, the traditional center-mount slide requires face-frame cabinet construction. Although you could mill a slide like this in your own shop, it requires quite a number of machine setups. This style of slide is better suited for use in a bedroom dresser rather than in a busy kitchen. For extra-wide drawers, consider using two slides, each spaced at one-third of the drawer's width.

The three-roller design (also called a single-track slide) is another style that requires face-frame construction. In my experience they are invariably squeaky and I've never had any long-term success with these slides.

The Accuride 1029 series is one more center-mount design that requires face-frame construction, but its ball-bearing action is very smooth. Coupled with the supplied nylon tack glides you attach to the face-frame rail, the hardware produces a drawer that doesn't wobble or shimmy. The load rating is light—only 35 lb.—but it somewhat offsets that liability with the asset that you can't see the slide from the side. That's an important consideration when you've worked hard to produce good-looking joinery to hold together the drawer box.

Epoxy-Coated Slides

Some catalogs refer to this type of slide as a "Euro slide" because it easily attaches with screws into the holes drilled in typical 32-mm system cabinets. Another widespread description is "epoxy coated" because of its durable low-friction coating. One other name you might see is "low-profile" slide. Although it's classified here as a side-mounted slide, the drawer member is actually an angle that also fits around the bottom edge of the drawer box's side. As a result, it can be attached to the bottom of the drawer box, its side, or both. You'll find a variety of installation jigs that speed the installation of the cabinet members inside your cabinet's carcase.

This slide design is extremely versatile, one that you can mount in frameless or face-frame cabinets, or team it with right-angle brackets to make pullout trays inside a cabinet or to hang a drawer from the underside of a counter or table. Like all side-mounted slides, the drawer or pullout must be a specific width in relation to the carcase width for good operation.

Match the Socket and Slide

Sometimes, a cabinet's design doesn't permit you to mount slides to the sides of the

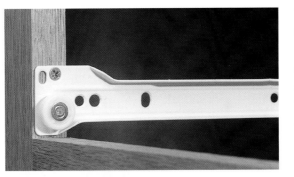

The epoxy-coated slide is popular because it's economical and adaptable to face-frame or frameless applications.

After you've installed pullout trays in your lower kitchen cabinets, you'll wonder how you survived without them.

> ### ► LEFT AND RIGHT

Some drawer slides are unhanded, meaning that you can use them on either side of the drawer. But other slides have members that are mirror images of each other. You determine the handedness of a drawer as you look at the front of the cabinet. The left-hand drawer member and cabinet member install to your left. Some manufacturers stamp the hand designation onto each piece of the drawer slide, which can be a time-saving feature during installation.

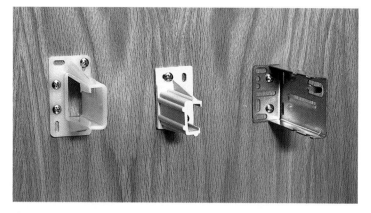

One manufacturer, three rear-mount socket designs. Make sure that you select sockets to match your slides.

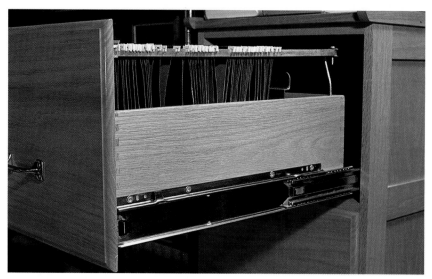

For total access drawers, particularly in heavy-duty applications, choose full-extension or overextension slides.

To make sure that sockets will stay put, you need to create a secure mounting location where you can drive screws that are at least $3/4$ in. long. You can use several different strategies to accomplish that. Use a thicker back for the entire cabinet, or simply add strips of plywood in the front or rear of the standard $1/4$-in.-thick back. If you add strips inside the cabinet, make certain that you'll still have enough interior cabinet depth for the slide and socket combo that you're using.

Side-Mounted Slides

A full-extension or overextension slide is often a side-mounted unit with impressive load ratings: from 90 lb. to a truly astonishing 500 lb. per drawer. Steel ball bearings enable the slide to carry heavy weight with smooth action. Whether you want to craft a carcase—the nearest support surface is the back of the cabinet. In that case, you'll need to find out whether the slides you want to use have rear-mounting sockets available.

Many types of slides offer the rear-mounting option, but you still need to shop carefully to make sure you end up with a slide and socket team that works together. I found three different sockets from the same manufacturer next to each other at a local home center. I then had to match their numbers against the drawer-slide packaging to ensure compatibility.

Check the slide's specification sheet for the required side clearance, and you'll be rewarded with smoothly operating drawers.

lingerie drawer or create a slide-out tool storage unit for your work truck, these are slides that combine full access with durability. File cabinets and office furniture are other popular uses for heavy-duty full-extension slides. If you're building lateral files—with drawers that are wider than they are deep—look for slides that are specifically rated for that application, and respect the stated limits on drawer dimensions and weight.

To prevent file cabinets from tipping or falling, you can purchase an interlock system that allows only one drawer to open at a time. The lock bar fits in the front of the cabinet, and the system can be retrofitted into existing cabinets.

Not surprisingly, side clearances are a critical dimension for side-mounted slides. Typical full-extension slides require a $\frac{1}{2}$-in. clearance on each side, so the overall drawer box width is 1 in. less than its target opening. You can cheat the size of the opening slightly larger, perhaps as much as $\frac{1}{16}$ in. per side depending on the slide's manufacturer, but you simply can't make the slides fit into anything smaller than $\frac{1}{2}$ in. per side. I usually make the drawer $1\frac{1}{16}$ in. narrower than its opening to avoid binding without introducing sloppiness.

Bottom-Mounted Slides

Drawer slides that hide under the box let you show off fancy traditional joinery and still have the convenience and smooth operation of modern hardware. The Tandem model from Blum can be used on face-frame or frameless cabinets, and with a drawer that's inset (its finished face flush with the front plane of the carcase) or with an applied front that overlays the carcase. The bottom recess and the bottom clearance are critical dimensions.

SLOTS FOR ADJUSTMENT AND HOLES FOR FIXING

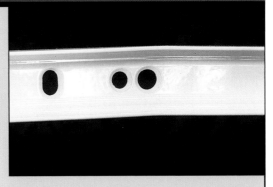

You'll notice that the parts of a drawer slide typically have both slots and holes. For initial installation, it's usually best to first drive the screws at the midpoint of the slots. That way, you can adjust the hardware's position by merely loosening the screw to permit movement fore and aft or up and down. But after you have the slide positioned perfectly, fix its location by driving screws through the holes. This slide by Blum has two different hole sizes—the smaller one accepts a no. 6 screw, and the larger takes a no. 7. Both holes have ample countersinks to fully seat flat-head screws—a sign of a high-quality slide. Other slides that look similar at first glance lack this refinement, so that the flat-head screws sit proud of the hardware, reducing their bearing surface and becoming a potential obstruction.

Drive a screw at the midpoint of a slot to permit adjustment, and then drive screws into the holes to hold the setting.

Drawers to Go

When you want to add a pencil drawer to a table or work counter, buy a ready-made unit, and you'll have it installed faster than you could even clear off your workbench to begin to make your own drawer. If you can adapt one of these to your kitchen table, you'll multiply its usefulness as a temporary home office, homework station, or crafts center.

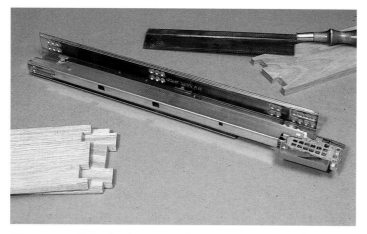

Choose a slide that's concealed under the box, and nothing distracts from the craftsmanship of the drawer's joinery.

You also can purchase ready-made metal drawer sides with the slide already built into them. Buy the length you want, then cut the front, back, and bottom from your own wood to make the exact width you need. This drawer assembled quickly, but I wasn't impressed with the less than snug fit where the plywood bottom meets the sides. If it were used as a kitchen drawer, that area would quickly fill with crumbs and other bits that spill out of boxes or leap from the countertop. Check out the designs from a variety of manufacturers.

Metal box sides with built-in slides can be a quick route to building durable drawers.

If you want nearly instant storage and organizational satisfaction, install a molded plastic drawer below a table or work counter.

Center-Mount Slide in a Face-Frame Cabinet

One of the first things that you need to know about this drawer slide has to do with the construction of the drawer itself. The Accuride model 1029 slide requires that the drawer bottom extends all the way to the front of the drawer (flush with the front plane of the carcase). There are many different ways to accomplish this, but the simple construction method I used involves identical sides and identical pieces for the front and back (see the drawing at right). You then add an applied front to the drawer box. This particular slide also requires a ¼-in. bottom recess: the distance from the lower surface of the drawer bottom to the lower edge of the drawer side: I used a clearance of ⅛ in. on each side of the drawer box, making it ¼ in. narrower than the face-frame opening.

After you build the drawer, turn it upside down on your workbench and draw a centerline from the front of the bottom to the back. Separate the drawer-slide pieces by extending the parts and then pull them apart hard enough to overcome the friction resistance that holds them together. Center the drawer member on the bottom, and drive a screw through one of the holes into a pilot hole in the back of the drawer **(A)**. The holes didn't match with the center of the back, so I drilled an extra hole in the slide so I wouldn't split the back. I also upgraded from the supplied #8 x ½-in. screw to a ¾-in. screw for additional holding power.

Secure the front of the slide by driving the screw through the angled slot into the drawer bottom and front **(B)**. Add a clamp from the front of the drawer to the back so that driving the screw won't separate the parts.

(Text continues on p. 148.)

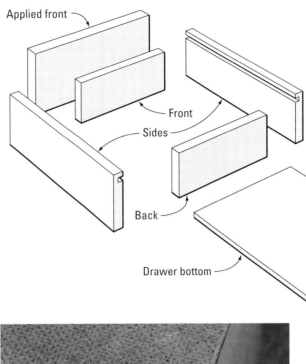

Applied front
Front
Sides
Back
Drawer bottom

A

B

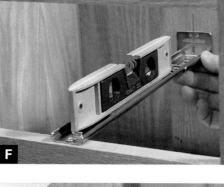

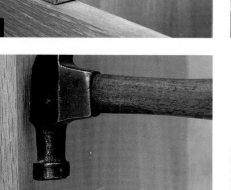

By measurement, determine the side-to-side centerline of the drawer opening, and mark this line on the face-frame rail **(C)**. Measure from this centerline to the side of the cabinet, and make a note of the measurement. Transfer this dimension to the cabinet's back, and mark a vertical centerline **(D)**. In this cabinet, I had enough room to add a ¾-in.-thick plywood strip, gluing it to the back and driving screws through the back into the strip. Adding this strip allowed me to drive longer screws through the rear bracket of the slide, strengthening the assembly.

Engage the rear-mounting bracket by sliding it onto the cabinet member, and drive a screw to attach the front end of the cabinet member to the center of the drawer rail **(E)**. Notice that the member is set back about ⅛ in. from the front of the rail to avoid interference with the drawer box.

Use a level on the slide to position the rear-mounting bracket **(F)**. It's a simple matter of matching the center of the bracket with the marked centerline on the back while the slide is level. Attach the bracket with a screw.

Use a hammer to tap the nylon glide tacks into the front rail **(G)**. Make sure that you position them so they will support the bottom edges of the drawer sides to prevent the drawer box from rocking. Engage the two halves of the drawer slide, and the installation is complete **(H)**.

Utility Slides in a Frameless Cabinet

Some drawer slides, like this set from Blum, have each component clearly marked to avoid possible confusion **(A)**. The first letter indicates whether it is the cabinet or drawer member, while the second identifies left and right. (For photographic purposes, I darkened the marks.) Position the drawer members flush with the front end of the box, and drive screws through the slide into the bottom of the drawer, the side, or both **(B)**. Driving screws into the bottom edges of boxes made from some plywoods requires carefully matching the pilot bit with the screw to avoid splitting the laminations. Driving screws into the sides of plywood boxes is usually less risky.

With Blum slides, you can use a jig the company makes to simplify installation **(C)**. (The jig accommodates several models of Blum slides, and the following directions apply to the Model 230 slides I installed.) Simply snap a cabinet member into the gun-shaped jig, making certain that its front end butts against the nubs that automatically produce a 2-mm setback. Following the pictorial instructions packed with the jig, mark the front edge of the cabinet with lines indicating the top and bottom of each drawer. Aligning the 20-mm mark on the jig with the drawer bottom mark positions the slide perfectly inside the cabinet **(D)**. The mark at 22 mm indicates the top of the next drawer.

Drill pilot holes, and drive screws to secure the cabinet member to the carcase **(E)**. When you've driven all the screws, simply twist the jig to separate it from the drawer slide. All that remains is to test-fit the drawer and apply its false front. The photo **(F)** shows the upsweep at the front of the drawer member that serves as a self-closing feature for this slide.

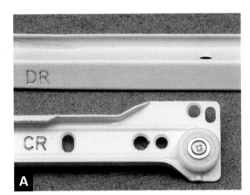
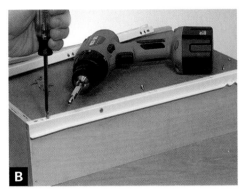
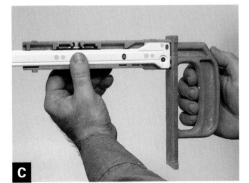

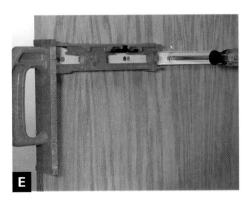

A

B

C

D

E

VARIATION

Utility Slides in a Face-Frame Cabinet

Attach the socket by pushing it onto the back end of the cabinet member **(A)**. Each style of drawer slide requires its own type of socket, so be very careful that you purchase sockets that match your slides. With the Blum installation jig shown in the photo **(B),** you simply snap in a cabinet member and the jig automatically produces the correct set-back on the face frame's stile. If you don't have a jig, you can position the cabinet member by measurement.

Visually check that the slide is straight, and drive screws to fasten it to the cabinet's back **(C)**. I made this cabinet with a ½-in. back and added a second thickness behind the cabinet in the target location of the drawer sockets so that I could use ¾-in. screws. The fully threaded shank of a sheet-metal screw provides excellent holding power in this application. Fasten the drawer members by driving screws into the sides of the drawer box **(D)**.

Install the drawer, and check that it moves freely without binding. The photo **(E)** shows the clearances between the drawer box and the opening in the face frame. Looking along the length of the drawer slide, you can see the socket in the back of the cabinet.

VARIATION **You'll sometimes run into situations where using a rear socket isn't practical. In that case, you can usually add blocking to the side of the carcase so you can screw on the cabinet member. For job-site work, consider using the plastic block shown in the photo at left. It's available in three thickness ranges—from ⁵⁄₁₆ in. to 1 in. thick. By adding the supplied ¹⁄₁₆-in. or ⅛-in. shims, you fine-tune the fit.**

Pullout Tray

Position the drawer member flush with the front edge of the tray, drill pilot holes, and drive the screws **(A)**.

[TIP]   Substitute #6 x ¾-in. screws instead of the ½-in. screws furnished with the slides.

Using the metric machine screws furnished with the brackets, attach the cabinet members to the brackets **(B).** Set up the hardware on a flat surface to ensure that the assemblies are square. Rip a scrap piece of plywood to serve as a spacer between the carcase side and the bracket to produce the clearance you need. Insert the slide on one edge of the tray into its mating piece on the brackets, and slide the brackets against the spacer **(C)**.

Use a small try square to establish a clearance at the front end of the tray (I used ¼ in.) so that the doors won't make contact. When you have the bracket situated, carefully remove the tray, and drive #10 x ¾-in. screws through a pair of the slots. The pair of slots I chose in the photo **(D)** will permit adjustment forward and back. Select the other pair of slots if you want side-to-side adjustability. Install the other bracket, and test-fit the tray.

(Text continues on p. 152.)

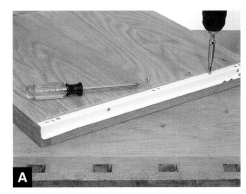

A

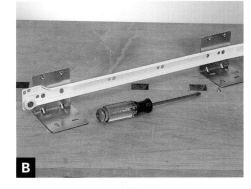

B

C

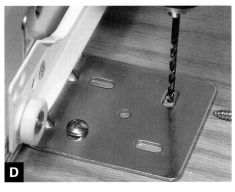

D

When you're satisfied with the fit, drill a ³⁄₁₆-in. hole through the center hole in the rear brackets, and drop in a 10-24 machine screw **(E)**. Add a fender washer under the shelf, and secure it with a nylon insert locking nut or separate lock washer with a plain nut. The fender washer shown has a ³⁄₁₆-in. center hole and 1½-in. overall outside diameter. This washer helps spread the bearing stress of the slide assembly when the tray is pulled forward. With a heavily loaded tray, this can be a considerable force, so the bigger the washer the better. If you can't access the underside of the shelf to install a fender washer, drive screws through all of the bracket's slots and center hole.

The completed tray **(F)** has a sleek appearance, and it effortlessly glides stored items within easy reach. To keep stored items from sliding, cover the bottom of the tray with a nonslip rubber pad from the housewares section of your hardware store.

Knobs, Handles, and Pulls

Knobs, Handles & Pulls

S ELECTING HARDWARE IS all about achieving balance and focusing attention where it belongs. When you choose the right hardware for a project—especially a period reproduction—the hardware will be the third or fourth thing that people notice. That's because tastefully chosen and appropriate hardware becomes part of the furniture, not merely a piece of metal tacked on as an afterthought.

On the other hand, contemporary cabinets and furniture sometimes cry out for a piece of hardware that will give them a design accent or a splash of color. A wall of stark white melamine frameless cabinets can make a kitchen look like a sensory-deprivation ward. But add bright nylon pulls in bold shapes, and you'll take a giant step toward creating a warm and inviting area.

Wood Knobs, Handles, and Pulls

Some furniture styles, such as Shaker, utilize wood for virtually all knobs and pulls. You'll even find movable Shaker latches whose only metal content is a tiny pin that secures the cam to the shaft. Other styles, such as Arts and Crafts, may use either metal hardware or wood knobs and pulls with a pyramidal face. One word of caution—just because a manufacturer has the machinery to produce pulls in a particular style doesn't necessarily mean that it will always use the wood

This selection of all-wood hardware has timeless appeal. The Shaker knobs and latch feature authentic profiles and wood species. The Arts and Crafts knob and pull feature pyramid styling.

For openers, this collection of contemporary wood products includes a jumbo 13-in. refrigerator handle and a sculpted shell pull. The other handles and knobs also feature sleek styling.

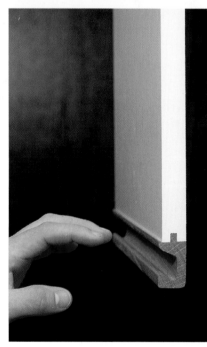

Get a grip on cabinet doors with a continuous wood pull. Neat installation requires precise machining of the groove.

that's exactly right. For example, genuine Arts and Crafts furniture used white oak almost exclusively, but you'll find pulls and knobs made today that are correct in form but in other species, such as red oak.

Contemporary knob makers are always turning out fresh shapes as well as new designs that meet current needs. You'll discover, for example, a selection of wood handles that are used in conjunction with wood-cladding kits to transform a metal refrigerator to look like a built-in cabinet.

Continuous Wood Pulls

If you want to add a wood feature to laminate-covered cabinets, you'll appreciate the continuous wood pull that's usually installed along the bottom end of wall cabinet doors and the upper end of lower doors. Of course, this technique will give a set of cabinets strong horizontal lines. If you'd rather accentuate the height of the installation, attach the continuous pulls along the vertical edge of the door. Although the pull is often used with laminate cabinets, you can certainly add it to plywood doors as well.

Naming Names

A knob has a single attachment point, which is sometimes a wood tenon but more frequently a wood screw or machine screw. The words "handle" and "pull" generally refer to items with two attachment points. The terms are used almost interchangeably, although it's interesting to note that a piece of hardware on a cabinet door is usually called a handle, while the identical item on a drawer is called a pull. The center-to-center spacing between the attachment points is sometimes called boring or centers. For

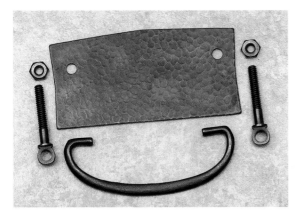

A traditional pull is a set of components: The threaded posts and nuts flank the baseplate, and the bail is at the bottom.

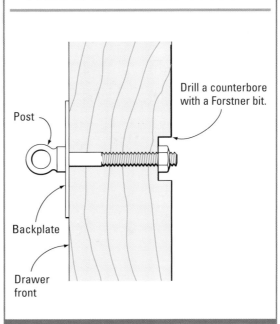

DRILLING A COUNTERBORE IN A THICK DRAWER FRONT

Post

Backplate

Drawer front

Drill a counterbore with a Forstner bit.

example, "handles with 3-in. boring" or "pulls with 4-in. centers."

A pull with a movable grip has a definite name for each of its components. The backplate (sometimes simply called the plate) is the flat piece of metal that lies on the drawer front. The threaded machine screw with a hole at the end is a post, and the movable part that you grip is called the bail. This multicomponent construction is the traditional method of making pulls, but some less-expensive modern pretenders join the tips of the posts and the backplate into a single unit. In this case, the factory permanently crimps the bail into position.

If the posts are too long, you can easily cut them, but if they are too short to reach

▶ See *"Shortening Screws"* on p. 162.

through a thick drawer, drill a counterbore as shown in the drawing at right above. When you install a traditional type of pull with separate posts, be careful that tightening the nuts doesn't twist the posts and bind the bail.

Pulls and Bin Hardware

If you're building a cabinet full of small drawers to organize your home or shop, you'll reach for the bin pull with a built-in cardholder. When you need a beefier pull for larger-scale applications, such as file drawers, purchase the cardholder and pull separately. If you need only a small pull, consider a sash lift. You can pair them on a drawer or let one work solo. For bins or drawers, check out the selection of rectangular and shell-shaped pulls that are available in either smooth-stamped profiles or with ornate cast designs. If you look closely at the top photo on p. 156, you may be able to tell that the screw heads visible in the center and right examples in the bottom row are part of the pull itself, not separate fasteners. The real attachment occurs via screws driven from inside the drawer.

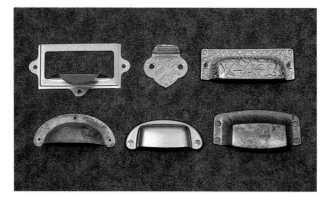

When you need some pull, consider this sampling of bin and drawer hardware. The first item shown at left on the top row is a bin pull with an integral cardholder and at center is a sash lift with cast design. The next item plus those on the bottom row are rectangular and shell pulls.

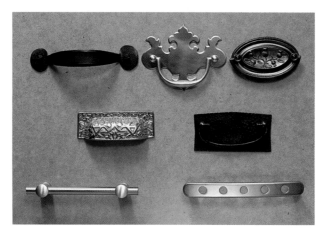

Top row, left to right: a hand-forged pull that you also can mount vertically, a Chippendale pull, and a Hepplewhite pull. Middle row, left to right: an Arts and Crafts pull and a sand-cast Victorian pull. Bottom row: contemporary fittings that can be mounted vertically or horizontally.

Pulls and Handles: Period to Contemporary

If you can't find the right piece of hardware for your project, it simply means that you haven't looked in the right place. Check the Manufacturers and Suppliers beginning on p. 214 to find the perfect period hardware to complement a reproduction or an up-to-the-minute look for a contemporary piece. In some cases, you'll contact a factory with the latest computer-controlled equipment, but other times you'll talk to an individual who set a hammer down on his anvil so he could pick up the telephone.

Mounting Handles and Pulls

Mounting door handles and drawer pulls is one of the last steps in building a cabinet, and it's a time when I'm not willing to leave very much to chance. In addition, individually marking each door or drawer is a time-

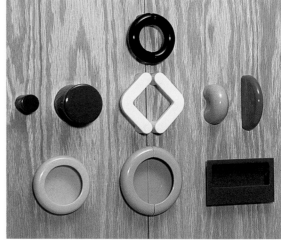

Whether you build cabinets from wood or laminate-covered materials, durable nylon hardware lets you project a colorful personality. Install the pulls on the bottom row by routing recesses into the doors or drawers.

consuming nuisance. So it's a good idea to buy a jig for its dependable accuracy. But even if an extremely tight budget prohibits the purchase of a factory-made jig, you can get far better results from a shopmade jig that you quickly knock together than you'd obtain by juggling a tape measure and subtracting fractions in your head.

One Word of Advice: Plastics

Plastics have come a long way in recent years and have arrived as a tough and stable hardware medium. HEWI is one company that combines function with fun in a line of pulls that can add style and color to contemporary furniture. Even if you scratch the rugged nylon hardware, the color goes all the way through the piece, so damage is barely noticeable.

The Backing Plate Cover-Up

Changing the pulls in a kitchen is an inexpensive way to give the cabinets a facelift. If you add a backing plate, you'll cover up scratches in the old door and also be able to switch to pulls that have a different center-to-center distance from the old hardware. In new construction, the plates add more metallic gleam, prevent scratches, and cover the sin of misdrilled holes.

> ### ➤ SPARE YOURSELF SOME TROUBLE
>
> **When you buy** pulls for a kitchen full of cabinets, buy at least two spares. Wrap them in paper and put them in a kitchen drawer so that you or your customer will be able to find them when one of the originals breaks. That way, you'll spare yourself the trouble of trying to find a replacement.

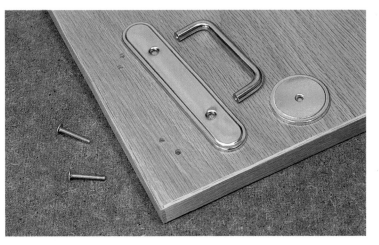

Backing plates are useful in new construction but really excel at covering up old holes during renovation work, letting you shift to pulls with a different boring.

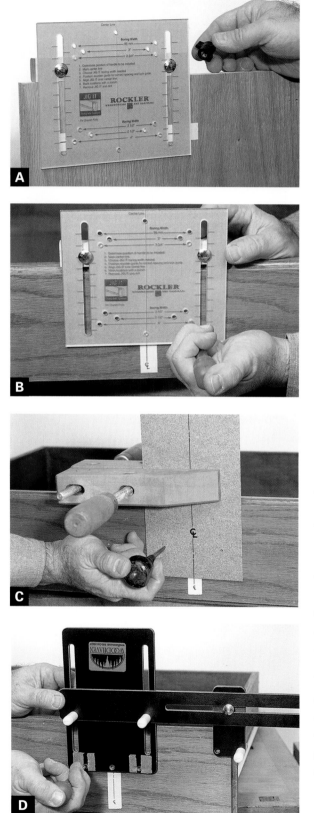

Mounting Pulls

You'll find a number of marking jigs on the market that range in price from economical to astronomical. The jig from Rockler (A) is very affordable, easily adjustable, and allows you to select from six different mounting-center dimensions. To set up the jig, draw a line parallel to the edge of a piece of scrap stock at the desired mounting distance from the drawer's top edge. Find the setting on the jig that corresponds to the center-to-center distance of the pulls you're installing, match the marks on the jig to the line, and tighten the locking knobs to secure the wood bar that rests on the top edge of the drawer.

To mark the drawer, put a vertical strip of masking tape at the approximate center of the drawer front, then draw the precise centerline on the tape. Match the centerline of the jig to the drawer's centerline, and you're ready to mark (B). You can use the spring-loaded punch like a scratch awl, gently pushing on it to make a small mark. But pushing harder on the punch loads up the spring mechanism, which then trips and makes a deeper impression into the wood. Turning the punch's barrel adjusts the amount of pressure that triggers the punch.

A shopmade version of the drawer-mounting jig is easy to build from a piece of 1/8-in.-thick hardboard or plywood. Simply lay out a vertical centerline, accurately mark the mounting centerpoints, and drill ⅛-in. holes to admit the point of your scratch awl (C). Calibrate the jig by using the method shown in photo **A**, and attach a wood handscrew clamp to act as the top stop.

To use either a purchased or shopmade jig on a drawer that uses two pulls, you simply mark a centerline at each pull's location. As an alternative, you can purchase a marking jig that has an adjustable end stop (D). To mark for the pull at the opposite end of the drawer, you simply rotate the jig 180 degrees. Cover the unused holes with masking tape to ensure that you get the correct spacing.

Once you have marked the drawers, use a guide for your portable drill to ensure that the holes are perpendicular to the drawer's face **(E).** Clamping a piece of scrap stock inside the drawer prevents tearout where the bit exits the wood.

Marking a door for a single knob is an easy job with a plastic jig that reverses to mark both right- and left-hand doors **(F).** To avoid mistakes, cover the unused holes with strips of masking tape. You also can use this jig to mark for pulls that use two mounting holes.

If you want to skip the marking and jump right to drilling, make a guide like the one shown in the drawing **(G),** tailoring the dimensions to center the hardware in the stile's width and matching the mounting centers of your pulls. The inserts shown (Lee Valley is one source) have ribbed sides that tightly grip the sides of a ⅝-in. hole to resist turning. Use a hammer to tap the insert flush with the face of the jig, then sink it 1/16 in. below the surface so it won't scratch your door when you reverse the jig. I put a 7/16-in. socket from a wrench set atop the insert, and sank it with a couple of light hammer taps. Screw in a bushing with a 3/16-in. hole, and you're ready to drill. Use a clamp to secure the jig to the front of the door and a scrap board behind the door to prevent tearout **(H).** Drill all of the right-hand doors, and then screw the bushings into the opposite side of the jig to reverse it.

Drill Guide for Mounting Pulls

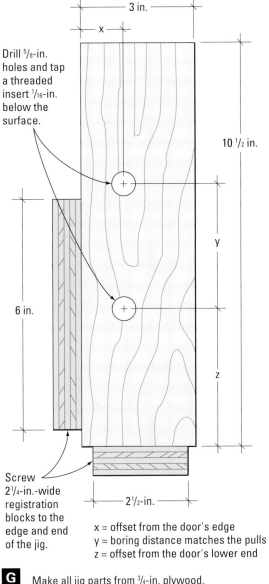

Drill ⅝-in. holes and tap a threaded insert 1/16-in. below the surface.

3 in.

x

10 ½ in.

6 in.

y

z

2½-in.

Screw 2¼-in.-wide registration blocks to the edge and end of the jig.

x = offset from the door's edge
y = boring distance matches the pulls
z = offset from the door's lower end

G Make all jig parts from ¾-in. plywood.

A

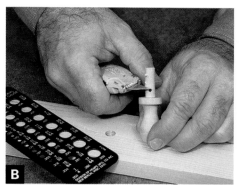

B

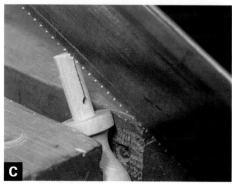

C

D

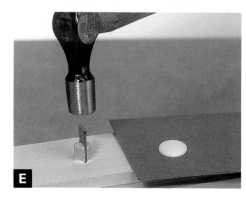

E

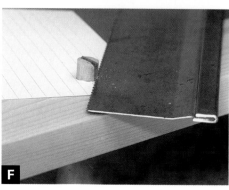

F

Installing a Wood Knob with a Tenon

Securing a wood knob by gluing a tapered wedge into its tenon is a traditional and secure technique. In fact, it's so secure that if you ever need to replace the knob, you'll need to drill it out.

Using a V-block at your drill press, drill a ⅛-in. hole centered in the tenon and ¼ in. from the shoulder of the knob. A brad-point bit helps to ensure accuracy **(A)**. To have a strong connection, you'll need a close fit between the hole and the tenon. Drill a test hole in a piece of scrap stock. If the fit is too loose, use a smaller bit for the hole in the door stile, and then shave the tenon to fit snugly into the hole **(B)**. Using a pencil, draw a straight line connecting the hole and the end of the tenon. Then draw a line on the end of the tenon through the center, meeting the line along the length.

To give your saw a starting place, use your utility knife to cut a small notch at this intersection of these lines. With a dovetail saw, cut a kerf from the end of the knob to the hole, using the marked lines as a guide **(C)**. Tilting the knob in your vise and starting your cut at an angle makes it surprisingly easy to make a freehand cut that follows both lines. Rip a square strip of stock, matching its end to the diameter of the tenon. For example, I ripped a ⅜-in. by ⅜-in. walnut strip to match the size of the ⅜-in.-dia. tenon and to contrast with its pale tone.

Use a scrollsaw to cut wedges into the end of the stock, tapering from 3⁄32 in. to zero over the length of the tenon's slot **(D)**. To do this, mark the length of the wedge onto the stock, and cut a number of wedges until you make one that will fit into the tenon's kerf. Apply glue to the tenon,

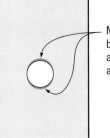

and place it through the stile with the kerf perpendicular to the grain **(E)**. Driving a wedge parallel to the grain could split the stile. Dip the wedge into glue and quickly tap it into place, making certain that the shoulder of the knob stays snug against the opposite face of the stile. Wipe away excess glue, and cut and sand the end of the tenon flush with the stile **(F)**. The offset backsaw I used does a good job of flush trimming, but its teeth can scratch the wood. To prevent that, I cut a hole through an index card and put it over the tenon to shield the stile. The completed installation utilizes traditional methods but has a clean, modern look **(G)**.

VARIATION 1 I sometimes file the back of the hole slightly oblong to give the tenon room to expand into a dovetail shape, creating a powerful wedging action. See the drawing at right for the details.

VARIATION 2 Driving a ½-in. screw through a ½-in. fender washer and into the back of a flush-cut ⅜-in. tenon creates a joint that's quick and mechanically sound. To give the round-head screw an antique look, I temporarily drove it into the end of a board and filed facets that simulate a hand-wrought look. A quick mist coat of flat black paint on the screw and washer completes the illusion.

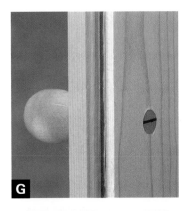

G

VARIATION 1

Make the hole oblong by filing away 1/32-in. at each end (shaded areas).

Back View

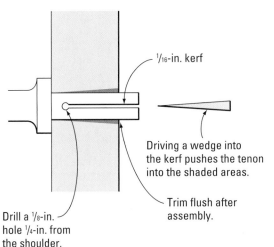

1/16-in. kerf

Driving a wedge into the kerf pushes the tenon into the shaded areas.

Trim flush after assembly.

Drill a 1/8-in. hole 1/4-in. from the shoulder.

VARIATION 2

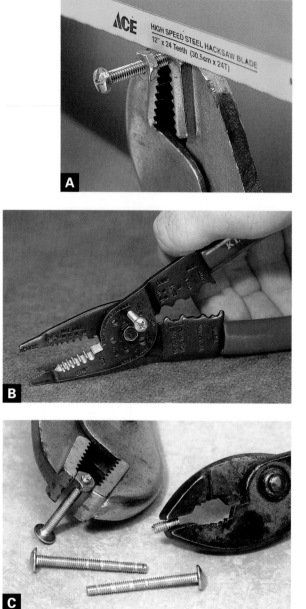

Shortening Screws

You'll use 8-32 machine screws to fasten the vast majority of knobs and handles on the market. But no matter what length the manufacturer furnishes, it always seems that you need a different size. When you're installing a whole kitchen full of cabinet handles, it's worth a trip to the hardware store to buy a box in the right length. But if you need to shorten only a few screws, there's more than one way to do it, and you'll be finished with the job before you could make the round trip to the hardware store.

Before you hacksaw a screw to length **(A),** spin on a nut, and then grab the waste end of the screw with a pair of locking-grip pliers. Snug the pliers into a vise, and you'll be able to saw easily. After you make the cut, removing the nut will restore the threads at the end of the screw.

A quicker method utilizes the holes in an electrician's wire stripper **(B).** You simply thread the screw into the hole, and squeeze the handles to cut the screw. As you withdraw the screw, the tapped hole reshapes the threads. When I have to cut more than a few screws, I'll gain leverage by putting one handle onto the workbench and pushing down on the other handle.

You can purchase 1¾-in.-long screws that have score marks that allow you to easily break them into shorter lengths **(C).** Some hardware distributors now furnish this type of screw with their knobs and handles. Spin a nut onto the screw, and position it just under the break point you want to use. Grab the nut with locking-grip pliers, and grip the waste end with pliers—locking grip or an ordinary slip-joint pair—and wiggle the screw back and forth until the metal fatigues and breaks.

Continuous Wood Pulls

As you can see in the drawing at right, the tongue of a continuous pull fits into a groove that you cut into the bottom end of the door. In this demonstration, I'll work with a kitchen cabinet door made from melamine-clad stock. First you need to carefully measure the dimensions of the pull stock **(A)**. The tongue is a nominal ¼ in. by ¼ in., but you will probably find that the actual measurement is different. In this case, the height of the tongue was 0.26 in., a very reasonable variation, but the width was only 0.22 in., representing 12% undersized. To handle this width, I decided to make two cuts with my standard table-saw blade.

Attach an auxiliary fence at least 6 in. tall to your table saw's rip fence to help hold the door panel vertical while it's being cut. Mark the inside face of the door panel with a piece of masking tape, and run a test panel over the blade **(B)**. Check that the back of the pull will be flush with the rear of the panel and that the test cut's depth matches the height of the tongue. When you're satisfied with the setup, make this cut in all your doors. Move the rip fence to widen the cut the required amount, and run the test panel over the blade again **(C)**. Using a hooked push block on its side keeps the stock tight against the fence and helps prevent chipout where the blade exits the stock.

Cut a 1½-in.-long piece of the pull stock to check its fit in the groove **(D)**. Cut each pull, matching is length to the width of the door. Identify each pull

(Text continues on p. 164.)

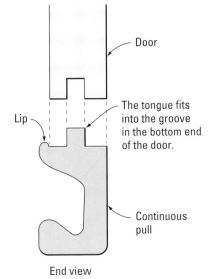

Door

The tongue fits into the groove in the bottom end of the door.

Lip

Continuous pull

End view

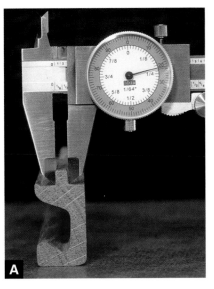

A

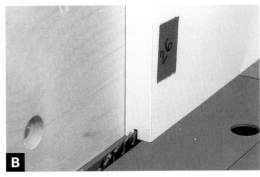

B

C

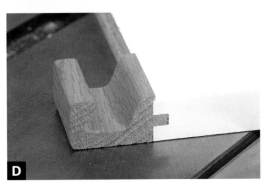

D

E

F

by writing an identifying number onto the tongue **(E)**. Mask off the portions of the tongue that will be glued into the groove (not the ends of the tongue), and apply finish to the pulls. Glue and clamp each pull into its door **(F)**. Don't be too generous with the glue, or you'll simply create a difficult mess to clean. Watch carefully for glue buildup between the lip and panel.

VARIATION 1 If you don't like the appearance of the tongue and groove on the edge of the door, here's one way to hide it. Use a router to cut a stopped groove into the bottom of the door, and then trim the tongue to fit. With this method, the depth of the groove is far less critical, so you can rout $\frac{5}{16}$ in. deep to ensure that the tongue does not bottom out in the groove before the shoulders are flush with the end of the door. When you cut off the tongue, be careful that you don't nick the lip.

VARIATION 2 Here's another way to eliminate the appearance of the tongue and groove on the edge of the door. Completely cut the lip and tongue off of the pull and you can then glue the pull directly to the raw end of the door panel.

VARIATION 1

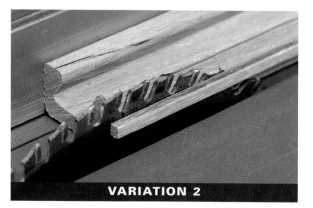

VARIATION 2

Glass and Panel Hardware

Panel-Retaining Hardware

➤ Installing a Panel Retainer in a Groove (p. 169)

Sliding Door-Tracks

➤ Plastic Door Tracks (p. 170)
➤ Aluminum Door-Track System (p. 171)

W HEN YOU INCORPORATE glass into a woodworking project, you'll want one of two opposites: either easy movement or no motion at all. If you're building a cabinet with bypass sliding doors, your goal will be smooth and silent sliding. But if you're putting a glass panel into a wood-framed door, you'll want solid and stationary stability. Either way, you'll find a good selection of hardware to help you complete your project.

Fixed-Panel Hardware

The traditional method of holding a piece of glass in a door frame is with molding strips made from the same wood species as the door itself. For high-end work, this is the only method because plastic strips or clips would cheapen the appearance of your work. For an absolute match of wood color and figure, or if you simply insist upon making everything yourself, you can mill square or quarter-round moldings in your own shop.

> ⚠ **WARNING** To make small quarter-round moldings, round over the edge of a wide board at your router table, then rip the strip on your table saw. Plan your rip cut so that the strip is on the outboard side of the blade at the end of the cut, not trapped between the blade and fence. A trapped strip can kick back with the speed and injury power of an arrow.

To safely rip a small strip of molding, use a zero-clearance table-saw insert and plan the cut so that the molding falls free on the outboard side of the blade.

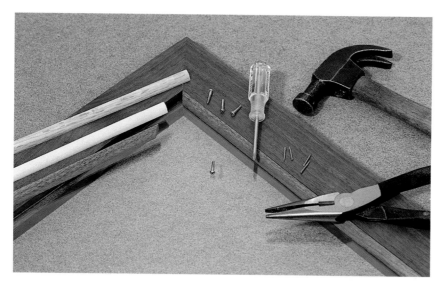

Purchased quarter-round moldings hold glass panels securely and install quickly with brads or screws.

Considering the hassle and dangers involved in making small moldings, you may want to consider purchasing ¼-in. quarter-round moldings. Available in walnut, oak, and birch, the factory-made versions will complement many of your projects. And at less than 60 cents per linear foot, 48-in. strips are a highly affordable convenience. With square shopmade moldings, you can cut butt joints, but the quarter-round moldings require miters in the corners. If you use

brads to nail the strips into place, it's a good idea to drill pilot holes to help prevent splitting. Personally, I prefer to screw the strips into place. It's less nerve-wracking than swinging a hammer near glass, plus it makes removal of the strips extremely easy.

There are two basic types of plastic panel-retainer strips: one you staple into position and the other fits into a groove. Both come in 25-ft. rolls, and you can easily cut them to length using a utility knife or heavy-duty scissors. The staple-in variety installs fast with either a manual or electric-powered staple gun but doesn't look quite as neat as the groove type. The groove type has the added advantage of easy removal, simplifying replacement of broken glass or allowing you to create reversible or replaceable panels that quickly change the look of a cabinet.

Panel Retainers

You can purchase several types of metal and plastic screw-in retainers to hold glass or wood panels. To select a retainer, you first need to know the relationship between the rear surface of the panel and the back face of the door. When the panel is in its rabbet, is its rear surface above the back face of the door, flush, or below? The S-shaped glass retainer with the threaded post covers the greatest range: above, flush, and below. On the negative side, this retainer is quite bulky in appearance. Plastic retainers come in several shapes and handle panels that are flush or recessed either ⅛ in. or ¼ in. When you install any of these retainers with a glass panel, advance the screws a little at a time, working around the perimeter. Stop when the glass no longer rattles. If you apply too much muscle, it's easy to crack the glass.

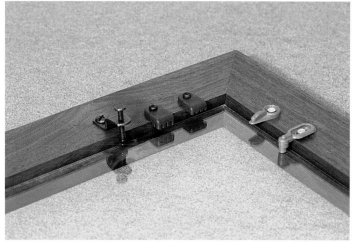

Plastic panel-retainer strips staple on or fit into a groove. You'll find the plastic strips in several wood tones, and the groove type is also available in clear, an especially good choice for installing glass panes.

The large retainer covers a wide range of panel thicknesses, from single-strength glass through leaded-glass panels. Select the smaller retainers based on whether the panel is flush or recessed.

Sliding Doors

Bypass wood doors are very space efficient because they don't require any room for the door to swing. Made from edge-banded plywood or with a solid panel, they are also excellent at hiding clutter. The hardware shown in the photo at right below lets you make sliding doors up to 26 lb. in weight. Installation is easy—cut 1/8-in. grooves into the carcase, and drill 30-mm mounting holes into the backs of the doors. The upper guides have spring-loaded tabs, and an eccentric cam on the lower rollers allows you to fine-tune the fit.

The following types of sliding door hardware are shown with 1/4-in. plate glass, but you could substitute plywood or hardboard panels to conceal the contents of your cabinet. Sliding glass mirrors—clear, smoked, or tinted—are another choice.

The least-expensive sliding door-guide system is a pair of plastic tracks sized for 1/4-in. plate glass. This system relies upon the slippery nature of the plastic to help overcome the friction generated by the weight of the glass. And you may find that it works well enough, as long as each door doesn't exceed a few square feet and provided that you don't need to slide the doors too often. But the economy approach will definitely lose its appeal as the size of the doors and the frequency of access increase.

This sliding-door hardware rides in discreet 1/8-in. grooves cut into the carcase top and bottom.

Plastic tracks are the low-cost route to sliding glass doors. Epoxy the tracks into grooves cut in the carcase.

With metal tracks and nylon rollers, even large glass doors glide smoothly and quietly.

The metal-track system is considerably more expensive—in bright aluminum, it's about four times the cost of the plastic guides; in bronze-finished aluminum, figure five times the cost of plastic. But your money goes a long way in eliminating friction. If you need to frequently access the contents of a cabinet, the convenience of easy sliding quickly outweighs the extra expense. The nylon rollers slide almost effortlessly along the metal-base track.

Installing a Panel Retainer in a Groove

Begin by cutting a rabbet that's deep enough to accommodate the thickness of the glass and the retainer—the rabbet in this demonstration is ⅜ in. by ⅜ in., cut with a dado head in a table saw **(A)**. Get ready to cut the groove for the retainer by putting a ⅛-in.-wide blade into your table saw. (I used one of the outer dado blades from a stack dado set.) The easiest way to position this groove for the retainer is by using a spacer that matches the thickness of the panel you're using. Place the spacer into the rabbet, and slide the rip fence until the spacer just touches the blade **(B)**. Lock the fence into position, and raise the blade to cut a groove ¼ in. deep **(C)**. Miter the frame, and assemble it. Cut the retainer to length with a pair of scissors, and use the rounded end of a marking pen or ½-in. dowel to push the retainer into its groove **(D)**. It isn't essential to take the retainer all the way into the corner; stopping each strip about ½ in. from the corner will give a neat look.

VARIATION If you're making doors or panel assemblies with butt or mortise-and-tenon joints, you'll need to follow a different sequence of cuts so that the rabbets and grooves don't show through the ends of the stiles. Do a series of test cuts to establish the relationship between the rabbet and groove, then use a table-mounted router to cut the groove in the assembled frame. Switch to a rabbeting bit to cut the rabbet.

A

B

C

D

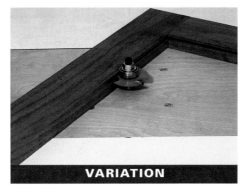

VARIATION

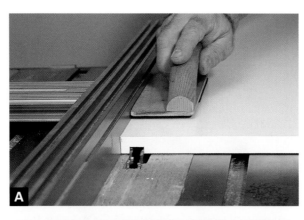

A

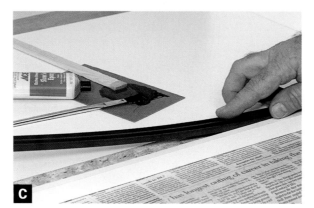

B

C

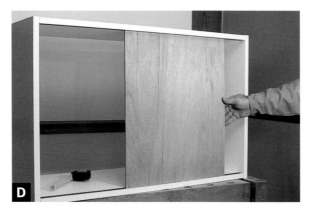

D

Plastic Door-Tracks

Use a dado head in your table saw (or a router for stopped cuts) to cut grooves to house the plastic track in the carcase members **(A)**. Make test cuts to ensure that the groove is wide enough to accept the track without pinching it out of shape, which could affect the fit of the glass. You'll have to cut a deeper groove for the upper track.

> **! WARNING** Don't assume that the upper and lower tracks are identical in width. With the set I got, the upper track was nearly 1/16 in. wider. Test cuts in scrap stock will ensure that you get the right fit.

After assembling the carcase and applying the finish, cut the tracks to length with a miter saw **(B)**. Mix up some epoxy, and use a few drops of it to secure the tracks into the grooves **(C)**. To determine the width of the glass doors, measure the overall opening, divide by two, and add half of the desired overlap. For example, if the opening is 36 in. wide and you want a 3/4-in. overlap, each door would be 18 3/8 in. wide. Cut 1/4-in. plywood as a pattern for the glass to be absolutely certain that vertical size is correct. Test-fit the plywood by first inserting it into the upper track, and then lowering it into the bottom one **(D)**. Be sure to check that the pattern slides easily along each groove of the track. Take the plywood pattern with you to the glass shop to eliminate any disputes over size.

Aluminum Door-Track System

Like the plastic tracks, this system is designed for use with ¼-in.-thick doors. After assembling the carcase, measure the width of the opening, and use a hacksaw to cut the upper and lower tracks to length **(A)**. Use a hacksaw blade with at least 24 teeth per inch (tpi) for a smooth cut. Remove any cutting burrs with a fine file. Using the supplied round-head screws, attach the tracks to the carcase. Drive the first screw 2 in. from each end, and then space the screws about every 8 in. along the track **(B)**. Be sure to carefully align the tracks so that they are in the same plane.

To determine the width of the glass doors, measure the overall opening, divide by two, and add half of the desired overlap. For example, if the opening is 36 in. wide and you want a 1-in. overlap, each door would be 18½ in. wide. Hacksaw the runners to length **(C)**. Use the tip of a screwdriver to press the rollers into the smaller groove in the runners, positioning them about 1 in. from each end **(D)**.

Next, determine the height of the glass doors. The instructions supplied with this set of hardware gave the following formula: rough opening height minus 1⁷⁄₃₂ in. Cut a piece of ¼-in. plywood as a pattern for the glass. Cut ¼-in. lengths of the rubber channel, position one near each edge on the plywood, and press the runner

(Text continues on p. 172.)

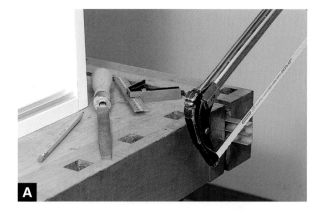

A

B

C

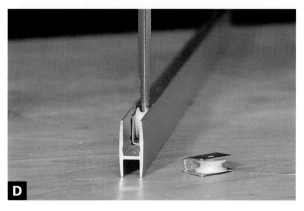

D

E

F

G

H

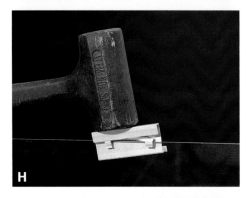

I

into place **(E)**. Attach the upper clear-plastic clips to the plywood **(F)**. Test-fit the assembly into the rear channel and then in the front to make certain that it slides easily. Make any adjustments necessary to the plywood pattern, and take it with you to the glass shop.

Cut the rubber channel ½ in. shorter than the width of the door, and center it on the edge of the glass. Press the runner into position **(G)**. You can add an extruded aluminum pull to the front glass door. Use the ¼-in. lengths of rubber channel to cushion the grip of the metal on the glass, and tap the handle into place **(H)**. If the channel of the pull is too tight to go onto the glass, widen the opening by gently twisting a screwdriver inside the channel **(I)**. To slightly close the opening, remove the pull from the glass, and give it a gentle tap with a deadblow mallet.

Hardware for Shelves

BUILDING STRONG SHELVES requires careful material selection plus a knowledge of strengthening strategies. Generally speaking, panels manufactured from little bits of wood pressed together, like MDF and particleboard, lack significant spanning ability on their own, but they are satisfactory for short, lightly loaded shelves. Plywood is a stronger structural choice, especially when you add a ³/₄-in. by 1¹/₂-in. hardwood strip along the front edge. For a heavyweight contender, add strips to both the front and rear edges. Solid wood is a good choice, although it can get pricey and still sag over time. The strength ranking shown in the top left photo on p. 174 is intended as a general guide only.

Another way to make a shelf stronger is by shortening it—design a bookcase with several short spans instead of a single long shelf. And when you start to fill your bookcase, concentrate stacks of books near the ends of shelves, placing lightweight items in the middle of the span.

For safety's sake, use glass shelves for supporting only lightweight decorative items, and consider using products such as tempered or laminated glass to further reduce risk.

➤ See *"Glass: The Clear Facts"* on p. 168.

Follow Up with Strong Supports

After you've invested time and money into building strong shelves, it doesn't make sense to trust them to the world's cheapest support

Cabinet Shelf Standards

➤ Installing Metal Shelf Standards (p. 178)

Shelf-Support Holes

➤ Shelf-Pin Drilling Jig (p. 180)

➤ Clamp-On Commercial Drilling Jig (p. 181)

➤ Shopemade Shelf-Hole Jigs (p. 182)

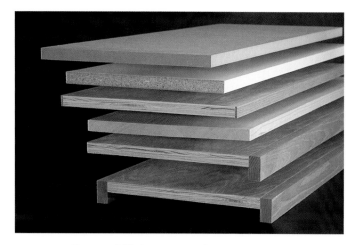

From pitiful to powerful, choose from this lineup of shelving options. Top to bottom: MDF, melamine-covered particleboard, edgebanded plywood, solid pine shelf, plywood with a strip on the front only, and a plywood shelf with support strips front and back.

system. Economics and aesthetics certainly play important roles in the decision-making process, but for the moment, consider the engineering realities behind your choices.

Without a doubt, steel clips that fit into steel standards make the strongest combination. Neither component is likely to wear out, bend, or break.

Shelf Pins: From Hardy to Hardly Enough

If you opt for pins that fit into line-bored holes, metal is obviously superior to plastic. And you can improve the performance of either metal or plastic pins by placing them into metal inserts that spread the bearing stress. Inserts that have a rolled lip have the added virtue of hiding chipout at the perimeter of the hole.

One other engineering reality is the larger the diameter of the pin, the stronger it will be. The selection of shelf pins in the top

photo on the facing page merely hints at the wide range of styles, materials, and finishes available. Some of the special features you'll find are screw-in pins that banish the dropout problem and pins that cushion or capture glass shelves. An L-shaped support with a hole in it lets you drive a screw into the shelf so it won't slide. A small paddle-shaped plastic support is designed for completely invisible service—it fits into kerfs cut into the ends of each shelf board.

Drilling for Shelf Pins

There are plenty of ways in which you can drill accurate lines of holes without investing in designated machines that do the job. Some woodworkers favor a jig that clamps to the workpiece and indexes a carriage with a plunge router at set intervals. The router can make cleaner holes than a drill, but it is also several times noisier, so be sure to wear hearing protection if you choose this method.

Combine a drill press or hand-held drill with either commercial or shopmade jigs, and you can produce columns of equally spaced holes quickly and efficiently. Some

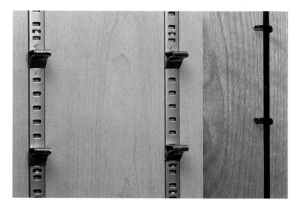

Steel standards and clips (the double row shown at left) combine low price with high strength. The plastic standard and metal clip of the low-profile system shown at right offer a more discreet appearance.

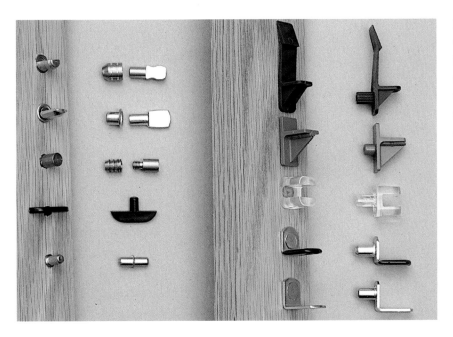

Left column, top to bottom: a ⅜-in. bushing with a ¼-in. paddle-shaped pin, a ⁹⁄₃₂-in. insert with a rolled lip and ¼-in. paddle-shaped pin, a 7-mm tapped sleeve and threaded post, a 5-mm shelf support that conceals in a ⅛-in. kerf cut in the shelf's end, and a 5-mm pin with a central collar. Right column, top to bottom: a plastic support thatfits into a ¼-in. hole and locks onto a ¾-in. shelf, an economy plastic pin that fits into a ¼-in. hole, a clear plastic pin that fits a ¼-in. hole and grips a ¼-in. glass shelf, a ¼-in. pin with a bracket plate with a rubberized coating to cushion glass shelves, and a ¼-in. pin with a bracket plate that has a hole in it to permit attachment to the underside of a shelf.

jigs must be clamped to unassembled components, whereas hand-held versions allow you to drill holes even after the cabinet has been hung on the wall. For clean holes, use a brad-point bit whenever possible. When you drill for a shelf-pin insert, carefully measure its outside diameter (O.D.), and choose a bit that will give a snug fit in the material you're using.

Utility Shelving

When you need utilitarian shelving in a hurry, consider brawny standards and supports that can even offer no-tool installation. End-join the standards with special connectors to create floor-to-ceiling shelves, make sturdy lumber racks, or even build a work surface as quickly as you can lift a sheet of material onto the 22-in. brackets with outrigger supports. Click hooked ends onto the standards, and you can hang them from the edge of a foundation or the top plate of a stud wall. With another style of end fitting, you can screw the standards to studs or hang them from joists.

Hang the standards from a foundation wall, and you'll rack up yards of utility shelf space without breaking a sweat.

The hooked end (left) works great on foundation walls or top plates, while the fitting shown at right lets you attach to studs or joists.

WARNING Carefully check the top of the wall before placing the hooked ends. Electricians sometimes run wiring along plates, and you don't want to accidentally place the metal supports where they could cut into the insulation.

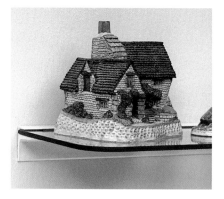

With no visible fasteners, glass-shelf kits have clean lines that keep the focus on the items you're displaying.

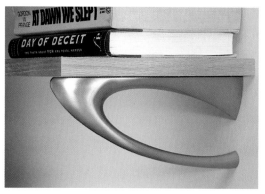

The sleek curves of this bracket support a shelf in style. The installation procedure is straightforward and the mounting hardware is invisible.

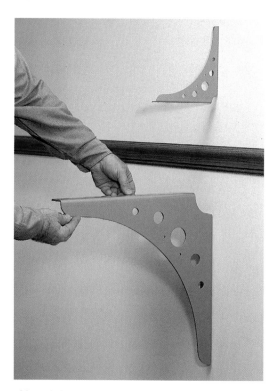

No trick photography here—that's a steel bracket upscaled to support a work surface in the office or shop.

Wall-Mounted Shelves

You'll find plenty of choices in wall-mounted shelves, from individual glass units for light-weight displays to standards strong enough for your heaviest books and collectibles.

Hardware stores and home centers stock glass-shelf kits that include an extruded metal support that you screw to the wall through holes in the channel. Slip the glass shelf into the channel, and the fasteners disappear. Some kits cushion the glass with a continuous rubber U-channel, whereas others rely on short wedges of clear silicone.

You'll discover other styles of brackets for single shelves that range from purely practical to stunningly sculptural. To mount the bracket shown in the photo at left, you install a dowel screw into the wall, then spin on a threaded stud that has a groove milled around it. Slip the stud into a hole in the back of the upper part of the bracket, then tighten a setscrew into the groove to secure the shelf.

When you want to set up an office in a hurry, consider using giant brackets that are strong enough to support a countertop. Projecting 18½ in. from the wall and made from ³⁄₁₆-in.-thick steel, these brackets are something you'll probably never be able to overload. The companion 8-in. bracket can be mounted as shown to cradle the end of a shelf in its flange or in the same posture as the big bracket for a long run of shelving.

Screw steel standards to wood studs, and you have the basis for a powerful shelving system. Choose from arms that have plain ends or with upturned hooks that restrain the edge of a shelf or fit into holes you drill in the bottom of the shelf. Standards that have a double row of holes accept arms with

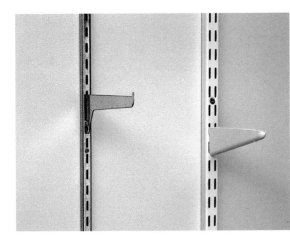

Choose between steel standards with a single row of slots (left) or the brawnier double-row design (right).

Swooping from below your desk, a stylish bracket makes a design statement while helping to keep you organized.

superior shear strength plus resistance to twisting. Those arms have holes along the sloping lower edge that allow you to drive screws upward into the shelves.

Add a Shelf to a Desk

If you ever wished for a desk stretcher, you may have just found it. The brackets in the top photo at right add to your workspace without subtracting even a square inch from the desktop. Have a glass shelf drilled for display or light-duty storage, or choose a wood shelf for more serious holding tasks.

Dividers Organize a Shelf

Building shelves creates the space you need to get organized, but adding wire dividers to a shelf takes efficiency to the next level. The inexpensive organizers eliminate the need for pricey bookends, and you can rearrange your shelves simply by moving the dividers to a new set of holes. An installation tip—after drilling the holes in the shelf, I use a countersink to cut a $\frac{1}{32}$-in. chamfer around

Shelf organizers help you divide and conquer storage problems. Choose from a variety of shapes and finishes.

the rim of each hole. The chamfer makes it easier to insert the dividers and also helps prevent tearout of the wood when you remove them.

Installing Metal Shelf Standards

If you're simply building a storage cabinet for the shop, you may choose to surface-mount these standards, but housing them in a groove is an easy job that makes the completed project look much better.

Use a dado blade to cut a groove that matches the width of the shelf-support standard **(A)**. The standards I used are ⅝ in. wide, but my initial test groove was about 1/32 in. too narrow, so I added dado shims between the chippers to widen the cut. (You can make your own dado shims, but a purchased set is inexpensive and highly accurate.) You have the width right when the standard goes into the groove without forcing but also without any sideways play. The standard is 3/16 in. thick, but I cut the groove only ⅛ in. deep so that the metal is 1/16 in. proud of the side panel—the offset helps prevent the ends of the shelves from scraping the inside of the carcase. (Of course your shelves have to be cut to length accordingly.)

Carefully align the lower factory end of each standard flush with the bottom end of the carcase side, and mark your cutline at the top. Positioning each standard so that the numbers stamped on them are right side up will help ensure that all of the shelf-clip holes will be level, and that means shelves that don't rock. Using a hacksaw, cut the standard to length **(B)**. Be sure to clamp the standard close to the cut to prevent the metal from bending. Choose a fine-toothed hacksaw blade, one with at least 24 tpi or even 32 tpi. If the teeth are too coarse, the blade can catch, bending the standard.

Next, apply the finish to the carcase. After it dries, drive nails through the standards to hold them in place **(C)**. The nails, which have annular rings to increase their holding power, are usually in the bag with the shelf clips you purchase. These fasteners are a hefty gauge, so you may need to drill pilot holes prior to driving them in tough materials. For maximum strength, drive a nail through every round hole in the standard. After you install the shelf clips **(D),** you're ready to add the shelves.

VARIATION **If you're installing low-profile standards, apply the finish to the wood before cutting the grooves. Otherwise, finish could pool inside the groove or the standard itself. Cut a ¼-in.-wide slot ½ in. deep in the carcase side. Cut the standard to length using a fine-toothed handsaw or power miter saw. If you are using a power miter saw, cut very slowly to keep the plastic from shattering. Make sure you are consistent in the orientation of the standards so that the shelves will be level. Apply glue sparingly inside the groove, and press the standard into place. To ensure that the standard is flush with the surface of the side, press it down with a wallpaper seam roller or laminate J-roller.**

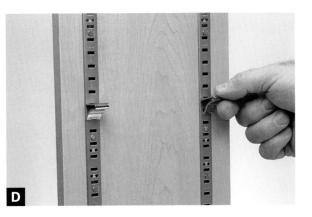

D

VARIATION

A

B

VARIATION

Shelf-Pin Drilling Jig

The Rockler jig in this demonstration has a simple appearance but is surprisingly versatile. You can use it on components or drill the shelf-pin holes after assembling or even after mounting the cabinet on the wall. The large holes in the jig capture the end of special self-centering bits that drill either ¼-in. or 5-mm holes and stop the holes at the correct depth for the shelf pins.

Assemble the jig by installing the wood strip along the edge of the jig. When placed along one edge, you can drill holes with a 32-mm offset, whereas switching to the opposite side produces a 64-mm offset. In this case, the offset is measured to the edge of the hole, not its centerpoint. Choose the holes you wish to use, and cover the other column with a strip of masking tape to prevent accidental use. Carefully place the jig at its starting position, and hold it firmly while you engage the tip of the bit into the holes in the jig and drill **(A)**. When the jig is brand new, you may have to push onto your drill to get the self-centering lip on the bit flush against the jig. To make sure that the jig doesn't shift while you're drilling, clamp or tape it securely to the carcase member.

To drill a line of holes longer than the jig, use the indexing holes near the ends of the jig **(B)**. Simply slide the jig in the desired direction, and insert a shelf pin through the jig and into a hole you already drilled.

VARIATION **To use the jig inside a face-frame cabinet, simply turn over the jig and butt the wood strip against the inside of the frame.**

Clamp-On Commercial Drilling Jig

This jig from Veritas does an excellent job of eliminating uncertainty because it ensures that the holes are exactly opposite each other, perpendicular, and equally spaced.

Assemble the jig and clamp one end flush with the end of a carcase side **(A).** Position the two rails (with the holes) parallel to the edges of the carcase to establish the offset you want. I used a gauge block to set the rails so that the shelf-pin centerpoints are 2 in. from the edge **(B).** Whatever dimension you choose, it must be identical for each rail. That's because you'll turn the jig to drill the mirror-image carcase side. Tighten the thumbscrews to secure the rails.

Select a guide bushing, and install it in the bushing carrier by tightening the setscrew with an Allen wrench **(C).** The jig comes with a wide selection of hardened bushings: 5 mm, 6 mm, 6.75 mm, 7 mm 7.5 mm, 8 mm, and 9 mm, as well as $\frac{7}{32}$ in., $\frac{1}{4}$ in. and $\frac{3}{8}$ in. (You can use the 8-mm bushing to guide a $\frac{5}{16}$-in. bit.) In addition, you also receive an unhardened bushing (silver colored in the photo) that you can drill to virtually any size you need.

Set the guide bushing into one of the holes in the rail, and use your portable electric drill to make the parallel columns of holes **(D).** Use masking tape to blank out any holes you don't want to drill. A masking-tape flag can also serve as a makeshift depth indicator if you have only a few holes to drill. If you need to continue the chain of holes for a long carcase side, simply loosen the clamping nuts and slide the jig forward. Slip a registration pin through each rail and into a hole you have already drilled, and tighten the clamping nuts.

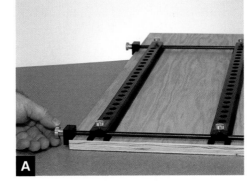

A

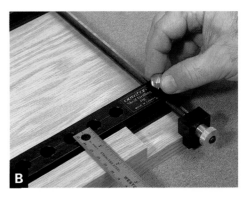

B

C

D

Shelf-Hole Drilling Jig

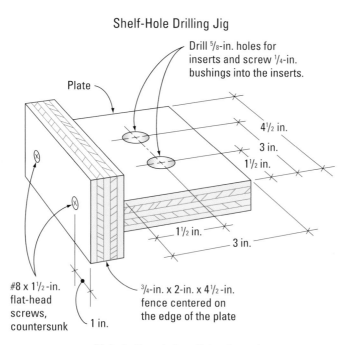

Drill ⅝-in. holes for inserts and screw ¼-in. bushings into the inserts.

Plate

4½ in.

3 in.

1½ in.

1½ in.

3 in.

#8 x 1½-in. flat-head screws, countersunk

1 in.

¾-in. x 2-in. x 4½-in. fence centered on the edge of the plate

Make both parts from ¾-in. plywood.

A

B

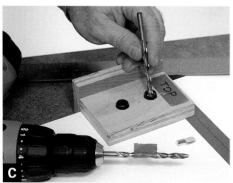

C

D

Shopmade Shelf-Hole Jigs

One of the primary advantages of making your own shelf-drilling jig is that you can easily create groupings of holes where they will be most useful. Another plus of the two-bushing jig I designed is that it's small enough to fit into your toolbox for job-site work. When you're working in the shop on a large project, you can use the same jig or scale it up to any desired size by simply adding more inserts and bushings.

To make the jig, cut the plate and fence from ¾-in. plywood to the dimensions shown in the drawing at left. Drill ⅝-in. holes through the plate, making their center-to-center distance any dimension you wish. Place the tapered end of the insert into one of the holes, and tap it with a hammer until it is nearly flush. To make the jig reversible, you need to sink the insert 1/16 in. below the surface of the plate. A couple of taps on the end of a socket from a wrench set will do the job quickly **(A)**. After you glue and screw the fence to the plate, screw the ¼-in. bushings into the inserts **(B)**.

▶ See *"Mounting Pulls"* on p. 158 for another jig featuring inserts and bushings.

To use the jig, first lay out the location of a starting hole near each edge of a cabinet side. Use a framing square to make certain that they are aligned. Place the line so that it coincides with the top of the jig; it is difficult to accurately judge the location looking through the hole. Hold the jig flat and firmly against the edge and drill the top hole **(C)**. Insert a bit into the hole to lock the jig into position, and drill the second hole **(D)**. To drill the third hole in the series, remove the bit, slide the jig down, place the bit into the second hole, and drill. You can continue this process—called step and repeat—for as many holes as you need.

To drill the line of holes on the opposite side, unscrew the bushings from the jig and turn it over. You will want to swap the top and bottom bushings to equalize the wear. The top bushing is used to drill only the first hole, and after that it's used just for alignment. However, the bottom bushing is used for drilling every hole in the series except the first. As it gets more wear, the hole size increases, and that decreases accuracy.

The completed line of holes **(E)** shows proves that even a small jig can produce accurate results.

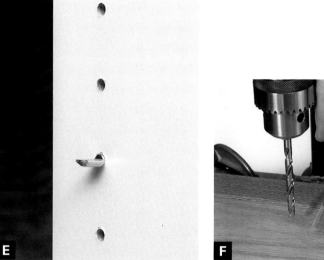

VARIATION 1 The drawing at right and photo **(F)** show a drill press version of the step-and-repeat concept. You can buy ⅛-in. plastic (it's used for break-resistant windows and doors) at virtually any hardware store. With this jig, you're not limited by the size of commercially available bushings, so buy two identical bits, and you can drill the size you need. In this case, I used the jig to drill a line of 9/32-in. holes for lipped inserts that hold ¼-in. shelf pins.

Drill Press Sheet Hole Jig

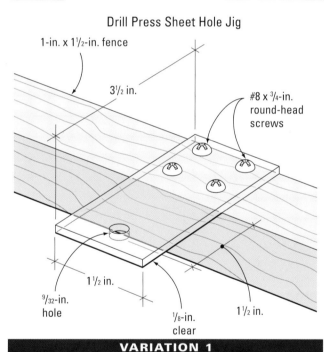

1-in. x 1½-in. fence

3½ in.

#8 x ¾-in. round-head screws

9/32-in. hole

1½ in.

⅛-in. clear

1½ in.

VARIATION 1

VARIATION 2 Using the holes in ¼-in. pegboard is a quick and inexpensive way to lay out a pattern of shelf-pin holes. The jig has a limited life span, but the material is so inexpensive that you can make a new jig for each project. Define the lines of holes you want to drill with strips of masking tape. Using a portable drill guide will ensure that the holes are perpendicular and consistent in depth.

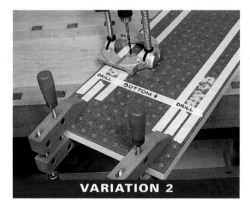

VARIATION 2

Bed Hardware

Bed Assembly

➤ Bed Bolts (p. 190)
➤ Bed-Bolt Covers (p.192)
➤ Bed-Rail Fasteners (p. 193)
➤ Bed Irons (p. 195)

Disappearing Beds

➤ Murphy Folding Bed (p. 196)

Bunk-Bed Accessories

➤ Bunk-Bed Ladders (p. 198)

EXCEPT ON MOVING DAY, most people don't give their bed hardware any attention. In some ways, that's appropriate, because a properly built bed does absolutely nothing: no shaking, no rattling, and no rolling. One exception to the absolutely stationary bed is a category that folds against the wall to give you extra space when you're awake, but even this type has sturdy hardware to prevent unwanted motion.

To attain dependability when you build a bed, you need to thoroughly understand all your options. After all, you certainly don't want to lose any sleep wondering whether you've made the right choice.

Post-to-Rail Connectors

When you build a bed, you can choose between two general construction techniques. In the first method, you build four bedposts, two side rails, a head rail, and a foot rail. In this case, you need two sets of rail-to-post fasteners for each post. The second method involves the same parts, but this time you permanently join two posts with the head rail, creating the headboard assembly, and the other two posts with the foot rail, making the footboard. For this construction method, you need only one set of post-to-rail fasteners for each post.

You'll find two styles of bed bolts. The traditional type has a square head that requires a special wrench. The bolt mates with a square nut mortised into the rail. The more modern version of the bed bolt has a hex head that allows you to use a standard socket wrench. It couples with a threaded steel dowel that you insert into the rail. Although both styles of bed bolts make strong joints, neither fastener is particularly good looking. The usual solution is to hide the bed bolt's head under a cover made from stamped or cast metal.

Bed-Rail Fasteners

The photo at right below shows three styles of interlocking fasteners, each available in two sizes, that give you additional ways to assemble a wood bed frame that has a headboard, footboard, and two rails. Although all of the fasteners appear different, they share two virtues—putting more weight on the bed tends to draw the joint tighter, and they are completely concealed when the bed is assembled.

In the first style, you simply screw mating halves of the fasteners to the rail and headboard and footboard. Position the tab upward on the headboard and footboard, and the tab downward on the rails. This style is available in two sizes, $3^3/_4$ in. or $5^{11}/_{16}$ in. long. Choose the larger size if your bed rails are wide enough. Select the largest-diameter and longest screws your hardware and lumber will hold.

The second design requires you to cut mortises into both the bedposts and the rails. Mortise the female plate into the bedpost and the hooked plate into the end of the rail.

The third style of fastener utilizes a bedlock, which is mortised into the bedpost, and a hooked plate that is surface mounted to the rail. The long bedlock is specifically designed for a sleigh bed. The extended mounting plate helps to strengthen the joint.

The square heads on traditional bed bolts require a special wrench, whereas you use an ordinary socket wrench with the newer style. Choose bed-bolt covers from dozens of available patterns and finishes.

Bed Irons

To support the box spring, you can attach a wood cleat along the lower edge of each rail and span between the rails with individual wood slats or pieces of plywood. Another choice is the bed iron, which looks like a corner reinforcement bracket that took massive doses of steroids. Mortise three irons into each rail, and you'll have a strong support for the box spring. You also can add an iron or two to the head and foot rails for extra security. If you're wearing both a belt

Interlocking post-to-rail connectors gain rigidity by wedging action. The three types shown here are each available in two sizes.

L-shaped bed irons support a box spring, eliminating slats. Mortising the irons into the side rails is not a difficult task.

and suspenders as you read this, install the extra irons.

Beds That Disappear

Most people sleep only eight hours a day, but the bed consumes a large amount of space all the time. By making a bed disappear into an enclosure, you'll suddenly gain more usable space within the same number of square feet.

Among the various styles of self-storing beds, you'll discover a full range of sizes and styles: from single to king, beds that fold vertically or horizontally, beds that hold only a mattress, those that also accommodate a special thin box spring, and even those that utilize a standard mattress and box spring set. Each of those choices influences the height of the mattress above the floor as well as the depth of the enclosure required. In addition, you'll base part of your decision on whether you're shopping for personal comfort or whether you want to give houseguests a subtle motivation to move on.

Some manufacturers of folding-bed hardware offer an extensive line of prefinished surround kits, many of which include bookcases and lighting options. Other suppliers provide plans so that you can build your own cabinetry.

Murphy-Type Beds

One type of folding bed utilizes a piston-lift system similar to the type that holds open the rear liftgate on a car or van. Choose between a double or queen bed, mounted either vertically or horizontally, as shown in the drawing on the facing page. One manufacturer includes extensive construction notes with the hardware so you can build the framing from plywood or particleboard—solid wood isn't recommended.

Making a bed disappear has more to do with physics than wizardry. But you'll enjoy the extra living space that magically appears. (Photos courtesy Rockler Woodworking and Hardware)

TWO STYLES OF BED MOUNTING

Vertical lift

Horizontal lift

► MURPHY'S DISAPPEARING BED

The Murphy bed is designed to fold against the wall when not in use, freeing up the floor space for other uses. By utilizing a Murphy-bed mechanism, you can transform a little-used guest bedroom into a home office or hobby room. Over the years, the Murphy name has also been used to describe competitors' products, in the same way that many people refer to all brands of plastic laminate as "Formica." So when you shop for a folding-bed mechanism, you'll find Murphy beds and Murphy-type beds. Some mechanisms, including the genuine Murphy, attach to the floor, and the surrounding cabinetry is completely independent of the hardware. However, floor mounting is impractical in most apartments, unless you have a very understanding landlord who will allow you to cut away carpeting and drill holes into the floor. Other folding-bed mechanisms attach to wood studs in the wall and utilize either springs or piston power to raise the bed.

Still another type of disappearing-bed mechanism consists of a pair of spring boxes. As shown in the drawing on p. 188, each box has two parts: a spring mechanism that you attach to the bed frame, and a heavy-duty sheet-metal socket that you screw to the wall-mounted frame. When you slide the spring mechanism into the socket, it securely clips into place. A screw on the spring mechanism lets you adjust the tension to match the weight of your mattress. These boxes are substantial pieces of hardware— each pair weighs more than 23 lb.

Powerful pistons lift wall-mounted beds to create valuable floor space during the day.

Baby's Crib Demands Careful Thought and Work

Some enthusiastic woodworking fathers and grandfathers can't resist the urge to build a crib for their offspring. But before you succumb to that temptation, do a quick reality check. You need to understand that today's

The spring box packs a lot of bed-lifting power into a 9-in. by 13-in. package. It's available in two sizes, for a twin or double bed.

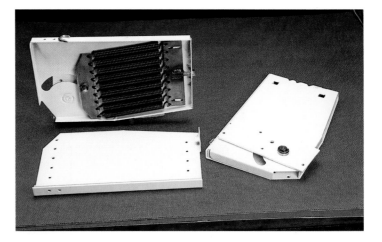

SPRING-BOX BED HARDWARE

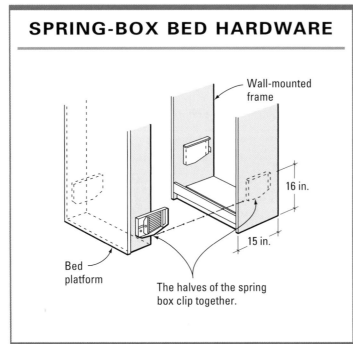

Wall-mounted frame

16 in.

15 in.

Bed platform

The halves of the spring box clip together.

helpless little armful will soon unleash a relentless destructive force to escape the confines of your workmanship: kicking, jumping, screaming, and even gnawing at the wood like a giant termite. Every child, regardless of gender, has an aptitude for damage that makes Attila the Hun look like a sissy.

That said, a handcrafted crib can be more than a satisfying project; it can even become a treasured family heirloom.

When you're ready to build a crib, you can purchase several different woodworking plans and hardware kits. One hardware style allows both sides of the crib to lower. This feature simplifies construction, but the design is not as sturdy as the type with one fixed side. Another kit lets you convert the crib into a youth bed, then into the headboard and footboard of a full-sized bed. Whatever style you choose, absolutely insist that the hardware and design meet the regulations of the United States Consumer Product Safety Commission (CPSC). As you assemble the hardware, look for opportunities to substitute longer screws whenever possible to increase the strength of your project. When the crib is in use, periodically check that all fasteners remain snug. See the sidebar on the facing page on safety.

Welcome an addition to the family by building a crib. But before you buy hardware or plans, make certain that they meet the latest safety regulations. (Photo courtesy Rockler Woodworking and Hardware)

Beds for Older Children

Some people believe that moving a child from a crib to an adult-sized bed is too abrupt a change, so they opt for a juvenile-sized bed. You can find plans to build a bed in this size, but it's always prudent to buy the mattress and box spring before you start cutting lumber. Bunk beds are a perennial favorite. For children, they satisfy the urge to climb, and for parents, they fulfill the need to save space. The ladder on a bunk bed is a potential problem area, but there are several pieces of hardware that firmly anchor it to help prevent accidents.

Whether you're building a bunk bed from scratch or adding a ladder to an existing bed, inexpensive hardware simplifies construction and makes a sturdy connection to the safety rail. The fixed-hook bunk-bed-ladder connector can adapt to rails of various thicknesses and widths, but once you've attached it to the rail, you're committed to that spot. The adjustable-hook style requires a $7/8$-in. by $4^1/2$-in. safety rail, but you can move it to a new location on the rail by simply loosening the lower clamp.

> ## ▶ SAFETY, SAFETY, SAFETY

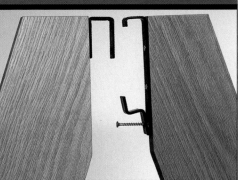

Keep a bunk-bed ladder firmly attached with either a fixed-hook style (left) or an adjustable hook (right).

People say that there are only three important things in real estate: location, location, and location. With a baby's crib, the only three important factors are safety, safety, and more safety.

When you're shopping for crib plans and components, you'll find some variations, such as whether one or both sides can be lowered. But many other items, such as the height of the mattress, the design of the posts, and the spacing of the slats, are covered by guidelines issued by the United States Consumer Product Safety Commission (CPSC), an independent Federal regulatory agency. Be sure to ask the supplier whether its product and design meet current CPSC regulations. And unless you're absolutely familiar with the regulations yourself, don't alter the woodworking plans you purchase. If you have any doubts, contact the agency directly: U.S. Consumer Product Safety Commission, 4330 East-West Highway, Bethesda, Maryland 20814-4408; phone: 800-638-2772; www.cpsc.gov.

Traditional Bed Bolt

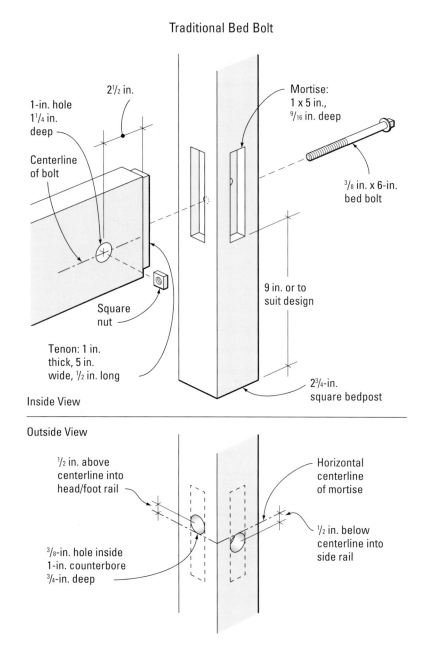

Inside View

1-in. hole
1¼ in. deep

2½ in.

Centerline of bolt

Mortise:
1 x 5 in.,
⁹/₁₆ in. deep

³/₈ in. x 6-in. bed bolt

Square nut

Tenon: 1 in. thick, 5 in. wide, ½ in. long

9 in. or to suit design

2¾-in. square bedpost

Outside View

½ in. above centerline into head/foot rail

Horizontal centerline of mortise

³/₈-in. hole inside 1-in. counterbore ¾-in. deep

½ in. below centerline into side rail

Bed Bolts

In the demonstration shown here, you'll learn how to use two types of bed bolts. The old-fashioned style of bed bolt has an integral washer below the square head and requires a special wrench. The tapered tip of the bolt makes it somewhat easier to locate the square nut captured in a recess in the rail. The modern version of the bed bolt has a separate washer and a hex-head bolt that you drive with an ordinary socket wrench. It mates with a threaded dowel that fits into a hole drilled into the rail. Except for the size of the hole for the nut, the installation steps for both types of bed bolts are identical.

Referring to the drawing at left, use a square to lay out 1-in. by 5-in. mortises centered in the width of the bedposts (these measure 2¾ in. square, a common bedpost size) **(A)**. A plunge router is my weapon of choice for forming the mortises **(B),** and I cut them ⁹/₁₆ in. deep to ensure that the tip of the tenon doesn't bottom out in the mortise and prevent the tenon's shoulders from drawing up snugly to the post. Wood hand-screws clamped to the post serve as stops that

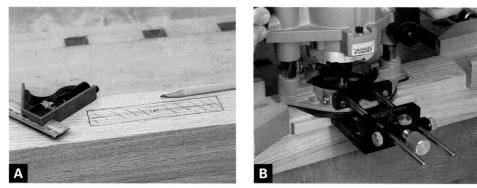

A

B

register against the router fence. Square up the corners of the mortise with a chisel **(C)**.

The hardwood rails are 8/4 stock, milled to a finished size of 1¾ in. by 6 in. Use a dado head in your table saw to cut a tenon that's ½ in. long, 1 in. wide, and 5 in. high centered on each end of the rails **(D)**. Use a square to transfer the horizontal centerline of the mortises to the opposite faces of the bedpost. Draw the vertical centerlines on these faces, then mark the bolts' centerpoints: ½ in. above the horizontal centerline for head and foot rails, and ½ in. below the horizontal centerline for the side rails **(E)**.

Take the post to your drill press, and drill 1-in. counterbores ¾ in. deep and ⅜-in. holes centered in the counterbores **(F)**. Clamp the rails to the posts, and using the holes through the posts as guides, use a bit that's at least 8 in. long to drill 3¼ in. deep into the end of the tenon **(G)**. If you're making a single bed, you can clamp the head and foot rails vertically as shown in the photo, but you'll drill horizontally into the side rails. Lay the rails with their inner faces upward on your workbench. Use a square and pencil to

(Text continues on p. 192.)

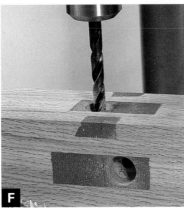

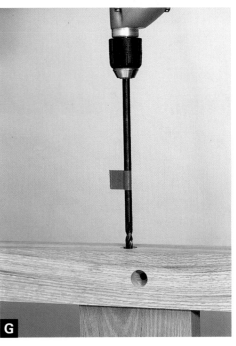

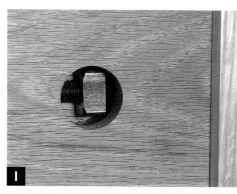

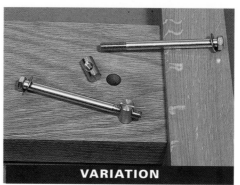

VARIATION

draw the centerline of the bolt on the rail, and mark a centerpoint 3 in. from the shoulder of the tenon. Use a 1-in. Forstner bit to drill a hole 1¼ in. deep **(H)**. When you tighten the bolt, the nut will seat itself into the hole in the rail **(I)**.

VARIATION The modern version of the bed bolt utilizes a threaded metal dowel instead of a square nut in the rail. Install it by drilling a ⅝-in. hole 1½ in. deep. The line on the dowel indicates the centerline of the threaded hole. The threaded dowel is ⁹⁄₁₆ in. in diameter, but you'll have a tough time finding a brad-point or Forstner drill bit in this size, so the ⅝-in. hole is acceptable.

Bed-Bolt Covers

To conceal the counterbored bed bolts, install a bed-bolt cover. Some covers have a single tab, allowing you access to the bolt by simply swinging the cover **(A)**. The two-tab style requires you to remove one of the screws. Base your choice on aesthetics and whether you need quick bolt access to disassemble your bed with the speed of a NASCAR pit crew. Choose your bolt covers to coordinate with the style of bed you're building. The covers are available in a wide variety of patterns and finishes **(B)**.

Bed-Rail Fasteners

Lay out the location of the mortise for the bed-lock onto the posts of the headboard and foot-board **(A)**. With the 2¾-in.-square posts and 1-in.-thick rails I used for this bed, I positioned the edge of the rail flush with the post to pro-duce a ½-in. reveal on the outer edge of the rail. As you can see in the photo, the mortise is 1 in. longer than the length of the bedlock's body to allow entry of the hook plate you'll later attach to the side rail.

Plunge-rout the ⅜-in.-wide mortise **(B)**. I posi-tioned handscrew clamps on the post to stop the travel of the router at the ends of the mortise. Drive a 1-in.-wide chisel straight down along the lines at the upper and lower ends of the bed-lock's location **(C)**. At this point, you don't need to chisel away any wood near these lines—you're simply using the chisel to mark the lines into the wood. Use a ¼-in. chisel to square up the bottom end of the mortise so that the bedlock will rest solidly **(D)**. You don't need to square the upper end of the mortise. Strip away the masking tape.

Next, mortise the plate of the bedlock into the post. To do this, set the depth of your router bit 1/32 in. deeper than the thickness of the plate **(E)**. I used a ¼-in. bit in a laminate trimmer because it's easier to handle than a big router for a small-scale cut like this. Rout the mortise freehand, cutting as close as you dare to the chiseled end lines, and remove the remaining waste with a 1-in. chisel **(F)**. The bedlock curves from the plate into the mortise, so you need to chisel a radius

(Text continues on p. 194.)

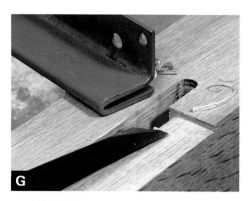

G

I

K

H

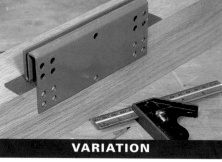

VARIATION

J

along the edge of the mortise **(G).** An exact fit isn't necessary—simply shave away enough wood to allow the bedlock's plate to fit into its mortise. For a neat fit, check that the plate doesn't project above the surface of the bedpost.

Drill pilot holes, and drive screws to fasten the bedlock to the post **(H).** To maximize holding power, I used #10 x 2-in. sheet-metal screws. Lay the bedpost onto your workbench, and insert the hooked plate into the bedlock. To position the bed rail flush against the hooked plate, put a ½-in. spacer (equaling the reveal) under the rail **(I).** Double-check that the hooks are fully engaged in the bedlock, and mark the centerline of the two large mounting holes parallel to the rail's length. Mark the intersecting line for the centerpoint along the edge of the mounting hole that's away from the hook. This procedure moves the hooked plate toward the center of the rail, ensuring a strong joint because the hooks can't bottom out in the bedlock. Drill ³⁄₁₆-in. pilot holes ⅞ in. deep into the rail for the ¼ x 1-in. lag screws, and drive them **(J).** To make certain that the tip of the screws would not penetrate too far, I used a flat washer under the head of each screw. With installation of the hardware complete on both the post and the rail, you're ready to assemble the joint **(K).**

VARIATION If you're building a sleigh bed, you can choose the longer bedlock to reduce the risk of splitting the curved bedpost. This bedlock is shaped differently, with its mounting plate designed to attach to the inner side of the bedpost.

Bed Irons

Bed irons resemble corner braces, but they are 1¼ in. wide and ¼ in. thick. Lay out the location of three irons on each side rail, positioning an iron 12 in. from each end and centering the final iron **(A)**. In this demonstration, I'm installing the irons flush with the lower edge of the rail, but you can move the iron up or down to expose more or less of the box spring to alter the finished height of the bed's surface.

Here are a couple of quick tricks that will help prevent tearout when you rout the mortise for the bed iron. Before routing, use a backsaw to make cuts at each end of the mortise, angling them to the ¼-in. mortise depth **(B)**. Using a router or laminate trimmer, make a light cut no more than ⅛ in. wide, moving from right to left along the lower edge of the mortise **(C)**. This technique, called climb cutting, reduces the risk of blowing out chunks of wood.

Clear out the rest of the mortise, freehanding your cuts as close to the layout lines as your confidence takes you **(D)**. If you're making a batch of beds, you can save time by making a jig that will guide your router to produce a mortise the precise size of the bed iron. But if you're crafting only one bed, you can probably rough-rout and chisel faster than you could make the jig. Finish the mortises with a chisel, then drive the screws **(E)**. For maximum holding power, use the largest-diameter and longest screws your iron and rail will hold: #12 x 1¼ in. is typical.

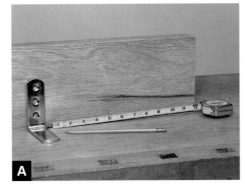

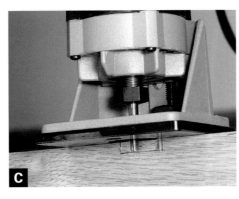

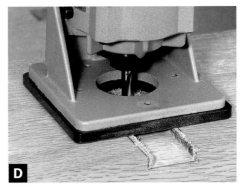

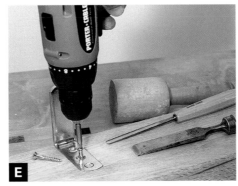

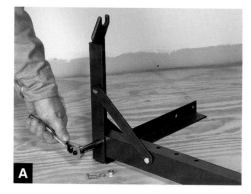

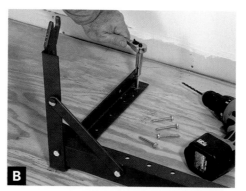

Murphy Folding Bed

Begin with the base assembly. Bolt the angle iron, with its spring holes facing upward, to the L-shaped base brackets **(A)**. I added split-lock washers under the nuts to keep the joints solid. Position the base assembly with the legs of the base brackets pointed toward the wall. For this particular model, the standard mounting distance puts the vertical angle iron supports 19 in. from the wall. This position provides enough clearance for an 8-in.-thick mattress and a wall-mounted headboard up to 2 in. thick. If you have a thicker mattress or if the headboard is more than 2 in. thick, move the base assembly 1 in. away from the wall for every inch of additional thickness. I used a 10-in.-thick mattress, so I moved the base assembly 21 in. from the wall.

Drill ³⁄₁₆-in. pilot holes, and screw the base assembly to the subfloor using the 10 ¼ x 2-in. lag screws furnished **(B)**. If you can easily access the underside of the floor, you can gain holding power by adding blocking as a target for the screws or by substituting bolts. For installation to a concrete floor, drill holes for plugs with a hammer drill, and drive the screws. (There also are screws available that you can drive directly into the concrete, but the hole you drill must be a specific diameter in relation to the screw's diameter.)

Attach the U-shaped mattress holder to the frame with ¼-in. nuts **(C)**. This photo also gives you a good view of the 3-in.-thick foundation that substitutes for a box spring in this model. Set the factory-assembled bed frame onto the base assembly **(D)**. The pins on the frame simply slide onto the slots on the base brackets. Pivot the frame into its upright position, and attach the leg control bars to the base brackets. The control bars automatically open the legs as you lower the bed and close them when you raise it. Be sure to position the nylon bushing where shown **(E)**. The manufacturer supplied ¼ x 1-in. machine screws for this purpose, but my addition of a flat washer under the head plus the substitution of a nylon-insert locking nut meant that I had to switch to a machine screw 1¼ in. long.

Don't overtighten the fasteners—this is a pivot point that must rotate smoothly. Bolt the metal bar with plastic feet between the two leg control bars **(F).** The Murphy name on the bar plus the word "Pull" instantly tells you which way this bar attaches. Have your helper make sure that the frame stays upright against the wall while you attach the springs.

> ⚠ **WARNING** **Wear eye protection and keep your fingers away from the springs during installation!**

Hook one end of a spring through a hole in the angle iron of the base assembly, then use the shank of a long and strong screwdriver to work the other end of the spring to the mating hole in the angle iron of the bed frame **(G).** Putting the tip of the screwdriver into an adjacent hole helps you get the leverage you need. Place an equal number of springs on each side of the frame. Twin and double beds usually require four springs, whereas a queen bed will balance with six springs. Add the mattress and linens, and you're ready for a well-deserved nap. Before you raise the bed, secure the bedding with the strap attached to the frame **(H).** The counterbalanced bed raises and lowers easily **(I).**

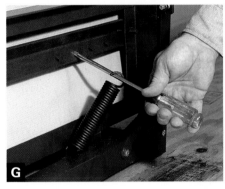

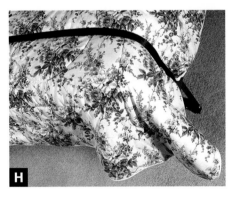

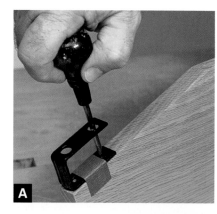

A

B

Bunk-Bed Ladders

Securing a ladder to the safety rail of a bunk bed can help prevent accidents. The fixed-hook style gets its name from the fact that it's secured to a stationary location on the rail. The hooks can be shimmed to fit a variety of rail thicknesses, and the width of the rail is not a critical factor. For those reasons, it's a good choice for retrofitting an existing bed.

Tape the U-shaped hook flush with the top end of the ladder, and put a scratch awl through the large-diameter clearance holes to mark the centerpoints of the smaller mounting holes **(A)**. Drill pilot holes, and screw the hook to the ladder **(B)**. I used #6 x 2-in. screws. Choose the location on the rail for the ladder, and then secure it by screwing on the horizontal strap **(C)**. The dimple in the strap fits into the upper clearance hole to immobilize the hook.

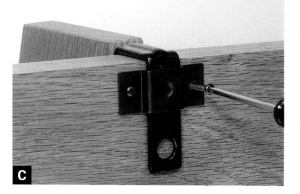

C

VARIATION The adjustable-hook style can be easily moved to a new location along a ⅞-in. by 4½-in. safety rail by loosening the lower bracket. It is *not* designed to allow a child to slide the ladder along the rail, so choose a location, then tighten the clamp. For added security, the larger hook style fits over both the upper and lower edges of a ⅞-in.-thick rail that's 4½ in. wide. Because this style is not adaptable to other rail sizes, it is typically used for new bed construction rather than retrofits.

VARIATION

Technology Hardware

Wire Management

Keyboard & TV Hardware

THE LAST TIME I LOOKED under my desk, I saw enough wire to set up a power-distribution grid for a third-world country, and the back of my entertainment center is choked with even more cables and cords.

Fortunately, hardware manufacturers have been hard at work on the problem of organizing your wires, so you'll find plenty of products to support, swivel, hold, slide, stack, power, rack, clip, bundle, route, cool, hide, and clamp away your problems.

Wiring Solutions

One of my favorite wire organizers doesn't come from a hardware store but from local Radio Shack stores, where they sell inexpensive packages of printed and blank markers. The printed markers go all the way through the alphabet and then up to 15 in digits, so you can hook up a complete home-theater system. The best part is that you can later take apart any of the connections and hook them back without consulting a single manual. Simply wrap a lettered strip around a cord, and cover it with a length of clear tape for security. Identify its terminal on the equipment with a matching individual letter. The write-on strips are self-laminating, meaning that the white surface is already attached to a piece of clear tape.

There is a wide selection of products that can help you bundle together wires for a neater appearance. Grab some twist ties out of a box of trash bags, purchase cable ties in

Cable organizers made from springy plastic keep your work area tidy.

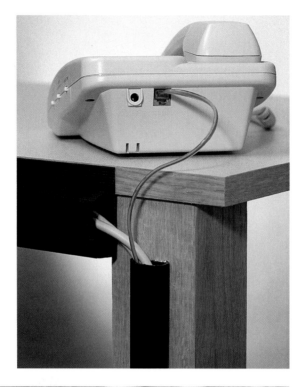

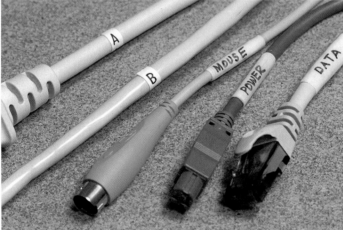

Identify wires and terminals with inexpensive labels, and you'll be able to unhook and reconnect a computer or entertainment center without anxiety.

the electrical aisle of the hardware store, or buy split tubing or spiral wrap at an electronics or auto parts store.

Purchasing high-quality shielded cable can help minimize data that jumps from wire to wire, but it is no absolute guarantee. So exercise some moderation—in computers and in life, you can create problems if you're wired too tightly.

You can purchase a plastic trough to capture wires at the rear of your work surface and a channel that can attach inconspicuously to a table leg to route them down to the floor. In both cases, double-faced tape is a quick and inexpensive attachment method.

One of my favorite low-tech methods of accommodating wiring in a cabinet involves a simple miter cut at a rear corner of the shelves. It's small enough that's it barely noticeable but large enough to handle speaker cables and even power cords. Best of all is its price tag of zero. One caution— be sure that you don't cut away the bearing surface for a shelf pin. A three-point landing is great if you're in an airplane, but it's an unstable setup for shelves.

Powerful Solutions

Tracing extension cords all over the workplace creates tripping hazards and is unsightly. Organize your power needs by choosing a power outlet that you can conceal in a desktop or on a conference table. The model shown in the right photo on the facing page has four grounded outlets and a power cord that can supply 15 amps. The gently domed lid sits nearly flush with the table when you don't need power, but turn it 180 degrees, and it elevates itself $3/8$ in.—high enough to prevent pinching the cords that are plugged in but low enough to conceal the plugs. The enclosure can also handle up to three data ports in an add-on panel.

If you need both power and a data port in a compact package, consider a pop-up that hides the idle outlets but lets you plug in whenever you need them.

Snip a 1½-in. cut at the corner of a shelf, and you'll have plenty of room to route wiring—even a heavy-duty grounded plug.

Put power precisely where you need it by recessing a gang of outlets into a tabletop.

Grommets and More Grommets

Grommets used to be like Model T cars: available in any color you want, as long as you want black. Now you'll find grommets that color-match trendy computers, sport metallic finishes, blend almost invisibly into your laminate work surface, or showcase natural wood species. In addition, brush grommets let you literally drop plugs through the opening, and the bristles instantly close around the wire for a neat look.

Some grommets have an opening that can snap shut when it's not needed, and others have a wire retainer on their rim to prevent an unplugged cord from disappearing down the hole.

Keep Cool with Vents

All electronic equipment generates heat when in use, so you'll need to perforate equipment enclosures with vents. Some plastic vents pop into round holes from the outside, whereas while the square version shown in the middle photo on

p. 202 presents a finished look on both the inside and outside of your cabinet. The unfinished wood grille adds a traditional look and admits a generous amount of cooling air.

It's a good idea always to use at least two vents in an enclosure. Position one vent low on the cabinet to inhale cool air and another vent up high to exhaust the heated air. Another approach is changing the ventilation system from passive to active by purchasing an equipment-cooling fan.

Home-Office Hardware

Working at home can be a delight or dreadful. If you set up your office to achieve efficiency and comfort, you'll improve the odds in your favor.

A good place to start is with a keyboard support that can fully retract under the work surface to free up precious desk space when it's not needed. You'll actually find two categories of supports—one is essentially a drawer and the other is a fully articulated arm.

The drawer type of support is economical, and although the lack of adjustability can

This rugged power and data port is ready for business when you are, but the extruded housing self-stores into your desktop when it's off duty.

limit your choice of work postures, it may be more stable than some of the arm types. You'll find some keyboard drawers that are ready to install, or you can purchase drawer slides and brackets to mount below your work surface, allowing you to make your own tray. If you want to conceal every vestige of technology when the drawer is closed, look for slides that also incorporate a hinge at the front end. These allow you to add a flip-down front to hide the contents of the drawer. Carefully check the depth required by the drawer to make sure that you'll still have enough knee room.

You can purchase the slide and support as a "package" system or purchase the components individually. If you purchase only the slide hardware, you can design and craft your own support tray.

The drawer type may be a good choice if you use a home office to pay bills and to occasionally access the Internet, but if you work full time at home, you should seriously consider the advantages of a keyboard arm. The variety of working positions you can choose with a fully adjustable arm does more than offer relief from monotony—the change may also help prevent carpal tunnel syndrome or other ailments caused by repetitive stress.

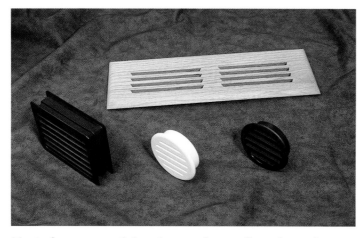

Vents form essential pathways for cooling air to circulate through cabinets that house electronic gear.

Take Your Computer to the Next Level

In the surreal realm of roadside America, there are several tourist sites that claim to have the world's largest hairball extracted from one species or other of mammal. And if you think that sounds disgusting, you'd probably find its identical twin inside your computer's case.

No need to settle for the ho-hum when it comes to grommets. You can choose one that virtually disappears or others that nearly stand up and shout for attention.

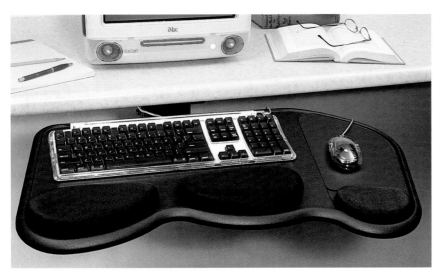

A full-function keyboard arm offers a wide variety of working positions and stows neatly beneath the work surface when not in use.

The tiny fan (sometimes several of them) inside the box of the central processing unit (CPU) works full time sucking in human and pet hairs, fibers from clothing, furniture, and carpets, as well as vast quantities of airborne dust, dirt, and other things so strange that they would stump even the forensic geniuses on the television crime shows.

Some of this fuzzy gunk blows into your workspace where you can inhale it, and some settles on components inside the CPU where it may reduce cooling efficiency to the point that circuit boards can fry themselves to death. Another danger from the buildup is the potential for creating alternate current paths—these are called short circuits.

Lifting your CPU off the floor may not instantly transform the air quality in your home or absolutely ensure that you'll never burn out a component, but it's a step in the right direction. A CPU holder will also prevent you from accidentally knocking over the unit, and you may be able to slide it backward to improve knee room. As a huge bonus, many CPU holders also swivel to bring all of the wiring connections within easy reach.

Lifting your CPU off the floor will help it stay cooler and cleaner by improving air circulation around it, and the swiveling slide also gives access to the back without crawling around with a flashlight.

Position Your Monitor

Placing your computer's monitor in a comfortable position can improve your productivity while easing eyestrain caused by glare on the screen. The tub that recesses into a workstation can set your home office apart from the ordinary, and it is also worth considering in job environments where you must simulta-

Installing a monitor tub requires planning and careful support of the work surface, but it can give your workstation a sleek custom look. (Photo above courtesy Doug Mockett & Co.)

A monitor arm is the next best thing to levitation—it magically clears your work area.

neously talk to a client and work on the computer.

The swiveling and extending monitor arm shown in the photo above clamps to the edge of a work surface, and its retractable wire support can hold a keyboard when it's not in use. You'll also find monitor arms that mount in the center of a work surface or to a wall. Reinforcing the underside of the table by screwing on a plywood plate (the larger and

▶ For information on working with nylon straps, see *"Television Pullout and Swivel"* on p. 211.

thicker, the better) will help prevent your work surface from damage. For safety, never swing the monitor past the edge of the table. It's also a good idea to secure the monitor to the arm with a safety strap so it can't be accidentally knocked off its platform.

Organized Media Storage

The compact disc (CD) may be the hardest-working medium in show business but it also performs a variety of jobs around the modern office, storing programs and data. Fortunately, there are a number of CD storage racks that let you create custom systems that are either freestanding or an integral part of office furniture or an entertainment center. Choose from units that store single or double CDs in tracks that lock the case until you push in with your finger. The plastic springs at the rear of the unit then pop the case forward so you can easily grip it. Another style of CD holder is adaptable for vertical or horizontal installation in 5-mm holes or $\frac{1}{2}$-in. saw kerfs.

Storage for Videotapes and DVDs

The rush is on toward DVDs, but videotapes will probably be part of your entertainment collection for a number of years. Similar in design to the CD holders you just saw, the spring-loaded videotape storage unit shown in the top right photo on the facing page handles tapes with or without a cardboard sleeve. The DVD tray can be used freestanding but is more secure when mounted inside

Videotapes pop in and pop out of the spring-loaded rack (left), while the more passive tray (right) holds DVDs.

The spring-loaded unit shown at left stores single CDs in their cases, while the unit shown at right does the same thing for double cases. The divider shown at center can be ganged for vertical or horizontal applications.

From left, a 7-in. square chair swivel, a 6-in. square lazy Susan bearing, and a 3-in. square version inside the 12-in. round.

a cabinet. Its design allows side-by-side placement along the full length of a shelf. Mounting could hardly be easier—double-faced tape works fine. You also can use the tray as a shelf (5-mm shelf pins are included), locking the tray between vertical uprights.

Position a Television

You can use a lazy Susan bearing to easily make a swiveling platform for your television. The 12-in.-dia. round bearing shown in the middle photo at right has a colossal 1,000 lb. load rating. You'll gain some additional stability by choosing a 17½-in.-dia. round bearing (not shown) that's similar in design, but its weight rating drops to 330 lb. But even that is plenty to handle most televisions, even the oversized variety.

The instruction sheets that are sometimes supplied with lazy Susan bearings describes a blind-mounting technique, but that's not the method I use. See the sidebar on p. 206 for a

A swiveling slide can position your television for great viewing, but you'll also need to anchor your cabinet and beef up its construction.

system that I developed so you can see what you're doing.

A heavy-duty chair swivel with a 7-in. square base is thicker than most lazy Susan bearings but usually has a stiff enough action to hold its setting without modification. Its reduced footprint makes it more suitable for smaller televisions.

AN EASY WAY TO MOUNT LAZY SUSAN BEARINGS

This simple mounting technique works for both square and round lazy Susan bearings.

After you've shaped and applied finish to both the base and top, lay out the location of the pilot holes in both parts and drill them. If you have a square bearing, screw it to the base, and rotate it 90 degrees. Put a scratch awl through the mounting hole in the top plate, and mark its position on the base. Create the access hole by drilling through the base at that centerpoint with a ⅝-in. Forstner bit. Referring to the drawing at right, you can now place the base on the top and use the access hole to drive screws into the top. Don't torque down on the screws until you have them all started. Complete the assembly by adding a cork or nonslip rubber foot at each corner of the base.

When you're mounting a round bearing, simply position the bearing on the base and mark the centerpoint of the access hole. Remove the bearing to drill the hole, then complete the procedure described above.

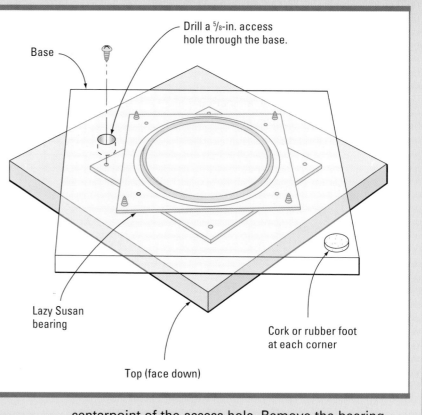

Base

Drill a ⅝-in. access hole through the base.

Lazy Susan bearing

Cork or rubber foot at each corner

Top (face down)

Downscaled lazy Susan bearings, such as the 3-in. and 6-in. sizes, are too small to safely hold a regular-sized television, but you'll find them handy for making rotary storage units.

A swivel that also pulls the television out of the recesses of your entertainment center is a helpful accessory that makes any seat in the room a great place for viewing.

In addition, you can swivel the television 90 degrees to make it easy to hook up accessories such as a DVD player and auxiliary speakers.

The heavy-duty slide shown in the bottom photo on p. 205 can handle a television that weighs up to 225 pounds. But the strength of the hardware itself won't be your biggest concern. Cantilevering the center of gravity of the television past the edge of the cabinet creates a powerful levering action that will attempt to rip the rear edge of the shelf out of the cabinet or tip over the entire entertainment center. For those reasons, I wouldn't suggest using a television slide in any cabinet that isn't securely fastened to the house.

Laminate-Covered Grommet

With a special grommet, you can cover its cap with plastic laminate, matching your work surface for a virtually invisible installation. When you adhere the laminate to the work-surface substrate, also put some adhesive on the top of the cap and an oversized piece of laminate **(A)**. If you use solvent-based contact cement, be sure to work in a well-ventilated area.

After you've adhered the laminate, place the trim ring onto the cap, and use a flush-trim bit in your table-mounted router to cut the laminate to size **(B)**. I use a rubber-covered grout float (from the ceramic tile department of a home center) to keep my fingers away from the bit. Use a ½-in. drill to power a 3-in.-dia. hole through the work surface **(C)**. You may want to test-drill in a piece of scrap to ensure a good fit. While drilling, be sure to remove the bit periodically and clean the teeth using a brass wire brush. Once the pilot bit penetrates the work surface, complete the hole by drilling from the underside of the work surface. If necessary, use 100-grit sandpaper in a block to fine-tune the edge of the cap so it fits. I held the block steady on its edge and lightly rolled the cap. Use household cement or epoxy to adhere the liner into the hole **(D)**. Be sure to adjust the liner to the proper depth so that the cap is flush with the work surface **(E)**.

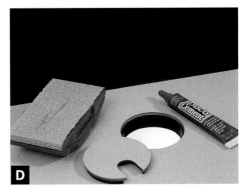

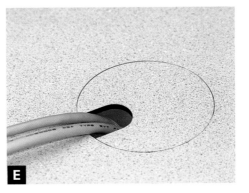

VARIATION To install a brush grommet, decide on its location, and trace the perimeter onto the work surface. Mark in ⅜ in. from each corner to locate the centerpoint to drill with a ¾-in. spade bit. Cut the opening with a jigsaw. Cut to the center of the lines to allow clearance for the tape that holds together the grommet assembly.

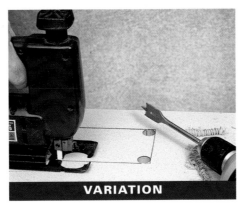

VARIATION

A

B

Data and Power Port

The housing for this pop-up port requires a 2⅞-in. hole through the work surface. If you're able to get the surface to your drill press, you can drill the hole with an adjustable fly cutter **(A)**. Make certain that the tip of the cutter is positioned as shown in the photo. If you have it reversed, you'll get a straight-walled plug, but the hole through the work surface will have a tapered ridge at the bottom.

[TIP] **If you can't maneuver the work surface to the drill press, you can still use a fly cutter to make a router template. To do that, drill the 2⅞-in. hole through a piece of scrap ¾-in. plywood, and clamp it to the desired location on the work surface. Use a spade bit to drill a 1-in. starter hole within the template's opening and through the work surface. Chuck a flush-trimming bit with a top-mounted bearing into your router, and rout the hole.**

Press the housing into the work surface, making certain that the rectangular slot faces the direction that you want for plug and port access **(B)**. If you need to slightly enlarge the size of the hole, use a rasp, but don't let its teeth drag across the edge of the laminate on the upstroke because that could cause chipout. If the fit is too loose, glue the housing in place with household cement (Duco is one brand).

Use a small flat-bladed screwdriver to pry off the data port retaining bezel (the orange plastic part in this case), and remove the data port **(C)**. Back out the Allen screws in the bottom of the extrusion, and put the end of a data cable through the hole in the bottom (I cut one end from a factory-made data cable). Do *not* put the wires through the housing in the work surface. You wire up the data port first, then push it up into the housing from below the work surface. Strip the jacket off of the cable, and attach the individual color-coded wires to the matching terminals on the data port by using a push-down tool. The blue plastic item shown in the photo doubles as a wire jacket stripper and its notched metal part is the push-down tool.

Attaching the wires is a quick and easy procedure, but if you are unsure about the process, take the cable and data-port assembly to an electronics-supply store or a computer retailer, and the people there can either show you how to make the connections or do the job for you. When you've completed the hookup, snap the connector covers (not shown in photo) over the wired terminals, and position the data port sideways inside the extrusion. Snap on the retaining bezel to hold the port in position. Replace the Allen screws to secure the bottom onto the extrusion.

Reach under the work surface, and push the completed assembly into the housing. Using an Allen wrench, drive the small screws that secure the cap to the extrusion **(D).** Don't try to tighten these screws too much, or you'll risk stripping the tiny threads.

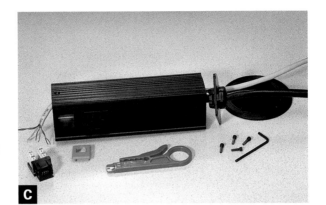

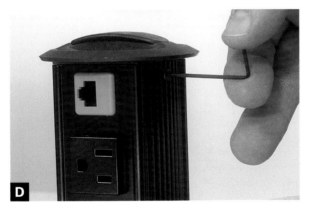

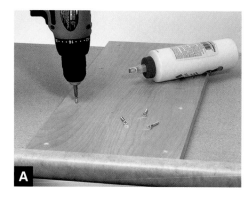

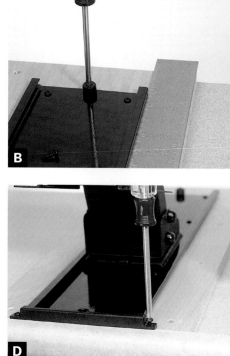

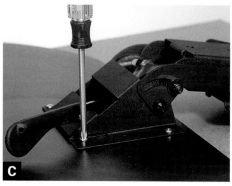

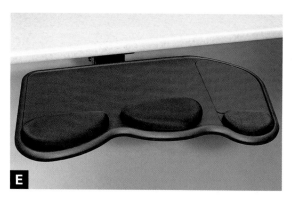

Keyboard Support

The ready-made countertop in this demonstration has the laminate wrapped around a built-up front edge, so I glued and screwed a piece of ¾-in. plywood to the underside to bring its level flush with the rolled edge **(A)**. At 9½ in. wide, the plywood is 4 in. wider than the metal track of the keyboard arm. Use a framing square to make certain that the track is square to the front edge of the countertop, and drive the supplied screws into pilot holes to fasten it. Install the stop bumper in the center rear hole of the track **(B)**, but omit the screw in the front center hole for now.

Place the keyboard tray face down on your workbench, and drive the supplied screws through the articulating arm mechanism into the tray **(C)**. Slide the arm mechanism about 6 in. into the track, and swing the keyboard tray to one side to provide access to the front of the track. Drive the three screws that secure the plastic track guard, which prevents the mechanism from being accidentally pulled out of the track's front **(D)**. (I temporarily removed the keyboard tray in photo **D** to show the track guard more clearly.)

Attaching the wrist supports is hook-and-loop easy. The completed installation **(E)** is ready for your keyboard.

VARIATION If you have a laptop computer, you don't actually have to juggle it on your lap. To install a laptop platform, follow the same steps as for the keyboard support. Some laptop platforms let you add a mouse pad on either side.

VARIATION

Television
Pullout and Swivel

If you're designing an entertainment center, I'd suggest that you do an initial test installation on a mock-up shelf on the workbench instead of inside a cabinet. That way, you don't have to calculate clearances—you can measure them directly to make absolutely certain that you'll avoid embarrassing and costly mistakes.

The manufacturer of this swivel suggests that you place the center of gravity of the television over the center of rotation or rearward. In many cases, though, you'll find that following the manufacturer's recommendation will place the television unacceptably far back on the swivel, so you'll need to cheat its position forward. To find your television's front-to-back center of balance, place a ½-in. square rod on your workbench, and rest the television on the wood strip **(A)**. When the set balances, you've found that center of balance. As you can see in the photo, I went one step further and also found the center of balance with the television resting on its back. The intersection of the two balance lines is the center of gravity, represented by the circle divided into quadrants.

I'm not really recommending that you need to find the center of gravity of your own television, but I did it with mine to make a point about the necessity of anchoring the TV to the platform. As you can tell, the center of gravity is only about 4½ in. back from the front of the screen and at nearly 60 percent of its height. The design becomes quite unstable when you put it into motion on a slide, or more correctly, when you try to stop it at the end of a sliding motion. The 80-lb. television will want to stay in motion, and its high center of gravity makes it a likely candidate to drop face first onto your floor. You'll find out more about the anchoring process later in the demonstration.

(Text continues on p. 212.)

A

B

> ⚠ **WARNING** Any hardware that moves equipment forward in an entertainment center can exert tremendous leverage upon the shelf, so make certain that it is strong enough and fastened extremely well. In addition, moving a television forward changes the center of gravity of the cabinet and could cause a freestanding cabinet to topple forward. To prevent this, bolt the cabinet to the floor, or use lag screws to anchor the cabinet to wood wall studs.

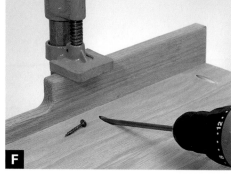

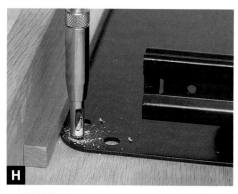

Next, you'll need to determine the size of the wood platform that you'll make and attach to the swivel plate. Although you could make the platform's length just slightly more than the actual contact surface of your television, that could produce an unnerving barely balanced appearance. I made the front-to-back depth of the platform 1 in. greater than the contact surface. (Some people make the platform much deeper, then chop off the corners for swinging clearance.)

Cut a piece of ¾-in. plywood to size for the platform, and cover the plywood's exposed core on the two ends **(B)**. I used iron-on edgebanding, but you could glue on thin solid-wood strips. Hold your utility knife blade flat against the end of the plywood and push down to cut the overhanging ends of the banding. Scrape and sand the edges of the banding flush with the plywood. Temporarily place the plywood on top of the swivel plate, measure to the shelf, and subtract ¼ in. to determine the width of the fascia board **(C)**.

Rip the fascia board to width, and crosscut it to length. Referring to the drawing on the facing page, lay out the centerpoints of the holes. After you drill the holes with a Forstner bit, draw lines tangent to their rims to complete the shape. Cut along the lines with a scrollsaw or bandsaw, and sand smooth **(D)**. Chuck a ¼-in. roundover bit into your table-mounted router, and round over the inner and outer lower edges and the outer upper edge. Do any touch-up sanding necessary **(E)**. Use glue and pocket-hole screws to attach the fascia board to the platform **(F)**.

▶ See *"Pocket-Hole Assembly"* on p. 17.

Place the completed platform upside down on your workbench, and place a ½-in. square spacer rod between the centered swivel and the fascia. Make sure that the slides are fully retracted to the hold-in position, and measure from the front end of the slide to the front of the fascia **(G)**. Add ¼ in.

for clearance, and make a note of this dimension. Rotate the swivel to mark and drill ⁷⁄₆₄-in. pilot holes into the platform for the supplied #8 x ⅝-in. screws **(H),** but do not drive them yet. Position the swivel right side up on the shelf, offsetting the ends of the slides by the dimension you noted earlier **(I).** Mark and drill ⁵⁄₃₂-in. pilot holes for the supplied #14 x ¾-in. hex-head screws in the first three holes on each slide, and drill ¹⁷⁄₆₄-in. holes through the rear holes for ¼-in. bolts.

Drive the screws that fasten the platform to the swivel **(J).** When the slide is fully loaded with the weight of the extended television, the rear bolts and the wood are under tremendous stress, so I decided to upgrade from the factory-supplied fasteners **(K).** I chose high-strength grade 8 bolts that you can identify by the six raised lines on their hex heads. Even more important is the ¼-in. x 2-in. fender washer that spreads the bearing stress on the lower surface of the platform. A nylon-insert locking nut keeps the assembly snug. The total cost of the upgraded hardware was less than $2.

Place the television onto the platform, and look for places to attach the restraining straps. On this television, I backed out a screw at each upper corner of the television cabinet and added a triangle hanger and a 1-in. D-ring **(L).** At each rear corner of the platform, I added another D-ring, securing it with a mirror hanger, flat-head ¼-in. machine screw, and nylon-insert locking washer **(M).**

Diagonally between these two points, add 1-in. nylon strapping (from the rope aisle of a hardware store). For photographic clarity, I used yellow strapping, but you'll probably pick black. Cut the strapping with scissors, and seal the ends by slowly passing them ½ in. above a candle flame **(N).** Adding plastic buckles makes installing and removing the television an easy task.

Don't overdo the tension on the straps—you merely need enough to prevent the television from rocking forward **(O).**

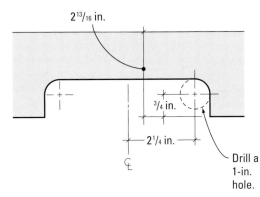

2¹³⁄₁₆ in.

¾ in.

2¼ in.

℄

Drill a 1-in. hole.

J

K

L

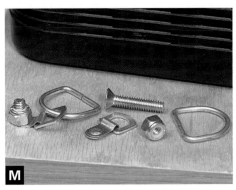

M

N

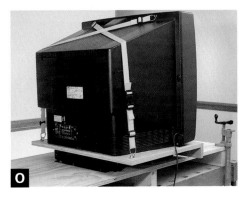

O

Manufacturers and Suppliers

Acorn Hardware
P. O. Box 31, Mansfield, MA 02048
Toll free: (800) 835-0121
Fax: (800) 372-2676
www.acornmfg.com
Manufacturer of classically styled hand-forged cabinet hardware in iron and stainless steel.

Amerock Corp.
4000 Auburn St., P. O. Box 7018
Rockford, IL 61125-7018
Phone: (815) 969-6308
Fax: (815) 969-6138
www.amerock.com
Manufacturer of cabinet hardware in a variety of finishes.

Architectural Products by Outwater LLC
22 Passaic St., P. O. Box 347
Wood-Ridge, NJ 07075
Phone: (800) 835-4400
Fax: (800) 888-3315
www.outwater.com
Distributor of plastic cabinet hardware and molded architectural elements.

Baldwin Hardware Corp.
841 E. Wyomissing Blvd., Reading, PA 19611
Phone: (800) 959-3568
Fax: (610) 775-5564
www.baldwinhardware.com
Manufacturer of decorative cabinet hardware in brass and other metal finishes.

Ball and Ball Hardware Reproductions
463 W. Lincoln Hwy.,
Exton, PA 19341-2594
Phone: (800) 257-3711
Fax: (610) 363-7639
www.ballandball-us.com
Manufacturer of a variety of 18th- and 19th-century reproduction hardware.

Belwith-Keeler
4300 Gerald R. Ford Fwy.,
Grandville, MI 49468-0127
Phone: (800) 453-3537
Fax: (616) 531-8515
E-mail: customerservice@belwith.com
Distributor of decorative die-cast and brass-plated hardware.

Blum (See Julius Blum, Inc.)

Brownells
200 S. Front St., Motezuma, IA 50171
Toll free: (800) 741-0015
Phone: (641) 623-5401
Orders: (641) 623-4000
www.brownells.com
Manufacturer of firearm accessories and gunsmith tools.

Brusso Company, Inc.
4865 Highland Rd.,
Waterford, MI 48328
Toll free: (800) 211-0158
Fax: (248) 674-5962
www.brusso.com
Manufacturer of solid-brass cabinetry hardware.

Create-A-Bed Inc.
4735 Poplar Level Rd., Ste. 3,
Louisville, KY 40213
Toll free: (877) 966-3852
Phone: (502) 966-3852
Fax: (502) 966-4979
www.wallbed.com
Manufacturer of Murphy-style beds.

D.I.G.S.
115 Wooster St., New York, NY 10012
Toll free: (888) 868-DIGS
Fax: (212) 966-9651
www.DIGS.com
Manufacturer of hardware and artistic cabinet accessories.

Dimestore Cowboys, Inc.
407 Second St. SW,
Albuquerque, NM 87102
Phone: (505) 244-1493
Fax: (505) 244-1496
dimestorecowboys.com
Manufacturer of hand-crafted forged-iron hardware.

Fagan's Forge
159 Cooney Rd.,
Pomfret Center, CT 06259
Phone: (860) 928-4020
Fax: (860) 963-4020
www.fagansforge.com
Manufacturer of hand-wrought iron hardware.

Gardner Screw Corporation
220 Union St., Gardner, MA 01440
Phone: (978) 632-0850
Fax: (978) 632-4606
www.gardnerscrew.com
Manufacturer of furniture hardware, metal fasteners, and stampings.

Garrett Wade
161 Avenue of the America, New York, NY 10013
Toll free: (800) 221-2942
Fax: (800) 566-9525
www.garrettwade.com
Distributor of woodworking tools, supplies, and accessories.

Grass America Inc.
1202 Hwy. 66 S.,
Kernsersville, NC 27284
Toll free: (800) 334-3512
Fax: (336) 996-5149
www.grassusa.com
Manufacturer of cabinet hinges, drawer slides, machinery, and accessories.

Hafele America Co.
3901 Cheyenne Dr.,
Archdale, NC 27263-4000
Phone: (336) 889-2322
Fax: (336) 431-3831
www.hafeleonline.com
Manufacturer of furniture fittings and architectural hardware.

HEWI
2851 Old Tree Dr., Lancaster, PA 17603
Toll free: (877) 439-4462
Phone: (717) 293-1313
Toll-free fax: (800) 827-3270
Fax: (717) 293-3270, www.hewi.com
Manufacturer of tubular plastic door handles and accessories.

Hager Hinge Company
139 Victor St.,
St. Louis, MO 63104-4736
Toll free: (800) 255-3590
Fax: (800) 782-0149
www.hagerhinge.com
Manufacturer of full-mortise hinges, spring hinges, and cabinet accessories.

H. B. Ives
62 Barnes Park N., P. O. Box 5035,
Wallingford, CT 06492
Toll free: (800) 766-1966
Toll-free fax: (877) 257-5032
Manufacturer of cabinet hardware and
accessories.

Hempe Manufacturing Co., Inc.
2750 S. 163rd St.,
New Berlin, WI 53151
Toll free: (800) 777-5981
Fax: (262) 797-7429
www.hempe.com
Manufacturer of tools and fasteners.

Hettich America
6225 Shiloh Rd.,
Alpharetta, GA 30005-2206
Toll free: (800) 438-8424
Fax: (800) 627-5152
www.hettichamerica.com
Manufacturer of cabinet accessories
and hardware.

Horton Brasses Inc.
Nooks Hill Rd., Cromwell, CT 06416
Toll free: (800) 754-9127
Phone: (860) 635-4400
Fax: (860) 635-6473
www.horton-brasses.com
Manufacturer of authentic reproduction
furniture and cabinet hardware.

Julius Blum, Inc.
7733 Old Plank Rd., Stanley, NC 28164
Toll free: (800) 438-6788
Fax: (704) 827-0799
www.blum.com
Manufacturer of concealed hinges,
drawer runners, and specialty hardware.

Kreg Tool Company
201 Campus Dr., Huxley, IA 50124
Toll free: (800) 447-8638
Phone: (515) 597-2234
Fax: (515) 447-2354
www.kregtool.com
Manufacturer of pocket-hole jigs, dis-
tributor of pocket-hole screws.

Lee Valley Tools LTD.
12 E. River St., P. O. Box 1780,
Ogdensburg, NY 13669-6780
Toll free: (800) 267-8735
Fax: (800) 513-7885
www.leevalley.com
Manufacturer and distributor of wood-
working tools, hardware, and accessories.

Liberty Brass
38-01 Queens Blvd.,
Long Island City, NY 11101
Toll free: (800) 345-5939
Fax: (718) 784-2038
www.libertybrass.com
Manufacturer of turned brass and alu-
minum products and hardware.

Liz's Antique Hardware
453 S. LaBrea, Los Angeles, CA 90036
Phone: (323) 939-4403
Fax: (323) 939-4387
www.LAHardware.com
Distributor of contemporary, reproduction, and antique hardware.

Londonderry Brasses, LTD.
P. O. Box 415, Cochranville, PA 19330
Phone: (610) 593-6239
Fax: (610) 593-6246
www.londonderry-brasses.com
Manufacturer of reproduction cast-brass
hardware.

Ludwig Industries, Inc.
133 Middleton St., Brooklyn, NY 11206
Toll free: (800) 527-2312
Phone: (718) 387-0947
Fax: (718) 387-0524
www.ludwigind.com
Distributor of hardware for metal, wood,
plastic, and paper applications.

Manasquan Premium Fasteners
P. O. Box 669, Allenwood, NJ 08720
Toll free: (800) 542-1979
Fax: (732) 528-5628
www.manasquanfasteners.com
Distributor of fasteners.

McFeely's Square Drive Screws
1620 Wythe Rd., P. O. Box 11169,
Lynchburg, VA 24506-1169
Toll free: (800) 443-7937
Fax: (800) 847-7136
www.mcfeelys.com
Manufacturer and distributor of fasten-
ers, tools, accessories, and hardware.

Mepla
909 W. Market Center Dr.,
Highpoint, NC 27260
Toll free: (800) 456-3752
Fax: (910) 410-7064
www.mepla-usa.com
Manufacturer of accessories, fittings, and
fasteners.

Misugi Designs
3276 Formby Ln., Fairfield, CA 94533
Phone: (707) 422-0734
Fax: (707) 425-2465
www.misugidesigns.com
Distributor of Japanese woodworking
tools, cabinet hardware, and designs.

Mockett
Box 3333, Manhattan Beach, CA 90266
Toll free: (800) 523-1269
Toll-free fax: (800) 235-7743
International phone: (310) 318-2491
International fax: (310) 376-7650
www.mockett.com
Manufacturer of architectural hardware.

Murphy Bed Company, Inc.
42 Central Ave.,
Farmingdale, NY 11735
Toll free: (800) 845-2337
Phone: (631) 420-4330
Fax: (631) 420-4337
www.murphybedcompany.com
Manufacturer of Murphy beds.

MyKnobs
217-14 Northern Blvd.,
Bayside, NY 11361
Toll-free phone: (866) 695-6627
Phone: (718) 352-9580
Fax: (718) 352-9586
www.myknobs.com
Distributor of decorative cabinet hard-
ware and accessories.

Nathan's Forge, LTD.
3476 Uniontown Rd.,
Uniontown, MD 21158
Toll-free phone: (877) 848-7903
Phone: (410) 848-7903
Fax: (410) 775-7902
www.nathansforge.com
Manufacturer of hand-forged ironware.

National Manufacturing Co.
P. O. Box 577, Sterling, IL 61081-0577
Toll free: (800) 346-9445
Toll-free fax: (800) 346-9448
www.natman.com
Manufacturer of builder's hardware.

Porter-Cable Corp.
4825 Hwy. 45 N., P. O. Box 2468,
Jackson, TN 38302-2468
Toll free: (888) 848-5175
www.porter-cable.com
Manufacturer of power tools.

Restoration Hardware
15 Koch Rd., Corte Madera, CA 94925
Toll free: (888) 243-9720
www.restorationhardware.com
Manufacturer of textiles, furniture, lighting, bathware, and hardware.

Rockler Woodworking and Hardware
4365 Willow Dr.,
Medina, MN 55340-9701
Toll free: (800) 279-4441
Fax: (800) 865-1229
www.rockler.com
Manufacturer and distributor of woodworking supplies, hardware, and tools.

Salice America Inc.
2123 Crown Centre Dr.,
Charlotte, NC 28227
Phone: (704) 841-7810
Fax: (704) 704-7808
www.saliceamerica.com
Manufacturer of furniture hinges.

Schlage Lock Company
1010 Santa Fe, Olathe, KS 66051
Toll free: (800) 847-1864
www.schlagelock.com
Manufacturer of door locks and accessories.

Smith Woodworks & Design Inc.
101 Farnersville Rd., Califon, NJ 07830
Phone: (908) 832-2723
Fax: (908) 832-6994
www.niceknobs.com
Manufacturer of wood and metal knobs and pulls.

SOSS Invisible Hinges (See Universal Industrial Products)

The Stanley Works
100 Stanley Dr., New Britain, CT 06053
Phone: (860) 225-5111
Fax: (860) 827-3895
www.stanleyworks.com
Manufacturer of tools and hardware.

Sugatsune America, Inc.
221 E. Selandia Ln., Carson, CA 90746
Toll-free phone: (800) 562-5267
Phone: (310) 329-6373
Fax: (310) 329-0819
www.sugatsune.com
Manufacturer of decorative hardware and accessories.

Sun Valley Bronze
706 S. Main St., Bellevue, ID 83313
Phone: (866) 788-3631
www.svbronze.com
Manufacturer of hand-finished solid-bronze door, kitchen, bath, and cabinet hardware.

Tool Crib
3002 Industrial Pkwy.,
Knoxville, TN 37921
Phone: (865) 525-6195
www.toolcrib.com
Distributor of woodworking tools.

Truth Hardware
700 W. Bridge St.,
Owatonna, MN 55060
Toll free: (800) 866-7884
Fax: (507) 451-5655
www.truth.com
Distributor of hinges, locks, and window systems.

Ultra Hardware Products
1777 Hylton Rd., Dept. HW 2000,
Pennsauken, NJ 08110
Toll free: (800) 426-6379
Phone: (856) 663-5050
Toll-free fax: (800) 858-7210
Fax: (856) 663-1743
www.ultrahardware.com
Distributor of residential and commercial hardware.

Universal Industrial Products
1 Coreway Dr., P. O. Box 628,
Pioneer, OH 43554-0628
Toll free: (800) 922-6957
Fax: (419) 737-2130
www.soss.com
Manufacturer of SOSS invisible hinges.

Van Dyke's Restorers
39771 S. D. Hwy. 34, P. O. Box 278,
Woonsocket, SD 57385
Toll free: (800) 787-3355
Fax: (605) 796-4085
www.vandykes.com
Manufacturer of antique furniture and vintage home restoration hardware and supplies.

Williamsburg Blacksmiths
Goshen Rd., Rte. 9,
Williamsburg, MA 01096
Toll free: (800) 248-1776
Fax: (413) 268-9317
www.williamsburgblacksmith.com
Manufacturer of hand-worked Colonial hardware.

Whitechapel Ltd.
P. O. Box 11719, 890 S. Hwy. 89, Ste. G,
Jackson, WY 83002
Phone: (307) 739-9478
Fax: (307) 749-9458
www.whitechapel-ltd.com
Manufacturer of cabinet, furniture, and architectural hardware.

Windy Hill Forge
3824 Schroeder Ave.,
Perry Hall, MD 21128
Phone: (703) 594-3092
Fax: (703) 594-3094
www.windyhillforge.com
Blacksmithing, manufacturer of ornamental iron, decorative, and architectural products.

Wm. J. Rigby Co. Antique Hardware
73 Elm St., Cooperstown, NY 13326
Phone: (607) 547-1900
Fax: (607) 547-5939
www.wmjrigby.com
Manufacturer of original, antique, and restored hardware.

Woodbury Blacksmith & Forge
125 Main St. S., Woodbury, CT 06798
Phone: (203) 263-5737
Fax: (203) 263-2388
www.blacksmithandforge.com
Manufacturer of period hand-forged iron ware.

Woodcraft
560 Airport Industrial Park, P. O. Box
1686, Parkersburg, WV 26102-1686
Toll free: (800) 225-1153
Fax (304) 428-8271
www.woodcraft.com
Distributor of woodworking tools and supplies.

Woodworker's Hardware
P. O. Box 180, Sauk Rapids, MN 56379
Toll free: (800) 383-0130
Fax: (888) 811-9850
www.wwhardware.com
Distributor of woodworking hardware and supplies.

Woodworker's Supply Inc.
1108 N. Glenn Rd.
Casper, WY 82601-1698
Toll free: (800) 645-9292
Toll-free fax: (800) 853-9663
www.woodworker.com
Distributor of woodworking tools and supplies.

Index

Index note: page references in *italics* indicate a photograph; references in **bold** indicate a drawing.